AMAZONS

The idea of the Amazons is one of the most romantic and resonant in all antiquity. Greeks were fascinated by images and tales of these fierce female fighters. At Troy, Achilles' duel with Penthesilea was a clash of superman and superwoman. Achilles won the fight, but the queen's dying beauty had torn into his soul. This vibrant new book offers the first complete picture of the reality behind the legends. It shows there was much more to the Amazons than a race of implacable warrior women. David Braund casts the Amazons in a new light: as figures of potent agency, founders of cities, guileful and clever as well as physically impressive and sexually alluring to men. Black Sea mythologies become key to unlocking the Amazons' mystery. Investigating legend through history, literature, and archaeology, the author uncovers a truth as surprising and evocative as any fiction told through story or myth.

David Braund is Emeritus Professor of Classics at the University of Exeter. An internationally acclaimed authority on the ancient Black Sea, his books include *Georgia in Antiquity: A History of Colchis and Transcaucasian Iberia*, 550 BC–AD 562 (Oxford University Press, 1994) and *Greek Religion and Cults in the Black Sea Region: Goddesses in the Bosporan Kingdom from the Archaic Period to the Byzantine Era* (Cambridge University Press, 2018).

'David Braund, in his rich and robust treatment of the topic, is throughout aware of the deficiencies of the extant ancient written sources and doesn't make the mistake of telling us what they would or should have said. He retells versions of ancient myths extremely well. He is particularly strong on the gender and sexuality dimensions of his subject. And he correctly sees and shows that the Amazons were fundamental to the Athenians' identity. This is a powerful and important study of an eternally fascinating and culturally significant subject.'

Paul Cartledge, Emeritus A. G. Leventis
Professor of Greek Culture, University of Cambridge,
author of *The Spartans: An Epic History*
and of *Thermopylae: The Battle that Changed the World*

'This engaging overview of the Greek Amazon myth from renowned scholar of ancient Black Sea cultures David Braund is an important corrective to "truth behind the myth" rhetoric which equates ancient Amazons with historical Scythian women. Braund treats the Amazon myth as a Greek male cultural product, but also brings out its potential to show complex appreciation of the way women's capacities can go beyond expected norms of femininity. Scrupulous attention to context and detail in ancient textual and material evidence enables an approach which both acknowledges the power of the myth's attractiveness and does not minimise feminine potential. The Amazons have long fascinated those who study Greek myth and culture: this richly accessible overview will set the baseline for future scholarship and be very useful for student readers.'

Helen Lovatt, Professor of Classics, University of
Nottingham, author of *In Search of the Argonauts:
The Remarkable History of Jason and the Golden Fleece*

AMAZONS

The History Behind the Legend

David Braund

University of Exeter

CAMBRIDGE
UNIVERSITY PRESS

CAMBRIDGE
UNIVERSITY PRESS

Shaftesbury Road, Cambridge CB2 8EA, United Kingdom

One Liberty Plaza, 20th Floor, New York, NY 10006, USA

477 Williamstown Road, Port Melbourne, VIC 3207, Australia

314–321, 3rd Floor, Plot 3, Splendor Forum, Jasola District Centre,
New Delhi – 110025, India

103 Penang Road, #05–06/07, Visioncrest Commercial, Singapore 238467

Cambridge University Press is part of Cambridge University Press & Assessment,
a department of the University of Cambridge.

We share the University's mission to contribute to society through the pursuit of
education, learning and research at the highest international levels of excellence.

www.cambridge.org
Information on this title: www.cambridge.org/9781108834490

DOI: 10.1017/9781108993418

When citing this work, please include a reference to the DOI 10.1017/
9781108993418

First published 2025

Printed in the United Kingdom by CPI Group Ltd, Croydon CR0 4YY 2025

A catalogue record for this publication is available from the British Library

Library of Congress Cataloging-in-Publication Data
NAMES: Braund, David, 1957– author.
TITLE: Amazons : the history behind the legend / David Braund.
DESCRIPTION: Cambridge, United Kingdom ; New York, NY : Cambridge
University Press, 2025. | Includes bibliographical references and index.
IDENTIFIERS: LCCN 2024043725 | ISBN 9781108834490 (hardback) | ISBN
9781108995122 (paperback) | ISBN 9781108993418 (ebook)
SUBJECTS: LCSH: Amazons. | Women soldiers – Greece – History – To 1500. |
Mythology, Greek. | Greece – Civilization – To 146 B.C.
CLASSIFICATION: LCC BL820.A6 B73 2025 | DDC 398/.45–dc23/eng/20250103
LC record available at https://lccn.loc.gov/2024043725

ISBN 978-1-108-83449-0 Hardback

CONTENTS

The plates will be found between pages 144 and 145.

v

PLATES

PREFACE

This is a book about the Amazons of ancient Greek culture – a whole people, consisting entirely or primarily of strong and resourceful young women. They were the daughters of the war-god Ares and a mysterious nymph, named Harmonia. They not only established themselves in their own state, but went to war as an army of women. With and without the support of Ares, they were a military force to be reckoned with. They are credited with a series of sweeping campaigns from their principal homeland around the Black Sea as far as the Near East and Africa. Their ruling queens played principal roles in the prehistory of the Mediterranean world and its environs, culminating in Queen Penthesilea. She took over Hector's role in the defence of Troy, until she too died at the hands of Achilles, who was profoundly disturbed in victory over her. Her striking beauty had enthralled him, even as she died. For the power of Amazons – and especially their queens – combined the talents of male-style warriors with the allure for men of exceptionally attractive women. A series of Greek heroes would struggle to deal with that extraordinary combination, but, where other foes of Amazons had failed, Greeks credited the best of their heroes with victory over these extraordinary young women – not only Achilles, but also Heracles, Theseus, and others.

This book explores the remarkable range of talents and achievements that Greeks conferred on these mythical females. We shall see how and why this myth mattered so much to Greeks. Why did the male-dominated society of ancient Greece create and develop such a myth of powerful, independent females? For what reasons did Greeks depict Amazons on some of their finest temples and other public buildings, while showing them repeatedly on pottery and other artefacts of everyday private life? Why did Greeks find Amazons appropriate decoration for burials and tombs? And why were Amazons key figures in various cult contexts, especially in regard to Artemis and Apollo, both in Greece proper and around the ancient world, from Marseilles to the coastlands of the Black Sea and western Turkey, for example?

The history behind Amazon legend is their use by Greeks to express and support the social roles and attendant issues concerning Greek women – whether considered by the men who dominated Greek society or by the women whose outlooks are so hard to find there. Opinions on Amazons rarely seem to be expressed by women themselves for the simple reason that we seldom have comment from female authors of antiquity, of whom very few have survived for us. We shall see that the success of Amazons tended to defeat and disaster in ancient accounts of their stories. However, even in defeat their contribution to Greek culture was acknowledged even by Greek men, who dreamed of emulating the greatest of the heroes who had conquered an Amazon. A major new finding of this study is the proximity and similarity of Amazons and Greek women according to that pattern of thought. We shall see that Greek women could become 'Amazonian', especially when driven to such lengths by unreasonable menfolk. They could not become Amazons, since the Amazons were a non-Greek people, who were rooted in a Thracian culture that

Greeks traced from the Danubian regions eastwards across northern Asia Minor even to the Caucasus mountains. However, when the need or desire arose, Greek women too could take up arms and fight for themselves. The Amazon myth thereby expressed an idea that has often been overlooked in the study of Greek male attitudes to women. Greek women were credited with the potential to take to the battlefield, and even use the weaponry and armour of their men. That was not only a potential to violence, but an ability to engage in the normally male business and ritual of armed combat. Of course, to do that much was exceptional, as also was the occasional Amazon who in one way or another made a transition to the role of a Greek wife and mother. Much more common, however, was the transition that Amazons en masse were held to have made to becoming agents and servants of cults of their closest deities, especially Artemis – herself Amazonian as a young female goddess who could kill with her favoured weapon (the bow and arrow) and roamed wild places in the hunt, rather as young Greek men did in their preparation for manhood and battle. For all their creativity and achievements – well beyond the battlefield – Amazons could expect an early death, while Greeks were not so foolish as to give much credence to claims that flesh-and-blood Amazons were to be found living at the margins of the world, even after one or two companions of Alexander the Great chose to write of his encounter with such women in deepest Persian territory. Greeks knew that Amazons were a myth, albeit an old and hallowed one, part of a distant prehistory before the emergence of archaic Greece around 700 BC. Crucially, however, myth retained significance precisely because it connected to human realities, as Amazon myth did for Greek men and women, whether individually and separately, or in the collective spirit enshrined in religion and its buildings.

Modern scholarship on Amazons (especially in the English-speaking world) has been idiosyncratic by the standards of the study of Greek myth in general. There has been a powerful urge to locate armed women in simple reality, and to declare them somehow to demonstrate that Amazons were 'real'. The fundamental problems of that kind of work are set out in Chapter 1. However, it should already be clear that the Amazons of Greek culture are not simply women with weapons. Moreover, their whole significance for Greek society is lost if we reduce the study of Amazon myth to such a wild goose chase, whether embedded in journalistic fiction (e.g. Man 2017) or presenting itself as academic research, after the manner of Mayor 2014 (on which, Porter 2020), to take two well-known recent works. Meanwhile, art historians in particular have been entranced by the recurrent modern claim that Amazons in Greek culture somehow represent Persians, especially after the Persian Wars of the early fifth century. No Greek text ever says so, but the notion will no doubt subsist as a way to explain why Greek artists liked to show Amazons – both before and after the Persian Wars, of course. Images of Amazons sometimes resemble Greek art's depictions of nomadic Scythians, leading to claims that Amazons were nomads and had a great deal to do with Scythians. However, Greek texts make clear that they were not nomads (for all their love of horses) and that they were quite unlike the women of Scythia, who were neither very active nor warriors, as Greeks saw them. Amazons were women who often fought as mounted archers, like Scythian men, and were shown accordingly at times. Structuralist analysis has often been blended with these claims of ethnic identifications, and has also encouraged the particularly misleading notion that Greeks (and perhaps especially Greek men) perceived Amazons as monsters. In fact, as with Penthesilea, Greeks usually saw Amazons as objects of desire, and a challenging objective in the emulation of their greatest heroes. It was only in later antiquity that new fictions about Amazons made them somehow monstrous. Earlier, already in the fifth century BC, we glimpse only attempts by some Greeks to explain the gaps in myth about Amazons by creating lurid explanations of how these women were so good at fighting or how they managed not to be taken over by their sons – never germane to the early myth, as far as our evidence suggests. These various red herrings will be dealt with in Chapter 1 and throughout the book as they arise. It is to be stressed from the outset, however, that this is not a work of polemic, designed to attack the work of others, whether scholars or writers of simple fiction. The book will proceed with its own agenda, to show how and why Amazons mattered so much among Greeks, and a considerable array of more sober studies and ancient evidence will be brought to bear throughout. Greek culture is very much our focus, so that Roman material is only considered insofar as it has a direct relevance to Greek matters, an important and (often enough) difficult distinction.

This book has emerged from several decades of teaching about myth and history in antiquity, both in general and with regard to Amazons. My students and colleagues have contributed a lot over the years, as have friends and colleagues at seminars and lectures around the world. Much of my research over the years has been devoted to the Black Sea region, where Greek myth located Amazon homelands. That Pontic focus has helped me to develop a broader sense of Amazons, including perspectives far from the Greek heartlands, while observing the interplay and similarity between Amazon myth in very different contexts and locations. I have incurred so many debts that I cannot acknowledge them all here. And I must stress that some of those who have assisted me with their insights, knowledge, and experience are likely not to share views expressed here. Most of my writing has been done in Greece, where I have especially benefited from discussion with Karim Arafat, Bill Huntington, and Olga Palagia. Barbara Isherwood and Mike Little have offered the perspective of 'general readers', which has made this book rather more digestible than many of my other publications. Meanwhile, Bulgarian colleagues have also assisted greatly in Thracian aspects of the book, notably Ivan Marazov, Daniela Stoyanova, and Yulia Valeva. On Thracian coins, I am deeply indebted to Vladimir Stolba in Berlin, not for the first time. The British School at Athens and its staff have provided a rare environment and library resource in recent years, with invaluable extra support from the Institute of Classical Studies in London, where I am very much in the debt of Sue Willetts. Meanwhile, my excursions into the world of fiction and the Greek novel owe much to the advice of Karen Ní-Mheallaigh. I have tried more physical excursions to as many of the sites mentioned as possible, often in the company of Robert Pitt. He has been a constant support and source of wisdom before, during, and after the completion of this book, and I thank him too for taking on a series of practical tasks, including the index.

It is also a pleasure to acknowledge here the advice of Ayşe of the Kalehan in Selçuk, especially with regard to modern Turkish attitudes to Amazons. At Cambridge University Press I have been fortunate to enjoy the guidance of Alex Wright and his team, and, in matters of scholarship, of various readers, among whom Paul Cartledge deserves my greatest thanks for his careful comments on a draft of my text. As for the illustrations, I am variously impressed and appalled by those I have met in the course of seeking rights and images, happily much more often impressed than not. I am grateful to all those who helped me with images, including Christina and Georgios of Kyparissia, who made a silk purse of my very myopic attempts at photography. All translations here are my own, and are designed to convey the meaning and texture of the original without any attempt at literary elegance. Throughout the travails of creation, Georgia has supported and sustained me, as in all matters.

Introduction

Amazons in Love, War, and Mind – Their Significance in Ancient Greek Culture

~

In what follows, we shall see a fundamentally new vision of Amazons. For that reason, it seems best to set out that vision in broad terms before presenting it in detail in the ensuing chapters. There we shall travel far and wide around the ancient Greek world, both in a geographical sense and in examination of large issues surrounding Amazon myth. For Greek culture was spread across the Mediterranean and Black Sea regions, with priorities and emphases that tended to vary a great deal from place to place as well as in time across the centuries from archaic beginnings around 700 BC into the Roman period and beyond. Amazon tales and cult-practices around them varied, and they were further complicated by the development of fiction-writing, especially from about 400 BC, untethered from civic traditions and sometimes apparently created in reaction to them. However, for all this fragmentation and the localism of Greek culture and religion (of which Amazons were only one aspect), there was also powerful unity. For Amazon myth certainly also had a general coherence and consistency, centred upon key traditions, especially the encounters of Amazon queens with Achilles, Heracles, Alexander, and other Greek male 'heroes'.

Amazons tend to be known in the modern world in terms of battle. They tend to be characterised as 'warrior women' or the like, and that in itself is perfectly reasonable, in tune with much that we hear from ancient Greeks. Indeed, we shall focus on that very aspect of their myth in Chapter 2, where we shall see that their weaponry, tactics, and weapons skills were imagined along the lines of Thracian military habit, from their characteristic crescent-shields to their love of horses. For, as we hear already in archaic times, they are themselves Thracian, and they speak a Thracian tongue. For these are the daughters of the war-god Ares, whose earthly home was Thrace, while the women of Thrace had a particular reputation for combative attitudes among many Greeks, as we see most clearly in Athens. Of course, Amazons' abilities in battle (physical and psychological) expressed far more than battle itself, not only in ethnicity, but more generally as a demonstration of their independence and capacities for strength and resourcefulness.

At the same time, however, this study also contends that modern focus on Amazons as warriors has diminished their significance in ancient Greek culture, while obscuring too the key importance of their enemies, insofar as they were deemed much more successful against non-Greeks than against Greeks of any kind. Crucially, the ancient Greek world was a world of war, at least until Roman domination imposed forms of peace across much of this world. We must be clear that the Amazon myth could only be credible at all if Amazons were able to defend themselves and their community against the warring neighbours around them. If this all-female phenomenon was ever to be imagined, the Amazons must be not only warriors, but also very good ones. They could not rely on male warriors and hope also to be independent, though they could and did engage in diplomacy and alliances with more normative male-led states in their vicinity. For Amazons were 'matches for men', as Homer calls them, but we rarely find Amazons as acting or even thinking in a hostile fashion against men for the reason that they were male. On the contrary, these independent women feature in traditions that make them sexually interested in men, while Greeks and other men are said to have been very attracted to Amazons in sexual terms, too.

Conflict with men, therefore, was an inescapable aspect of Amazon myth, but was only part of their stories. We do well to remember that Amazon myth was the creation of a Greek culture that was dominated by men. Amazon tales combine a familiar pair of opposites, namely love and war. The Amazons represented a challenge to Greek male culture that was powerful precisely because Amazons were imagined by those men as worthy opponents in battle, who were armed also with the weapons of love. In binary terms, the Greek male who aspired to heroism, emulating Heracles and the rest in the gymnasium and symposium, at the heart of Greek male society, saw Amazons as an especially dangerous and testing foe, at once in love and in war. Accordingly, the archetypal encounters of Greek heroes and Amazon queens are as much or more about love and sex than about war, while it was the combination of those two themes that dynamised these tales. Achilles fell in love with his Amazon as he killed her, troubled, regretful, angry, and soon to die himself. Heracles had agreed a deal with his Amazon queen, whereby he exchanged sex for the queen's special belt, until mischievous Hera used her divine power to turn their deal sour and bring on violence. As we shall see in art and text, these duels, as they are sometimes called today, were an opportunity – as was the myth itself – for the exploration of the relationship(s) between love and war in general, in actual society as well as in the imagination and local traditions. More disturbingly, these and other tales may, and perhaps must be set in a real world where warfare was about, and regularly entailed, the slaughter and abduction or seizure of females by male warriors. In and around Athens, Theseus' abduction of his Amazon queen (variously named Antiope, Hippolyte, or otherwise) told how this intelligent woman became a fighter for Athens through her love for her abductor, even at war against her fellow Amazons. Images of her abduction show her very passive during her violent removal from her homeland, whether or not she has a weapon to hand. Given the rest of her story, we must wonder whether artists have tried to show an Amazon who was happy enough to be taken away to a better life in Athens by her dashing hero, who somehow combines his violence and love.

A story related by Herodotus takes these issues to the northern frontier of Greek culture and beyond (see Chapter 6). Three shiploads of Amazons have been captured by Greeks from their homeland on the southern Black Sea. They prove to be a dangerous cargo and take over the ships in a manner not explained, but we may suspect that their considerable female charms were made the means to their mastery of these ships soon after they had set off for Greece. We shall see in Theseus' tale and elsewhere that Greek authors tended to present women on ships as a dangerous and disruptive distraction for the male crew. Shipwreck on the northern coast brought

4

them into the sphere of the local Scythians. While Scythian elders consider them excellent breeding stock, the Amazons rescue themselves by using their wits and allure to persuade Scythian youths to leave with them to create a new people to the north and east of their Scythian homeland, beyond the river Don. For this is an aetiological story to explain the existence of Sauromatians, their difference from Scythians, and specifically the unusual habits of Sauromatian women, who fight in battle and go hunting on horseback with their husbands. Of course, this is another take on the issues of love and war that recur in encounters with Amazons. However, the story has generated a series of claims about real Amazons which need to be tackled here, since they have gained some ground in recent years. There has been a sustained attempt to elide Amazons and Scythian women, driven by preposterous claims about the archaeology of Scythian pastoralists, whose burials sometimes contain bows and arrows, occasionally with signs of violent death, which was all too common in the ancient world for men and women alike (see Chapter 1 on archaeological method and problems of terminology). In fact Herodotus' story is clear that the wagon-based women of Scythia have nothing in common with the Amazon horsewomen. Indeed, it is on that basis that Scythian youths are persuaded by the Amazons to leave their Scythian mothers for a new life beyond the Don. As we shall see, a medical text of much the same period as Herodotus also shows Scythian women as notably inactive in similar terms, unless they fall into Greek hands as slaves and are made lean by hard work. Greek writers have provided us with many a text on Scythians and many, too, on Amazons, but there is no single text that ever states, or even suggests, that Amazons are in some sense Scythian women. The Herodotus story shows precisely that they were not considered in such a way, while we have observed ancient Greek texts which are explicit and consistent in saying that Amazons were Thracian by ethnicity.

The implausible identification of Amazons as Scythian women has a series of (similarly unpersuasive) corollaries, which we shall tackle, where appropriate. However, we must address from the first the attendant claim that in the equation of Amazons with Scythian women we have a key to the origins of Amazon myth. For we are asked to believe that Amazons spring from Greek dealings with Scythians. The notion deserves attention only because it has attracted the unwary, feeding the hunger for origins of myth in simple reality. That kind of quest does nothing to enlighten us about how and why Greeks may have been so struck by Scythian society that they created a myth that they showed on their greatest buildings and brought into their religious outlook, already in place by about 700 BC and Homer's *Iliad*. Even if we choose to ignore the fact that Amazons were not Scythians (why should we?), we must also do violence to established chronology, for around 700 BC Greeks were just beginning to have a presence on the north coast of the Black Sea (some would argue for a later date), while Scythians too were fresh to the region, as usually supposed on the basis of such little evidence as can be found. Unabashed, the unwarranted equation of Amazons with Scythian women proceeds to appeal to ancient Caucasian testimony, as it is presented. This is in fact quite modern literature among the Ossetians, which is far too modern to be of any relevance at all, since it seems to emerge in the eighteenth century AD in the context of Russian imperial expansion across the region, which revelled in all classical themes.[1] If we are serious about tracing roots of Amazon myth, we should probably pray for new discoveries of the Near East, where Hittite specialists have already started to perceive Amazonian echoes in the limited tales that have survived from Anatolia. These include what seem to be colonialist texts in regard to the city of Zalpa, evidently located somewhere in the close proximity of Themiscyra, the Amazon homeland, and already told about a millennium before Homer.[2]

We do better to leave nonsense aside and proceed beyond even love and war to observe the intelligence and subtlety that Amazons are accorded. Extraordinary achievements are imagined of them. Their concern for the creation of cities is particularly stressed, for they are not pastoralists either. We shall see them founding new cites for Greeks, while ancient explanations for their attack upon Theseus' new city of Athens include reference to their supposed jealous rivalry in respect of this impressive new city, which they came to wreck. Even in defeat, Amazons are credited with achievements, first among which was one of the principal religious and cult sites of the ancient world, namely the temple and sanctuary of Artemis at Ephesus. Accordingly, the Amazons were imagined not only as Ares' daughters, but also as adherents of both forms of Artemis, that is both the static deity

[1] Those attracted to these notions should consult Mayor 2014, with the extended review by Porter 2020.
[2] E.g. Zorman 2005, with bibliography, where we see a further search for origins in progress, as the infinite regress of origin-quests demands.

of her Ephesian form and the young huntress who appears widely elsewhere, too. We start to see how Amazons' lives were unlike the normative lives of most Greek women, who were largely closeted and under male control and who went about in public with their bodies well covered and their faces veiled, unless poverty and status demanded that they work for a living in public space. However, we shall see that Amazons might become Greek enough in their behaviour too, while Greek women could certainly become Amazons enough, as we shall see in detail on Lemnos (Chapter 9), where again we find love and war as well as the goddess Aphrodite, never far from Artemis, her counterpart. That transferability highlights the important and wholly neglected fact that Amazon myth acknowledges the potential and capacity of women to go to battle and do much else besides, from weaving to astronomy – two talents which Amazons combined in the tapestry at Delphi, as told in Euripides' *Ion*. Given that Amazons are so masculinist a construct, celebrated in male society, what we have here is a rare enough demonstration that ancient Greek men understood how much women – Greeks as well as Amazons – had to offer. As we proceed through this study, the extent of Amazon resourcefulness in mind and body will become ever more apparent, with all its implications that (as occasional Greek tales relate) Greek women can do the same.

Alas, we are in a poor position to understand what ancient Greek women themselves thought about all this. Unfortunately, the few Greek works authored by women that have come down to us simply do not address the issue of Amazons. That should not be thought a meaningful silence, but rather another example of a general problem of finding women's voices from antiquity. However, as we shall see, male authors have interesting things to say about women's response to Amazons. There is no specific reason to think that the women of ancient Greece saw Amazons in a way radically different from the views of their menfolk, but we are free to guess at differences that may have arisen by reason of their female gender. It is to be hoped that readers, both female and male, will ponder possibilities as they proceed through this book and reflect on its arguments and images.

I
Approaching Amazons

~

Amazons were everywhere in the ancient Greek world – and from very early on. Images and tales of Amazons were already embedded in Greek culture from early archaic days, around 700 BC.[1] As their stories developed across the ancient Greek centuries, and further Amazon images were created across Greek culture, we can trace a remarkable phenomenon. For we see that their substantial challenge to male-dominated order in Greek society and culture constituted a pillar of that same masculine establishment.

Accordingly, Amazons featured on at least three of the Seven Wonders of the World, as identified by ancient Greeks.[2] And as well as great buildings, statues, and the like, there were Amazons aplenty in the local traditions of many Greek cities, religious cults, and great swathes of Greek culture in its many forms, from hard coinage to fantastical fictions. The great cities of the Greek heartlands – Athens, for example – shared an obsession with Amazons not only with humbler communities (little Skotoussa in Thessaly, for example),[3] but also with colonies of the Greek periphery, like mighty Massilia (Marseilles) with its links to Ephesus, and

[1] The Tiryns shield may be the earliest image of Amazons, but see p. 83.
[2] A diverse trio – a major religious centre (Artemis' temple at Ephesus), a very special statue of the king of the gods (enthroned Zeus in ivory and gold at Olympia), and a vast tomb (the Mausoleum at Halicarnassus), with a newly found counterpart that also boasts Amazons: see p. 190; Jordan 2014.
[3] Hansen and Nielsen 2004, 706–7 summarises its history.

like faraway corners of the Black Sea, whether in southern Russia or the colonies along the modern Turkish coast, east from Sinope. In all these places and more, Amazons were also the decoration and social currency of everyday life, whether among the Greek youths of the gymnasia, at the parties of the prosperous, or in the women's quarters, where our vision is especially shadowy, an area obscure to public gaze. Amazons were in every part of life, and were made prominent too in death, as in the decoration of Greek tombs and on the goods deposited inside. In particular, the depiction of Amazons on great public buildings and inside them across the Greek world from archaic times demonstrates that Amazons were somehow acceptable even at the grandest, public, male-dominated level. In exploring Amazons, this book will explain how these formidable, independent females were so very acceptable and accepted, even on the Parthenon and in other special contexts, as at Delphi and Olympia.

Amazons have also survived into modern times, in the sense that they are one of a diminishing group of ancient names that continue to enjoy some recognition. There is a skin-deep awareness that they are females with independent attitudes and capacities. They can fight and are at home enough on the battlefield. Most readers will bring that knowledge to this book, which is very welcome. And yet the sheer importance of Amazons across Greek culture should already be a warning that much more is involved than that. While women might well (now and in antiquity) find something valuable in Amazons, the fact remains that Amazons were a male conception – treasured, enjoyed, and often respected by the men of ancient Greek culture. It was usually men who designed, built, and decorated public buildings, civic coinage, and the like. It was men too (slaves in many cases) who painted the many Amazons on ancient pottery, and very likely men who chose to buy these wares. While we have some female authors, these are very few in number, and often we have little of what they wrote. Regrettably, these few female voices from antiquity show little or no concern with Amazons. In consequence, Amazon tales are overwhelmingly told to us by men. In fact there is almost nothing that might be taken to indicate that the women of ancient Greece had any particular view of Amazons, for example at odds with the views of men. At most we may retain some suspicion that some Greek women (or even many) could have done so. Sadly, the evidence is just not there, while we may observe some loud silences on Amazons too – for example in the rallying cries of Lysistrata's peace-women in Aristophanes' famous play. In fact, Amazons are hardly mentioned there at all, and only by men joking about sex. Why do we not have more about Amazons in a play on female power and independence at Athens – a city as obsessed with Amazons as any we know?

So, who and what are these Amazons of the ancient Greek world? Why did Greeks make so much of them? This book will reveal the history behind the Amazon legend. It will show a pathway through the murky tangle of myth and reality which surrounds Amazons and obstructs our under-standing of them. As we take this path, we shall see that modern society has developed notions of ancient Amazons which routinely underestimate them, especially by over-concern with their abilities in battle at the expense of their wider qualities and fundamental significance for Greeks at all levels.

From the outset we must be clear about the sense in which Amazons are a reality in Greek culture. As most

Greeks appreciated, Amazons were the product of their imaginations, individually and collectively. While some moderns (on occasion, even scholars) long to find flesh-and-blood Amazons, no-one has yet done so, and surely no-one ever will (see below). The reality of Amazons is to be found in the power and significance(s) of their myth itself. Amazons are real in much the way Homer's Trojan War is real – and other major cultural fictions too. These tales are ripping yarns for sure, but they also express large concepts, problems, and dilemmas in human experience that really matter(ed) to real people, both individuals and whole communities. Myths develop and persist precisely because they continue to speak to real human beings across space and time. However, from antiquity onwards, that has not satisfied some, who have sought to turn Helen, Achilles, and the rest into flesh and blood, seeking a literal truth in great tales – in determined pursuit of banality.[4]

The Victorian age was notably prone to that kind of misguided endeavour. While Cnossos on Crete was dug in quest of the Minotaur, the Trojan War was 'found' on a hill in northwest Turkey. Excavations are welcome enough, perhaps. But so much of this effort misses the point. It is the mythical Troy that has resounded into the modern world. Valiant digging does not change the fact that the world cares about the myth and not much about 'reality' by the spade – which itself depends on Homer for such interest as it garners.[5] And so, Alexander the Great, for example, was drawn to Troy by myth. The mythical Achilles had caught the imagination of Alexander, real

---

[4] On this long-standing tendency, Hayes 2014.   [5] Dickinson 2005.

enough for him. Subsequently, those who made myth of the remarkable Alexander pursued the Achilles theme, so that each of these legends had a famous encounter with an Amazon queen – superman and superwoman made an obvious pair in each case. To obsess with banal forms of reality is surely to cheapen and obscure the deeper kinds of reality at work in these tales which bridge and transcend simplistic versions of truth and fiction. And yet that strange compulsion will no doubt abide, for some at least.

Amazons in a Nutshell: What to Know and What to Forget

A lot has been written about Amazons, but a great deal of it is misleading or simply nonsense. We need to sort the wheat from the chaff and chuff, without petty quibbles and squabbles. That will allow us to consider the 'secret history' of Amazons – that is, everything usually ignored about them, such as their intelligence and capacities as builders, astronomers, and much else. An initial sketch will clear a lot of ground. We need to cut through the jungle of verbiage, fantasy, and misinterpretation that has come to envelop Amazons and conceal so much that is most interesting about them.

Battle seems a reasonable place to start – their most famous capacity by far. But how so? These are women who can and do fight. They know how to use weapons and are ready to do so, though they favour particular kinds of weaponry. By and large they prefer battle at a distance, using bows and throwing-spears. In that form, they resemble the light-armed troops of real Greek armies. They often appear also on horseback, light cavalry. At closer quarters they can use spears, but show an unusual liking for the axe and a light crescent shield, also usable on horseback. They sometimes appear in heavy armour, which may obscure their female identities – a repeated issue. In attitude on the battlefield Amazons are indistinguishable from men, as in their militarism more generally. For they too may be imperialistic, while military ability was always a prerequisite for their survival and independence.

Their military success was renowned among Greeks, but it was largely located away from Greeks. Amazons (themselves not Greeks) are the conquerors of eastern peoples in faraway lands. Amazons show military talent against such men, but ultimately they are always failures in battle, especially against serious opponents – Greek men. In that way Amazons are given sufficient success to make them worthy opponents for Greeks, but also fodder for the ultimate victory of Greek men. Of course, in the maelstrom of battle some Greek men would die too, but while Greek battle scenes show instances of Amazon success on the way to defeat, we hear little of significant Greek deaths at Amazon hands.[6] There was no glory for Greek men in defeating women without some military credentials. Meanwhile, Greek victory not only brought credit to Greek men, but also explained how and why Amazons had long since ceased to exist – unless they or women like them persist in some secluded corner of the earth, far from their Greek nemesis.

Greeks tended to believe that Amazons had been annihilated in the passage from prehistory to history, if ever

---

[6] Sthenelus attracted attention, hit by an Amazon arrow as he sailed away with Heracles and the Amazon belt: Ap. Rhod. 2.911–29; cf. Amm. Marc. 22.8.22, centuries later.

they had existed. Greek heroes had put an end to them –
often led by Heracles, a role model for many a Greek
youth, the champion of the gymnasium. This mortal hero
would attain divinity, becoming a god by his achievements,
as approved by his divine father Zeus. Theseus sometimes
took his place, or accompanied him against the Amazons.
And later Achilles would despatch the mighty Amazon
Queen Penthesilea at Troy – heroes all. In result most
Greeks knew and accepted that Amazons had been great
in the days of yore, if ever they had existed, but had died out
as history began. Individually and collectively, there was
a special heroism to be claimed in extinguishing the female
challenge that Amazons embodied for Greek men.
However, Amazons played important roles in the creation
of the world of the civilised and familiar, but their special
lives and lifestyle had no place in history proper. While
Amazons sparked positive outcomes for Greek culture,
a miasma of death hangs over them – the deaths of many
enemies, but also their own destruction. Even in their
heyday Amazons did not make old bones – they are as
hard to find in old age as they are in childhood. They
exist and die in their physical prime, as energetic, talented,
and potentially dangerous young women – untamed,
unmated, and uncontrolled by men. In early death, their
tombs, and their appearance on the tombs of Greeks, form
a major aspect of their legend. For all their achievements,
Amazons have brief lives. Greeks who contemplated their
images on tombs, and in further tombs where they were
said to lie, might reflect on the brevity of life, but also on
more positive themes – lives of glory and the creation of
culture, however unwitting. There was also assurance that

their aberrant lifestyles – a greater threat than their weapons – had been discredited and defeated.

Amazons could stand against men in battle, but they were not in general man-haters.[7] There is very little indication in our texts that they had any particular sympathy for other women either. In fact, we have an occasional hint of their alienation from their sisters in other cultures.[8] Differences in lifestyles and life choices trumped shared gender, at least in Greek male imaginations. Contrary to popular notions, they were not lesbians either.[9] They share a desire (or at least a willingness) to have sex with men, and to have children too. They are independent of men, by and large, but they are by no means hostile to men in general. While it was sometimes said that Amazons had to kill in battle before they could properly have sex with men, and (in later texts) we sometimes find extreme tales of their abuse of men and boys, Amazons were considered heterosexual, and possibly like men in their active pursuit of sex. There was no obstacle either to alliances with men. They fought among the Trojan allies, for example, and were sometimes said to have brought men with them in their assault upon Athens.[10] Much of the power of Amazons rested on their combination of familiar female strengths with a capacity to take on men in their own masculine contexts, including the battlefield, agriculture, and more besides.

---

[7] On the confusing word *antianeira*, see pp. 85–86. If Aesch. *PV* 724 makes Themiscyra 'man-hating' (as usually supposed) and not 'hateful to men', men's sack of the city would be enough to explain the epithet.

[8] Alienation: notably Hdt. 4.114, albeit a clever gambit. Fellow-feeling: arguably *PV* 728.

[9] Disappointing many, e.g. Rabinowitz 2002.

[10] Petrakova 2020; Isocrates, *Panegyricus* 68; *Panathenaicus* 193.

Greeks were clear that Amazons were not nomads, despite modern claims to the contrary – confusion that arises from an ancient tradition that a pastoral people (the Sauromatians) were descended from shipwrecked Amazons who had children with Scythians, who were indeed largely nomadic.[11] Amazons dwelt in settled communities, albeit close to their beloved horses. Their principal homeland was in north-eastern Turkey to the east of Amisus (now Samsun, on the southern shore of the Black Sea). There, they were said to have three towns on the lush plain of Themiscyra, where horses would always find grazing. They had come there from Thrace and retained their Thracian language. Another absurd etymology built that language into an explanation of the name of the nearby city of Sinope.[12] They were ruled by a queen and had laws – an ordered monarchy. Amazons are not simply women who go to war, but a specific *ethnos*, a people whose identity was ethnic before it was a matter of gender. Theirs was a state of women whose warrior ways were vital to their survival – although (as we are sometimes told) war was not for all Amazons.[13] The ancient world was routinely at war or close to it. Any state must have an army. Women alone must fight or become the victims of the (male) warriors who were their neighbours. The logic was inescapable, even though the concept of women warriors was challenging.

Myth – including the myth of Amazons – does not demand completeness, coherence, or consistency. It can and does leave a host of questions – unasked and unanswered. Details

---

[11] See Chapter 6.   [12] pp. 175–76.
[13] Strabo 11.5.1 indicates Hellenistic accounts that limited military training (including hunting) to Amazons inclined in that direction.

and inconsistences were of marginal concern when huge issues were at stake – life and death, the creation of culture, female strengths, and the rest. Even in antiquity, however, there were Greeks who wanted a tighter story. The more pedantic might well ask, for example, how Amazons had come to exist, and how they could reproduce. For Amazons were by no means immortal, despite their divine connections. They are often identified as the daughters of Ares (different mothers are named), but we can hardly imagine that the god was forever fathering them, and we are not told that. The fleeting existence of Amazons relieved any pressure to imagine their long-term sustainability. However, in later centuries, some Greeks developed exotic tales of organised mass-intercourse with male neighbours on distant mountain-tops. Others imagined an exploited male underclass, abused by Amazon mistresses who dominated them, and used them for sex and reproduction. But questions like this were not much asked. They accrued in the later Greek centuries, after Alexander the Great, when more of Greek culture was characterised by pedantry and a taste for lurid fictions. From the first, to be sure, issues of sex and motherhood had been at the very heart of Amazon myth, but in a very different way, as we shall see. From the first, Amazons were characterised as females who would not reproduce, either successfully or at all.

Amazon lives were very truncated, hardly more than moments in most cases. They were all young women of stunning physique. If they had been Greek girls, they would be marrying, having sex, and giving birth – immediately snapped up as fine breeding stock. Their menfolk would be taking care of the fighting as well as other heavy tasks. But the nubile Amazons will seldom have children. They will not run the risk of death in childbirth, but will surely die in battle or from the wounds they have suffered – a favourite theme for Greek artists. For Amazons are caught at a transient stage of life, between girl and woman, and they will die at this threshold in life's journey. As we have begun to see, their deaths will be marked and commemorated around the Greek world, from Athens and the Peloponnese to the colonial cultures of the Black Sea, Italy, and the farthest shores of the Mediterranean. Their deaths – whether individually or en masse – will also be a beginning for new settlements and peoples, the creation of cults and sanctuaries. They had failed, but there had been moments of success and they had not existed in vain – they had left a colossal legacy, including a principal focus for male ambition as well as for the aspirations of Greek females too, in all probability.

Much modern analysis not only stresses differences between Amazons and Greek females, but claims that the two are polar opposites – a favourite trope of the structuralists.[14] However, Amazons had much more in common with Greek females than is usually understood or admitted – part of the reason for their importance in Greek culture. Even in their demise they shared a lot with myths of Greek girls on the brink of marriage.[15] There were many Greek traditions about maidens who bravely gave their lives for the benefit of their families and communities. Of course, Amazons were often enough characterised as enemies. But even as enemies they could be brought into Greek culture – enemies who in death

[14] DuBois 1982; Tyrrell 1984; cf. more recently, Schubert and Weiss 2013.
[15] See Dowden 1989.

become not only friends, but even stalwart champions of the Greeks who had killed them.[16] A good example is the evil tyrant Eurystheus of Mycenae, who was killed by the Athenians and transformed into their protector. No coincidence perhaps that Athenians tended to mention Amazons and Eurystheus in the same breath.[17]

In the 390s Aristophanes famously ridiculed the idea of women running classical Athenian democracy in his *Women in Assembly* (*Ecclesiazusae*). However, this area of anxiety had already been explored often enough by Greek writers. The great heroes had sometimes endured domination by females, whether Odysseus imprisoned by the nymph Calypso on her island, or Heracles under the command of an eastern queen. She was Omphale of Lydia, who has a direct link to Amazons, for Heracles had given her the axe of the Amazon queen. Achilles had also felt the power of women when he had been captivated by the dying Amazon he himself had killed – Queen Penthesilea. Achilles had himself spent time as a girl, brought to join the royal maidens of Scyros by his worried mother, the sea-goddess Thetis. She tried to force his fate. He would either die young in glory or old in obscurity (as his mother preferred). But Achilles was not suited to girlishness, and soon would win glory and early death at Troy. Immediately we start to see that there is something of the Amazon about this warrior and Amazon-killer – glory in early death, and a measure of gender-ambiguity in his behaviour.

At a supernatural level, the goddess Artemis was in many ways a model for Amazons, except in her immortality. She is

[16] Visser 1982.   [17] See Visser 1982.

often associated with them, as at magnificent Ephesus. Elsewhere the goddess commonly appears as a young female, armed with bow and arrow. In the company of young females she ranges through the wilds, killing or saving as she sees fit – quick enough to inflict death upon any mortal who offends her. She was a virgin goddess, linked with the moon, and identified with the deathly Hecate. And yet she was also attuned to the battle of childbirth, and helped women in its pain and real danger.[18]

Her counterpart was Aphrodite, a sexual force for reproduction across nature and human culture, whether inside or outside formal marriage. Aphrodite too might go to war and wield weapons, while her child Eros would contribute with his bow and arrows.[19] Euripides' play *Hippolytus* offers an extended take on the complex rivalry and cooperation between Artemis and Aphrodite. This is all the more intriguing because the protagonist is the son of an Amazon – Hippolyte, brought to Athens by the hero Theseus, soon a widower. As the Amazon Queen Penthesilea had shown against Achilles, the Amazons also wielded the weapons of Aphrodite. Euripides' play demonstrates the likely problems of Amazon mother-hood, as well as the need for balance between Artemis and Aphrodite, and especially in human treatment of them, as still more violently expressed in the murderous tale of the Lemnian women, where an angry Aphrodite causes all the males of the island of Lemnos to be

---

[18] Hall 2013. Amazons are associated with Leto's birthing at Ephesus, as we shall see.

[19] On Eros, hunting and sex, see Cyrino 2013. On Amazons and Eros in ancient poetry, see Borowski 2021, 63–84.

slaughtered by their militant womenfolk.[20] Aphrodite was no less deadly than Artemis, whether armed with weapons of love or with those of war. Lemnos will also illustrate how Greek women may become Amazons in everything but their ethnicity.

Meanwhile, the goddess Athena offered a further model of the woman warrior. She was a mature woman who avoided sex with men, but who had a motherly dimension nevertheless, notably in her city of Athens. Although her fine physique might well make her, like the Amazons, an object of male desire, whether in myth or in the fantasies of male writers, she had little to do with them. At Athens, her protection of the city placed her firmly against them. On the Parthenon, we shall see how Amazons featured not only as (defeated) enemies of her city, but more generally too as proponents of a deviant lifestyle.[21] Athena was the most martial of goddesses, routinely in full armour, and yet the mature and curvaceous Athena managed to be warrior, virgin, and mother – a further divine dimension to the interplay of women's roles in bed and battle. We should note too that Greek culture was evidently very comfortable with her kind of woman warrior – one of many reasons to reject and reformulate modern notions that Greeks had a problem with Amazons because they were good in battle. A more obvious mother-goddess was Hera, wife and sister of Zeus himself. As such she was a champion of marriage, regularly striving to control the rampant infidelities of her husband. We should note the cruelty, violence, and unconcern for consequences in her endless efforts to rein him in, with scant concern for the other females who caught his

[20] See Chapter 9.   [21] Chapter 8.

eye. Amazons might appear in the decoration of her temples too, as at Argos and probably Selinus in Sicily. We cannot reconstruct their role at such temples, but there is every likelihood that Amazons were not favourites of this queen of formal marriage – Amazons offered a very different exemplar, suitably crushed for Hera.

Moderns often declare that Greeks saw Amazons as monsters. But there is very little of that in antiquity. Their links to Artemis and other Greek deities (including her twin brother, Apollo) are an immediate warning against that mantra. Athenians celebrated the oaths that their hero-king Theseus had exchanged with the Amazons. For, after protracted battle, they had sworn peace together before the gods. Amazons were properly religious and orderly in their own way. Men could make agreements with Amazons, as Heracles almost did over the belt he had been tasked to fetch from their queen. Moreover, in the eyes of ancient Greek men Amazons were young women of beauty: they never looked monstrous in any obvious way, for their allure for ancient Greek men was key to the danger and heroic challenge that ancient Greeks saw in them, as will become ever clearer in the course of this book. Often enough too, the beauty of Amazons was matched by their noble natures and considerate conduct. There was room to wonder: Who was the monster? Amazons or the animalian Greek men who slaughtered them and sacked Themiscyra for no good reason? Consider Heracles in his lion skin and wielding a great club, the crudest of weapons. The Amazon queen, as some said, had been willing simply to give Heracles the belt he wanted from her. A deal could have been done, but something had gone wrong – some said Hera had intervened to destroy the Amazons.[22] True, we occasionally find a darker picture of Amazons – for example, as eaters of lizards and killers of babies. Crucially, however, these are not only uncommon, but also limited to writers of the Roman and Byzantine periods, not least Christian authors,[23] who seem to have had a particular aversion to Amazons. An especially unfortunate tendency in much modern work on Amazons is the lumping together of tales that are separated by many centuries, as if they are all the same story. If we are to grasp the historical significance of Amazons, we must at all costs maintain a sense of the chronology of the stories that have come down to us.

Talk of Amazon monsters is at best unhelpful, despite the challenges they clearly offered. The Amazon was much more a figure of erotic allure. Male sculptors were sure to depict these nubile girls in skimpy clothes that revealed far more flesh (possibly a breast) than any decent Greek female should – let alone on the battlefield. However, there was restraint and respect, for all that, since nudity was limited and was in any case a feature of Greek public art for men too. Meanwhile, it is usually in or after battle that we find sculpted Amazons, on public and private monuments, or in the great paintings that have survived only in ancient descriptions of their images. Sometimes vase-painters would add what would be an exotic touch or two for Greek customers, a little fur perhaps, or trousers or leggings – alluring attire in a Greek setting.[24] Such vases might decorate drinking-parties, while some would also find their way into

---

[22] Further, p. 115.   [23] Cf. Cuffel 2007.
[24] An Attic cup (attributed to the Eretria Painter and now in Naples) shows an exceptionally wide range of Amazon attire and armaments on a single

burials – parties of a sort. Real young women were also at hand, many from non-Greek cultures and some with the Thracian ethnicity of Amazons. The images on vases around them often showed heroic conquest – an expression of the sexual reality in progress, couched in the heroism to which Greek males aspired, and on which they might hold forth in talk and song at these events.[25] There is many an Amazon – sometimes dying – on such jugs, cups, and bowls used for the preparation, dispensing, and consumption of wine. In these contexts, the god Dionysus is never far away, and his links to Thrace and to Amazons were doubtless noticed.[26] There might even be women playing the Amazon at these symposia, dancing for the guests with weapons and armour. Xenophon has fun with Amazon-mad locals of the southern Black Sea. These Paphlagonians had Amazons in their regional prehistory. For that reason perhaps they assumed a girl to be a real Amazon when she performed an armed dance for them – a blurring of myth and reality that was both humorous and condescending.[27] We have images of such dancers, and we hear a good deal about the dancing of Amazons themselves – another of their skills, and not so different from the Greek girls who danced in rituals and celebrations.

Amazons were not involved with magic, by contrast with other powerful women from the Black Sea and elsewhere – alluring witches like Medea and Circe from Colchis. Rather they were close to principal Olympian

vessel, c. 450–400 BC: *ARV*² 1252.50; perhaps including Theseus' Amazon: *LIMC* s.v. Antiope (2).
[25] Arrington 2015; Keuls 1993 goes to town on this.
[26] Further p. 273 on Bosporan data.   [27] Braund 2019.

deities – far more cultured and correct. At Delphi we now understand that their presence was considerable – likely enough on Apollo's archaic temple there too.[28] Their prominence on the archaic treasury of Massilia (now Marseilles) at Delphi illustrates both their western extent and their archaic presence at this key cult-centre in Greece. The smashed fabric of Delphi's principal buildings offers limited evidence, but Euripides reveals a whole tale of an astronomical tapestry of the heavens. Heracles had brought it there from the Amazons. Their ability in science, building, and very likely weaving, is all too easily obscured by modern obsession with the battlefield. Amazons were champions of technology, not magic – including the technology of war – innovators in iron weapons and cavalry. The exception is their ignorance of sailing the seas, a kind of progress that was often considered a step towards degeneracy, insofar as it brought the sudden mixing of cultures and power to those who might not have the benefits of landed wealth. There was a measure of conservatism in their inventiveness.[29]

An influential quirk in modern talk of Amazons has a bearing on Delphi, Athens, and elsewhere – the fine fantasy that Amazons represented Persians, though no ancient text suggests they did. True, Athens had endured both Amazon and Persian onslaughts.[30] True, the main Amazon homeland near Amisus lay in a corner of the Persian empire. We can also agree that Athenians and other Greeks liked to see Persian men as sorry warriors, effeminate by nature and habits, as they routinely say. But

---

[28] p. 123.   [29] See pp. 140–41 on sailing.
[30] At length, Castriota 1992. Objections have been made, notably Arafat 2013; Veness 2002.

Amazons are tough, quite different from supposed Persian dandies. The Amazons' long siege of Athens was very different from the Persian experience. Amazon landlubbers had little in common with the seaborne Persians at Marathon in 490, cut down on the beach. A decade later, Xerxes' invasion had been a Persian walkover in Athens. There was no siege. The Persian army sacked an abandoned city and left the acropolis in ruins, until defeated at sea at Salamis and later on land in Boeotia, to the north. We struggle to find parallels between Amazons and Persians, and yet the modern fantasy of an important parallelism persists. Athenian writers make no attempt at comparison, let alone any suggestion that Amazons are in some sense proto-Persians or a metaphor for Persians, as moderns repeatedly assert. Instead, Athenians liked to list their great victories, which included Amazons and others and also came to include Persians. However, Persians get none of the respect shown to Amazons. And when Athenians wished to portray Persians, they did just that, without recourse to Amazons, in art and text alike. Aeschylus, for example, could write a whole play on the defeat of Xerxes' Persians without any mention at all of Amazons, who appeared often enough in his other works. At Amazon-rich Delphi it is remarkable that scholars have formed the habit of interpreting Amazons on the Athenian treasury as somehow Persians. The current reconstruction of Theseus and Amazon on a treasury metope seems to suggest that Theseus is doing violence to the Amazon. If so, she would be Molpadia, queen of the Amazons who besieged Athens, as on the so-called Elgin throne (below). For, while there is a much later story that Theseus and his Amazon wife ended their relationship in violence, that was not the story told usually in Athens, where his wife died and was buried at the city wall, fighting for the city, whereas Molpadia was buried elsewhere.[31]

Amazons are located at the beginning of things, before history had started. Even their issues with marriage suited prehistory, since marriage was regarded as a mark of progress in human development.[32] Amazons existed in the company of gods and heroes. They were players in the great events of their mythic world, the tales of the Golden Fleece, Troy, and the beginnings of particular Greek cults, festivals, and states – Artemis at Ephesus, the start of games at Olympia, Delphi, and probably elsewhere, Theseus' transformation of Athens into a city, and more besides. The Amazon contribution was often challenging, disruptive, and even revolutionary, but they created an order and history, not least in their own destruction and the failure of the alternative they seemed to offer. For their death and defeat ensured that their challenge to the patriarchal status quo was more alluring than threatening. Amazons tested the mettle of men and confirmed male heroism. Through their freedom from male control and their assertive independence, Amazons were good rebels, but failed revolutionaries. For they will not survive into history, except as a memory that tends to be constructed as an achievement for men, in sexual, political, and broadly ideological terms. After all, Amazons are men's myths insofar as they are the fantasy of a male-ordered Greek world. But what did Greek females think?

---

[31] Notably, Pausanias, 1.2.1 and below. Latin versions introduced new elements (Ovid, *Heroides* 4.117; Seneca, *Phaedra* 227, 927), leading to the imperial Greek farrago of Pseudo-Apollodorus, *Epitome* 1.16–17. For the Delphi metope, as now presented, see Plate 1.

[32] Blundell 1998 notes Greek views of marriage as progress.

Women's Amazons?

There are no ancient texts that give a clear female perspective on Amazons. That might have suggested female indifference to their myth – if only we had more female authors extant from ancient Greece. However, Greek women must have been interested in them, whether as fellow females or as a major part of culture. Greek women tended to enjoy most public prominence in religion and cultic contexts, where Amazons too were important – no coincidence, of course. And since Amazons existed on the threshold between girl and woman, all Greek females had a personal stake in them, barbarians or not. For example, Artemis' rites took young Greek females into the wild places of her cults, where fleetingly they tasted a kind of Amazon life, away from men and with only the protection of the goddess against the unseen terrors at the margins of their small world, often at night.[33] There is much to imagine in female thought and action regarding Amazons, though we should not proceed to groundless fantasy – for example, the recent claim that Athenian girls were given Amazon dolls to play with.[34] There is no shred of evidence for such a thing. We should better observe the absence of Amazons from the mass of terracotta figurines that have survived, largely in burials and sanctuaries. While it remains unclear how many of these

---

[33] Further, Cole 1998; cf. Blundell 1998; Dillon 2001; Larson 2007.

[34] Mayor 2014, esp. 32–3 (followed by Penrose 2016, 91). Her 'Scythia' is the Bosporan Kingdom and its Greek cities, on whose dolls see Muratov 2019. Mayor shows the Roman-period figure of a female gladiator, and a pyrrhic dancer, in fashion among the terracotta-makers of the fifth century BC (and with no archaeological context). On larger problems, including texts, see Gutschke 2019, with bibliography on these 'neglected' figures. Cf. also Chiarini 2018, esp. 197–202 for admirable discussion of related nonsense.

were ever children's dolls in the first place, we struggle to find any Amazons in this material at all. We can find Amazon images in women's domestic space, but in the boudoir, on perfume-jars and other containers. It is unfortunate that we know so very little about the soft furnishings and other décor of this women's world inside the Greek home.

Amazons could even feature in the most traditional occupation of domesticated Greek women – woolworking, which expressed all the wifely virtues.[35] In this process, women used thigh-guards, or *epinetra* – the 'armour' of domesticity, perhaps. On occasion we find terracotta examples of these thigh-protectors that depict Amazons in action, arming themselves (Plate 2). Arming-scenes captured the transition from Greek-like, 'normal' woman into the woman warrior (even hoplite), setting out for battle – or are these Amazons even returning to domesticity, taking off their gear, without wounds for once? And were these – heavy – thigh-guards for use or only decoration?

Whatever a woman thought as she looked at these Amazons on the woolworking device, she was likely reminded of her own latent powers, and the existence of an alternative lifestyle – however deadly for her. Did Amazons even suggest a sense of protection, commensurate with the function of the device itself? Some women may also have recalled the arming-scenes of men, frequent in art and heroic tales, such as Homer's arming of Achilles. The very image of female arming shone a spotlight on women's capacity for male-style heroism. And yet Amazons were not always far from wool themselves, as we noted in the tapestry held at Delphi. Unresolved issues

---

[35] E.g. Harlow and Nosch 2014.

around Amazon woolworking were part of a fundamental question in any understanding of Amazons, ancient and modern. How different were Amazons from Greek women?

When Greeks tried to make sense of Amazons in historical terms, away from myths, they offered explanations which bridged the gap between the two. Already in the fourth century BC Greeks had perceived in Amazons a warning and guidance for men. The historian Ephorus of Cyme claimed that Amazons were abused women, some said. For it was in response to the abuse they suffered that they organised themselves and seized power from their men – even being ready to fight them in armed battle, so that the men preferred to leave them to their new future. Such was the story told at Cyme, not far from Ephesus. The concern with Amazons there went far beyond the historian himself, as its civic coinage shows. The (male-run) city put the normative portrait of a respectable lady on its coinage – the portrait of such a reluctant Amazon, it might seem. This was Cyme, the Amazon from whom the city had its name, though only her diadem marks her out (Plate 3). That kind of story warned men to behave better towards their women, and maybe even gave women a small measure of defence against abuse in that way. After all, quite apart from Amazons, Greeks (and perhaps Greek men in particular) kept returning to the theme of women's potential for violence (direct and indirect) in the face of oppression – from Penelope's artful handling of the 'suitors' in Homer to the butchery perpetrated by the likes of Medea and Clytaemnestra. This kind of Amazon moral had a context in Greek thought well beyond the local story at Cyme.

Sadly, the details of Cyme's civic tradition are largely unknown, but we should notice that together with the portrait of the city's silver coinage, there was also a rarer bronze coinage which shows Cyme in full clasping hands with the goddess Artemis herself, in her familiar guise as huntress-warrior (Plate 4). As a stunning mosaic from south-eastern Turkey now shows us (Plate 5), hunting persisted as a principal Amazon pastime into late antiquity, many centuries after our coin.[36] Presumably the goddess had played a key role in the events concerning the Amazons and the city's creation.[37]

There were also more extreme legends of female violence among Greek women, whose stories resonated with the Amazons in interesting ways. On the Greek island of Lemnos the women murdered their errant menfolk – husbands, fathers, boys. This mass murder was the greatest evil, as Aeschylus had it.[38] As we shall see, this Lemnian tale not only urged the decent treatment of women, but taught the need for proper balance in women's and men's lives between the conflicting priorities of Aphrodite and Artemis, rather as Euripides' *Hippolytus* would do. On Lemnos much of the point of the story was that Greek women could become women warriors too – each Greek woman might have an inner Amazon. As Jason and his Argonauts sailed into the island, these Greek women gathered in the armour of their murdered men to face the newcomers in battle. And yet they

---

[36] The mosaic was found recently outside Urfa (ancient Edessa), and is provisionally dated around AD 500 or so: see Dunbabin 2016, 382–6 (on Achilles and probably Penthesilea there, too); Loosley 2018 on four hunting Amazons shown in the same villa complex.

[37] See pp. 186–87   [38] See p. 213.

soon went to bed with the men (in some versions there was no battle at all) and offered them the lands and homes that had once belonged to their husbands. With some reluctance the Argonauts left anyway, with the women impregnated and a kind of balance achieved. However, while Greek women likely had their own perspectives on Amazons, that is not necessarily to say that their views were at odds with those of their men and their society at large. Our sources give no clear suggestion of any such tension.

Ancient and Modern

The appeal of Amazons for feminist movements – and others – is obvious enough in general terms.[39] Themes of female emancipation and empowerment are plain to see in their story. Deeper thought tends to complicate the picture, even so. Failure, death, and destruction are far more prominent in Amazon tales than their capacity for struggle and independence. Meanwhile, some might also question the desirability of male-style warriors as feminist models. Perhaps it is all to the good, therefore, that we can point out the many additional qualities of Amazons in Greek myth, for example their sharp intelligence and subtlety in word as well as action. All this has been overshadowed in much modern scholarship by notions of Amazons as alien brutes, which they very rarely are in ancient texts and art.

The pervasive and complex role of Amazons in Greek culture and history should have been enough to forestall

[39] Eller 2011 traces their intellectual history through Bachofen and beyond; cf. Stewart 1995.

anxieties and dissatisfaction that Amazons are a – very powerful – myth. To insist that Amazons must be real is a disabling error for several reasons. First, there can be no dispute that women can be militarily effective. Even in antiquity Plato mooted the advantages of bringing women into the Greek military and in battle action. We do not need 'real' Amazons to prove the point. Second, the demand for living Amazons has encouraged the misuse of archaeology.[40] It will suffice to observe that weapons in a woman's burial (where that can be shown for sure)[41] do not mean that she was a warrior in life. For weapons clearly had symbolic significance, as we sometimes hear in ancient texts – evoking the supernatural, local power, or even male connections. Third, there is a species of orientalism at work in these modern assertions too, since they invoke fantasies of the distant east.[42] Even if a people of 'warrior women' are one day discovered in the regions of Siberia and China (where modern writers tend to claim their reality among pastoralists and nomads), what possible relevance might they have for the ancient Greek myth of Amazons? The myth was already embedded in Homeric epic and elsewhere at the outset of the archaic period, well before Greeks can be

---

[40] On methodology, see Sofaer 2006; Stutz and Tarlow 2013. On the north Pontic material, see Kramberger 2017, with Hasanov 2018, who includes some Caucasian material, and observes modern reliance on ancient Greek texts (usually misinterpreted) and/or misrepresented, with the absence of armed females from the art of the broad region, while powerful women (goddesses?) often feature there.

[41] At the scholarly end of such claims, see e.g. Fialko 2017, tagging any woman with a weapon as an Amazon, whatever her likely ethnicity or burial-location.

[42] At its extreme, Penrose 2016, considering his fantasies to be postcolonialism.

imagined to have had significant (or any) contact with these distant regions. Fourth among the objections to the attempt to make the ancient Amazons 'real' is the outrageous misuse of Greek texts, and especially Herodotus' report of a story about the origin of the Sauromatians, who were located to the east of the lower Don in southern Russia. The story has a great deal to tell us about the Amazon myth, but it says nothing about Amazons living in the area.[43] In fact, as we shall see, this is an ancient attempt to explain why the women of the Sauromatians enjoy hunting and even fighting, like and with their menfolk. They had inherited these habits from a group of shipwrecked Amazons, the story tells us. But these women are not themselves Amazons; they are simply the imagined descendants of refugee Amazons who are long dead – another example of Amazon-disaster as a stimulus to cultural innovation.

The reality of Amazon myth is to be found not in the far-off soil of Siberia or the like, but in its expression and agency within the Greek culture that created it. It is myth about strong women with a rich mix of capacities – war, of course, but also love; force but also intellect; creation as well as destruction, including the construction of cities, sanctuaries, and more. The heavens and Hades are never far away. It is usually through death that Amazons achieve most and are made monuments, either in their own right or on the tombs and other monuments of Greeks, as we saw with the extraordinary Mausoleum at Halicarnassus. Amazon combat may well have appeared on Greek tombs already in the seventh century BC, perhaps exemplified by

---

[43] Cf. Ivantchik 2013.

a terracotta plaque which decorated the surface of a tomb in Attica which belongs to the period.[44] These special young women almost never proceed to marriage and the battles of birthing and motherhood, but in death they leave a varied progeny across much of Greek culture, society, and politics, as this book will show.

[44] Richter 1942 made a plausible case for that, but much depends on slight epigraphic remains that we struggle to understand; cf. Bothmer 1957, no. 3. We see Achilles, but not his opponent, who may or may not be an Amazon (Penthesilea?), nor the fallen warrior, from whom only a foot has survived.

2

Amazons in Battle

Weapons, Mind, and Body

~

Amazons are the daughters of Ares, the war-god. Their ability in battle is key to their myth, setting them apart from other women. While Ares had very many sons, his only daughters were the Amazons, exceptional in their militarism[1] – a whole society of females, whose only real choice was to become warriors. In the warring world of antiquity – real and imagined – no society could survive independently unless it could defend itself in battle. Otherwise, death, subjection, or enslavement were to be expected. Crucially, Ares' paternity did not make Amazons immortal, any more than most children of the gods. Although we glimpse Amazons at rest, and even in peace, their stories and images usually place them on the battlefield or close by – nursing tasteful wounds that hint at the grim realities of violence. Their female anatomy is always a key concern, their bodies on display. We begin to see their physical similarity to other women, primarily those of the Greek culture that imagined them – but these are young, exercised bodies, not much like most such women, whose athletic activities were marginal.[2] Amazon lifestyles were unlike the experience of Greek females, as their bodies showed, but they too were females, and in their physical prime. For they enjoyed the hunt, and prepared for battle, in

---

[1] Unless we count also the goddess Roma: Bowra 1957.   [2] Kyle 2014.

a youth from which violent death would soon release them. Their designer wounds[3] and alluring deaths attract the male gaze, for which their bodies are laid quite bare. This is the context for Amazons shown battling in floating dresses or mini-skirts (Plates 5, 6, 7, 11, 22, and more), even if their wardrobes contain other outfits, at times, more practical for fighting.[4] Older Amazon bodies, perhaps scarred by battle, are nowhere to be seen. Instead we have the Amazon tomb.

These are women warriors of exceptional qualities, characterised as ripe not only for battle, but also for sex, marriage, and motherhood – or so it seemed. Yet their independent society and martial abilities (mental as well as physical) created most of the distance that divided them from the finest women of Greek culture, whose closeted and controlled lives did not anticipate the battlefield. Helen of Troy was never going to take up weapons, beyond the very special weapons with which she was born. Amazons were not Greek women, of course – exoticism and fame further enhanced their charms for many. The powerful attraction of Amazons for Greek and other men is a recurrent theme of Amazon myth. We must be clear that battle-readiness did not make Amazons less alluring to the men of ancient Greece – very much the contrary, while Amazons themselves were often characterised as being as ready for sex with men as they were to do battle with them. Amazons were a myth for men, primarily, so that we should not be surprised to see a strong sexual atmosphere around their battles with Greek men, although (and because) such battles were dangerous. These were conquests for heroes.

---

[3] Ridgway 1965 surveys the theme in Greek art, contextualising wounded Amazons.
[4] Veness 2002.

For heroes went to fight Amazons precisely because they were a challenge on multiple levels – a worthy opponent, a special conquest that might transform a man into a hero. It was a short step from battle to bed and breeding, and from formal conflict and victory in battle to the informal conflict and conquest of relationships between men and women. In this context, too, Amazons provided a female collective to meet and match the collective male culture that was centred in Greek society around the gymnasium and symposium. The prime male figure there was Heracles, whose expedition of virile youths would – it was claimed – bring an end to the Amazon community of nubile virgins at Themiscyra, and scatter its parts near and far. The Amazon lifestyle must be replaced by forms of marriage, but there would also be Amazon victories in the consequent creations of this extraordinary Amazon diaspora – most obviously, the cults, cities, and tombs that followed.

A capacity for battle distinguished Amazons, but in many ways Greek women could battle too – and not only in a metaphorical sense. Athenian drama, in particular, brought many a resilient and dangerous female on stage, with or without a miasma of war – Clytaemnestra, Hecuba, Medea, and more. There was also the principal tale of Greek 'Amazons' – the militant women of Lemnos, who killed their men, created an all-female state, and made ready for battle in its defence.[5] In fact, there was a scatter of Amazonian women among Greeks, sometimes even on the battlefield. Taken together, this range of viragos and heroines demonstrate that the contrast between Amazons

---

[5] Chapter 9.

and Greek women is less stark than usually acknowledged. Amazons are foreigners – barbarians, if you will – and yet they are far from alien to the Greeks, who created and made so much of them. Among the divine, Amazons strongly resemble the Greek goddess to whom they are most devoted – Artemis herself, and the female deities associated with her – Thracian Bendis, for example.[6] She too is a mistress of the bow and arrow, mistress too of the wilds and the hunt, and mistress too of the animals she could protect, kill, or ride – from bull to flying griffin. She brings her twin with her – Apollo. For her brother is seldom far away, himself also an archer and builder, his archaic temples bedecked with Amazons. Among mythical mortals, there were also exceptional females in Artemis' mould.

A spectacular case is Atalanta, the Arcadian princess, herself a deadly challenge for amorous youths. As myth has it, she outdid the greatest warriors of her day in making the first strike on the massive Calydonian boar.[7] She was first to draw blood, though the mighty beast would not die easily. This was the greatest of heroic hunts, retold in poetry, painting, and stone. Like Artemis and the Amazons her lifestyle was far removed from the usual experience of a Greek girl. She was an untamed creature of the wilds, and all the more desirable for that. She had been brought up by a she-bear and hunters, after her father (hoping for a son) had ordered her to be abandoned in the wilds. She was committed to Artemis and virginity, which she killed to defend. Later, back with her father, she blocked his demand that she marry by insisting on one

[6] Braund 2017. [7] Barringer 1996.

condition – only if, she said, a man could defeat her in a footrace; failures would be executed. Many tried and died, until a devotee of Aphrodite was able to slow her down by dropping golden apples in the race, supplied by Aphrodite. For Atalanta's story is caught in the rivalry of the goddesses, as were the more mundane stories of all Greek girls at the threshold of marriage. But Atalanta was a phenomenon. Her exploits included a wrestling match in which she bested the hero Peleus (Achilles' father, who was also at the Calydonian hunt). She was a match for anyone, as her name declared in Greek, for it evokes weightiness and an equivalence to (in this case) men, rather as the Amazon epithet 'matches for men'.[8] She was Amazon enough. As a woman alone, her path was still harder. She did all she could to join the crew of the Argonauts in quest of the Golden Fleece. Accounts vary, but in our fullest version Jason turned her down.[9] There was no doubt about her abilities, which would make her a great asset. But she was just too alluring, and perhaps too good. She would divide and disturb the all-male crew on the voyage. Her success against the boar had caused enough mayhem, when some of the men resented the award of its huge hide to a woman. All this, and a Greek female – indeed, an Arcadian, arguably the oldest people among the Greeks.[10] Amazons were a match for men (*antianeirai*), but Atalanta – as her name announced to Greek-speakers – was simply Matchless.

[8] Cf. Hom. *Iliad* 5.576 (King Pylaemenes of Paphlagonia), described as *atalantos*, here 'alike to Ares'. Atalanta (or in Greek, Atalante) is the grammatically feminine form of the word. She is a match for anyone, including the men among whom she often appears.

[9] Ap. Rhod. 1.768.

[10] See Ní-Mheallaigh 2020. Cf. Blok 1995, 285 on Atalanta and Amazon images.

There were stories too of other Greek women who had
sufficient military prowess to defend their communities.
They were not virgins of the wild like Atalanta and
Artemis, but resembled Athena – more mature women of
courage, who could at least be taken for warriors, despite
their lack of martial training. While Amazonian females
like Atalanta constituted a challenge to normative society
and its roles for women, such women (like Athena) upheld
traditional values. They went into action only in time of
exceptional crisis, and without sustained or specialist training in weapons or tactics – but with daring and courage.
For the battlefield was very much male space in Greek
thought and practice; even Atalanta had not gone quite
that far. Greek women did not appear there – seldom
even in support roles.[11] Aphrodite's venture onto the
battlefield at Troy illustrates the strong Greek sense that
most females were out of place in battle action. This most
feminine of goddesses sustained a wound there, coming to
the battle only to rescue her son from certain death. The
Greek hero Diomedes had broken her immortal flesh, if
only near the wrist. As Homer tells it, he had seen that this
was an immortal out of place in battle – no Athena or
Artemis. The injured goddess fled to find Ares.[12]
Aphrodite might bear weapons (and her son Eros, with
bow and arrows), but her forte lay elsewhere.

At the interface of history and legend, there was also
Telesilla. She came from Argos, where she wrote love
poetry – closer to Aphrodite than to Athena or Artemis, no
doubt. However, she went into emergency action for her

---

[11] Schaps 1982 gathers texts on women digging defences, tending the
wounded, and so on.
[12] Hom. *Iliad* 5.330–51; Stamatopoulou 2017.

city, it was said. With Argos' army destroyed by the Spartans in 494 BC, Telesilla swiftly organised a militia of the stronger women of the city. Her new force drove off the enemy and saved Argos. Her monument was placed in the sanctuary of Aphrodite, in whose sphere lay her poetry. Telesilla was no creature of the wilds. She was a sophisticated urbanite, with no military credentials. Her success was a tribute to her agility of mind as well as her courage. As Pausanias has it (c. AD 170), the Spartans abandoned the battle, because there was no glory in fighting against women – only a bad name. And yet he stresses too that the women had fought bravely, and had not crumbled on hearing the battle-cry of the mighty Spartan army.[13] The story gave credit all round, while no-one was asked to believe that a poetess and her women's militia could actually defeat the best heavy infantry in Greece. A miracle had occurred, and the women had in effect used their gender to achieve victory – clearly, Aphrodite had a hand in these events.

In southern Greece too, we find further traditions of this kind, centred on a brave woman at Tegea in Arcadia (home of Atalanta). She is usually named Marpessa. Her force of women, too, defeated an invading Spartan army in battle, though it was also said that her army contained men. By the Roman period, her supposed shield was displayed in the temple of Athena Alea at Tegea. And her victory was marked by a regular women's festival there. At this festival the women of Tegea honoured the war-god Ares – father of the Amazons, but rarely a recipient of female cult. Marpessa had sacrificed to him after her women's victory, it was said, giving rise to

[13] Paus. 2.20.8–9; Graf 1984; cf. Fabre-Serris and Keith 2015.

these orgiastic celebrations. For this was a highly sexual-
ised affair. Marpessa herself was known also by a name
that evoked a vagina in everyday Greek speech – Choera,
perhaps 'Pussy' (more literally, 'Piggy').[14] Our knowledge
is slight in detail, but the broad nexus of warrior women,
sexual desire, and sexual freedom is clear enough once
more. When women assert their prowess in battle, they
assert forms of freedom, especially from patriarchal control. Male-style freedom might save the city in one way,
but anxiety abided about (im)moral consequences. When
women can win a battle, how can they return to the loom
under male control? Tegea's festival both contained and
expressed that dilemma in carnival.

While Spartan men did not wish to fight Telesilla's
women, nor perhaps Marpessa's, it was said that the
women of Sparta had set out in arms to do battle against
an army from Messene, where their menfolk were busy
staging a siege. A Messenian force had managed to evade
the siege and attack Sparta itself. These warrior women of
Sparta soon drove off the Messenians and saved Sparta in
the absence of their men. However, the Spartan men
returned and mistakenly took their armed women to be
an enemy force. Quickly the women undressed. They
removed their armour and clothes too. The Spartan
men responded with such passion that promiscuous sex
broke out between the two armies of Spartan men and
women. Such was an origin-story for the famous statue of

<hr>

[14] Paus. 8.47–8 with Moggi 2005; Parker 2011, esp. 208–9, comparing the
bawdy atmosphere of another female festival, the Thesmophoria at
Athens and very widely elsewhere. The name Marpessa suggests the act
of seizing or overwhelming. In late texts, we find an Amazon queen
named Marpesia: e.g. Justin 4.1.

armed Aphrodite which stood in Sparta. We have the story largely as a late statement of outraged Christian sensibilities,[15] but the now-familiar nexus recurs – women in battle, freedom, and unbridled sex. Even the restrained Telesilla seems close to Aphrodite – out of place on the field of battle, but very much involved all around it.

Greek warrior women are also to be found in Greek culture – not only Amazon outsiders. These are stories of exceptional women and events – females forced to fight by circumstances, in the absence of their men. By contrast, Amazons were a whole people – all females – whose everyday life centred on the need to fight. However, that strong contrast soon loses much of its force when we take a broader view of why Amazons went to war. They too were said to fight because of need. Their need was not an emergency, because they were permanently without men – the tale was variously told. Accordingly, Greeks who sought to rationalise the myth could easily invoke male absence or expulsion from the Amazon state, rather as the Amazons shipwrecked near the Don, all these women – Amazon and Greek alike – did what they must to survive. Meanwhile, Greeks also regarded some societies as more military than others, for a range of reasons. There were inescapable consequences for the women of these societies. Sparta was the prime example. Ancient Greeks routinely held that the women of Sparta were especially attuned to militarism, perhaps the nearest Greek

---

[15] Lactantius, *Divine Institutes* 1.20 (c. AD 300), with Pirenne-Delforge 1994, 205–8.

women to Amazons, not because their men were weak but because their whole society was imagined as a military undertaking.[16] Geography plays a part, too. Amazons feature in southern Greece, but they are concentrated in the north-eastern Peloponnese, towards Athens. Is it coincidence that our Greek women warriors appear in an area where Amazons seem to have been much less important than in Greece above the Peloponnese? Perhaps we should see these two sets of female warriors as different, but complementary, taking on similar issues of gender and power.

Throughout, as our examples of Greek women and Amazons illustrate, there was a strong view – an assumption, even – that battling women were desirable and desiring. In such stories, when women behaved like men in this way, sexual activity would follow. For these women were not under male control or protection, as Greek society would usually expect and demand. On the contrary, they were in male mode, while the men were only too pleased – so long as free sex was not to become the norm – to threaten social order. War morphed into carnival, fuelled no doubt by the delight of survival and victory. At the same time, sex could also signal peace, and the return to more familiar roles. Our Greek examples here entail the saving of the city and its society, not the creation of a new order. Such conservative women might succeed, whereas the rebellious and deviant Amazons could confirm the social order and male domination only by their defeat.

<hr>

[16] Cartledge 1981.

Female Nature and the Face of Battle

Would real-life Greek women really fight? Thucydides – the hard-headed historian of classical Athens – expresses some surprise that women might actually stand their ground in battle.[17] He reports that women did that on Corcyra (Corfu) when battling from rooftops in civil war there in the 420s. Around the time he wrote, Lysias (an orator of Athens, whose family had come from Syracuse), explaining the Amazons' failure to conquer Theseus' Athens, offers a whole analysis in terms of their female nature. That nature is not suited to proper battle, he declares. These women warriors might beat some men, but they could not stand against the real men of Athens. In Lysias' words:

In the distant past Amazons were daughters of Ares. They lived by the river Thermodon. They alone of the peoples around them had military equipment of iron. And they were the first of all humanity to mount horses, on which they took their opponents by surprise, because they had no experience of cavalry – catching those who fled and escaping those who pursued them. They were thought to be men on account of their fine spirit, rather than women on account of their nature. For they were reckoned more to excel men in spirit than to fall short of them in physique. They ruled many peoples. They had actually enslaved those around them when they heard tell of this land (Attica) and its great renown. By virtue of their substantial reputation and the scale of their ambition, they gathered the most warlike of peoples and marched against this city (Athens). But when they encountered good men, they gained spirits like to their nature and acquired a reputation opposite to their earlier one. They were understood to be women through their hazards, not their bodies. And they – exceptionally – had no

---

[17] Further, Kearns 1990.

opportunity to learn from their mistakes and take better counsel in the future. Nor to go back home, and announce their misfortune and the valour of our ancestors. For, they died here and paid the penalty for their lack of reason. So they made the memory of this city immortal for its valour, while they made their homeland nameless, because of their disaster here. So, having unjustly desired the homeland of others, they justly lost their own.

(Lysias, 2.3–6)[18]

Lysias traces Amazon success to a mental strength that outweighed their physical disadvantages as females. He offers no direct explanation for that strength, but implies that the cause was Ares' paternity. Their success was bolstered by iron weaponry and the innovation of cavalry, again perhaps with Ares' support. Puffed up by success, ambitious, and ignorant, they sought to add Athens to their empire. Crucially, says Lysias, they now faced real men, not the pushovers of Asia Minor. That encounter broke their male-like mentality, so that they became women in mind and body alike. Their imperialism brought them disaster – a great theme in Lysias' day, not only around Amazons.[19] In sum, Athenian ancestors emerge with pride. They had inflicted a just defeat on unjust attackers, who had no moral case.[20] The deviance inherent in these masculine females had been expunged totally, for the Amazons died at Athens – even if that was not the general view of their history. Lysias claims Heracles' victory at Themiscyra for Theseus and his Athenians. He also evades the Spartan problem against

[18] Further, Roisman 2005. On early cavalry, Aristotle, *Pol.* 1289b.
[19] Recurrent in Herodotus' *Histories* and very much Athens' own experience with defeat in 404 BC.
[20] Lysias ducks Athenian faults: see p. 65.

Telesilla and her army of women. On his formulation there was indeed glory in defeating women in battle. In addition to the larger ethical issues he stresses, the Amazon army also contained – in this version – male allies from the strongest peoples available to the Amazons.[21]

The nearest we get to a female view on such talk is Medea's powerful comparison of battle with child-bearing – where women were warriors in a different way. While we have no hard statistics, death was all too likely an outcome for women in labour. Away from the battlefield of men, they nevertheless faced real danger, spilled blood, and died in childbirth. As Medea declares to the women of Corinth in Euripides' tragic *Medea*, 'Men say that we women live a life without danger in our homes, whereas they battle with the spear. But they are wrong. I would prefer to stand with my shield three times rather than give birth once'. Of course her words were written by the male playwright, but he strikes a convincing note.[22] A native of Colchis, there is a suggestion of the (neighbouring) Amazon about her, as her gory biography confirms. She is by no means a typical woman – the ever-resourceful granddaughter of the Sun himself. And she will soon kill her own children. But Euripides' words express a debate that seems realistic enough, including this response to male claims to bravery. Euripides will return to much the same theme elsewhere.[23] Another debate might also be had: Amazons usually died on the battlefield, but did that make them braver than birthing mothers? And what then of Lysias' notion of 'female nature'?

---

[21] Isocrates involves Scythians: see pp. 197–99.   [22] *Medea* 248–51.
[23] Notably at the end of his *Iphigenia in Tauris* where women's blood in childbirth matches male bloodletting.

Amazon Weapons

Amazons were a favourite theme of Greek artists, for women with weapons made startling images even without elaboration. Their visual potential was enormous – imaginary yet real, exotic yet familiar, sexy yet historical, long dead yet current and so alive.[24] Amazons were especially popular with the painters of Athenian vases, where we regularly see them with weapons – in battle or close to action. For the most part, their weapons were standard enough from a Greek perspective, albeit with a measure of idiosyncrasy. They had no magical weapons to give them an edge, though Lysias might claim (unusually) that they were early in the use of iron and horses.[25] Their equipment ranges across the gamut of military roles, at least on land, from the duelling heroes of Homeric style through the heavy armour of the hoplites (the hard core of most Greek forces)[26] to the light troops who fought as archers, javelineers, and the like, as well as the important cavalry that Lysias mentions. Amazons might fill any role in the familiar forces of a Greek army. However, the majority of images depicted Amazons as cavalry or light troops. As such they offered much more visual interest, and were clearly female. Where Amazons are more heavily armoured, artists strive to distinguish them from male warriors – for example, with enough pale-coloured flesh on show, as if they had lived the indoor lives of Greek young ladies, shielded from the sun.

[24] Veness 2002.
[25] Iron and violence were variously located in the Black Sea: e.g. Phillips 1968; Aesch. *Seven* 941–6.
[26] Van Wees 2013.

Meanwhile, without quite the same visual imperative, Amazons in ancient literature also tended to be cavalry or light troops. For Greeks usually imagined Amazons as armed and equipped in ways more thinkable of real women warriors. Of course, a Homeric-style duel might be imagined, where a very special Amazon (Queen Penthesilea, most obviously) might fight in heroic style, with adaptations to reveal a female identity inside the armour.[27] However, the heavy infantry – the hoplites – fought as a massed scrum, where weight and size mattered hugely. The boastful men of Medea's speech are precisely hoplites, with a great shield and heavy thrusting spear and sword – the most male of warriors. Amazons might be hoplites, as also Telesilla and the rest, or the Lemnian women who faced Jason's Argonauts.[28] But the idea was harder and artistic benefits less readily available – though hoplites best suited the literary trope of discovery through the stripping of Amazon bodies. As light troops and cavalry, Amazon flesh was already on show enough, even if the Amazon girls offered to Alexander were unusually naked.[29]

As light infantry and cavalry, Amazons would battle from a distance, though the small space on vases made that hard to show. Fine for women and non-Greeks perhaps, but battle from afar was not the heroic norm.[30] An archaic tradition from Euboea is helpful. During war there, the cities of Chalcis and Eretria made a formal agreement, it was said, about the battle they must fight for the valuable plain between them.[31] There were to be

[27] On Exekias, see p. 65.   [28] Chapter 9.   [29] See p. 241.
[30] Lissarrague 1990.   [31] Krentz 2002.

52

no distance weapons – no arrows, no javelins or the like. This was to be a hoplite scrum between gentlemen. For distance weapons could suggest cowardice. Euripides' *Heracles* shows that even Heracles might be denounced on that basis, since he sometimes used a bow. Real man's courage was tested only at close quarters, face to face in the press of battle.[32] In Homer the unsatisfactory Paris duly favoured the bow. When he wounded heroic Diomedes, he used his bow from a safe distance. Injured, Diomedes wishes for a proper fight, with the spear. Tellingly, he declares that it feels as if he has been struck by 'a woman or a witless child'. The wound was serious, but archery in battle was prone to implications of woman-ishness among manly men. Of course, archers need not be diminished in this way – no disgrace in itself. But where pitched battle was underway there was little glory in the bow. However, as wounded Diomedes indicates, archery is fine for women. When Plato mooted the training of women as a force of archers for the city, he immediately recalled Amazons, imaginary or not. If women were to fight, archery was an obvious path for them. There was a coherence in Greek notions of Amazons as archers, on foot or horse. Heroes might even need archery to deal with them, like Homer's Bellerophon.[33] Accordingly, the most famous man killed by Amazon weaponry was Sthenelus, a companion of Heracles, killed by an Amazon arrow shot from around Themiscyra when he was already at sea.[34]

---

[32] Reguero 2019.

[33] *Iliad* 6.184–6 with Ziskowski 2014 on the importance of his killing the Chimaera in early archaic Corinth.

[34] Ap. Rhod. 2.911–22; Borowski 2021, 86.

Amazon archers can look rather Scythian, with pointed caps and composite bow, for such were archers in art – including Trojan Paris.[35] Even in close-quarters fighting we are invited to imagine Amazons with the weapons of long distance. In the siege of Athens by the Itonian Gate, for example, we are told that Molpadia the Amazon killed Theseus' Amazon wife with an arrow or a javelin. Amazons show less taste for the sword – wielded by Athenian Theseus as he cut down Molpadia in her moment of glory.[36] Amazons sometimes appear with swords, especially the slashing sabre that suited cavalry – even at the Itonian Gate, in an area now dominated by the remains of the temple of Olympian Zeus (Plate 7). However, when an Amazon displays sword skills, she may well be dancing – perhaps the 'sword dance for Artemis', whether danced by Amazons or other (real) women.[37] The phallic nature of the sword (especially the stabbing weapon) may account for its relative rarity in Amazon hands.[38] The spear is more ambivalent, insofar as in Homeric battle it may be thrown as a javelin as well as thrust into the enemy. Penthesilea appears with such a spear on vases. More ordinary Amazons may have spears as part of hoplite kit, but they are more usually throwers of javelins. Much depended on the painter's fancy.

While most of the vase images are rather formulaic, some suggest a whole story, which viewers are left to imagine for themselves. On occasion the story is known, as with Theseus' abduction of his Amazon on the so-called Croesus vase (Plate 8). But other stories are obscure

---

[35] Ivantchik 2006.   [36] See Chapter 8.   [37] Further, Bron 1996.
[38] Greeks were well aware: Ar. *Lys.* 632 with Henderson 1991, 122.

to us, as with the melancholy Amazon who leads her horse past a tomb (if that is what it is) on a vase now in Ferrara (Plate 9). On a red-figure lekythos of the mid fifth-century BC (now in the Louvre), we see an Amazon kneeling at an altar. A prominent palm tree at the altar shows this to be an altar of Artemis. The Amazon's exotic costume includes a panther skin, which may always raise thoughts of Dionysus. Her bow and quiver hang close above her, ensuring that we identify her ethnicity – an Amazon, perhaps seeking refuge after escaping a battle, her familiar archer's gear laid aside, but not abandoned.[39] In effect there are two female archers in this image, the Amazon herself and the goddess of the altar. A host of evocations follow, not least about the favourite theme of Amazon battle and likely defeat. These images illustrate nicely how weapons and related features were key to artistic choices and the making of Amazon images. While the implied narratives here may lie beyond our knowledge, these images display a strong coherence with the literary accounts of Amazons and their equipment.

The Amazon axe deserves special attention – an idiosyncratic favourite of Amazons in a range of forms and under various names.[40] The Amazon axe was usually a light weapon, but with enormous destructive potential – useful at close quarters for infantry and cavalry. However, it was rather unusual in Greek armies, where it is to be found mostly in the possession of archers and other light troops. Among Greeks otherwise it was considered either a relic from the heroic past or a barbarian weapon of

[39] *ARV*² 663, 2. Louvre, Inv. CA1710; *Getty Museum Journal* 24 (1996) 74, fig. 6.
[40] See LSJ s.v. sagaris.

choice all across Asia and around the Black Sea. Xenophon, listing the gear of a Persian soldier, refers to his axe as 'the sort Amazons have'. He expected his readers to understand that it was light, and not the huge axe more familiar from hunting or household use in Greece.[41] On occasion, however, we may spot an Amazon queen (even Penthesilea herself) doing battle with an axe, which demanded both strength and good fortune in battle with a Greek hoplite.

The axe was not a weapon for the gentleman Greek, despite its occasional appearance in Homer.[42] It suited a savage melee.[43] Vase-painters loved its visual rarity – it recurs in scenes of Amazon battle. It was an emblem of Amazons;[44] after all, axes were in any case a weapon of women in Greek culture. We may recall the axe which (in most versions) Clytaemnestra used on her husband Agamemnon and others. Her lover Aegisthus, for all his faults, at least used a sword. Axes were usual in domestic space, the world of women. Axes suited Amazons all the more because these were barbarian women from a milieu where battle-axes were familiar – more specifically women of Thracian ethnicity, for the axe had a special place in Thrace.[45] Similarly, their crescent shield (or *pelta*) was particularly associated with Thrace, whence light infantry (called peltasts) were said to have emerged.[46] This light shield might come in many forms, but its classic shape was a crescent moon, a further delight for artists on pottery and stone (Plates 10a–b). In the hands of women – indeed the devotees of Artemis – the moon-like shield might evoke also

[41] Xen. *Anab.* 4.4.16.   [42] *Iliad* 13.613: Menelaus wounded by an axe.
[43] *Iliad* 15.711.   [44] For the *labrys*, see p. 161.
[45] Topper 2015; Braund forthcoming.   [46] Best 1969.

female biology,[47] though literary texts are more concerned with its geographical implications. The home of Amazons in Italy seemed destined by its crescent coastline.[48]

Greeks imagined the challenging concept of armed Amazon women with weapons that seemed more appropriate to women of Thrace – even realistic. It may have mattered too that – rather as stoning – there could be an impersonality in launching a shower of arrows against enemy forces. Certainly, Aeschylus stresses distance and impersonality when he makes Apollo compare Agamemnon's death at his wife's hands in his own home with the death he might have found at Troy from a shower of Amazon arrows launched from afar.[49] Amazons appear with equipment that trained young women might be expected to prefer, including the horse. Plato exemplifies that tendency in his airing of the potential value of training women for war. He assumes that they would be archers – they would fight from a distance, and with a weapon that needed no special physique beyond that of the everyday young woman, once trained in the use of the bow.[50] He shows no concern about their mental toughness, but these women would not be expected to fight in the hoplite scrum. He alludes to Amazons but does not include other forms of warfare – not a word about axes or even javelins. He says nothing of cavalry either, though Greeks not only associated girls and horses,[51] but also imagined Amazons as cavalry often enough. Possibly he included female cavalry in his focus on archers – mounted archers. Meanwhile, Greeks

---

[47] See further Ní-Mheallaigh 2020, esp. 26–7; cf. 257 on shields and mirrors.
[48] See p. 136.   [49] *Eum.* 624–8; cf. 685; further, Loraux 1981.
[50] Plato, *Laws* 804e–806b.   [51] Tsantsanoglou 2012.

also acknowledged the Thracian origins of Amazons by giving them the *pelta*, the axe, and their other light weapons. But they stopped short of making them stone-throwers or slingers – roles not grand enough for the daughters of Ares. There is scant mention of a battle-belt either, aside from the special belt that Heracles would take from their queen. To that extent ancient Greeks maintained a sense of grandeur among Amazons, who retain considerable respect and admiration even in defeat. While artists take advantage of opportunities to show Amazons in scanty clothing, there was a heroism in nudity in classical art, for men and perhaps women too. Accordingly, when we see a largely nude male warrior driving his spear into a fallen Amazon, we must contrast her clothing with that usual among the covered women of the Greeks, but must also reflect on the cruder scenes that the artist could have chosen to depict (Plates 11, 12, and 13). Presumably, the artist's choice matches in this regard the sensibilities of his customers.

Bodies, Wounds, and Mutilated Breasts

Equipment aside, there was an obvious physical element to the fighting Amazon – her body. But Amazon bodies were well exercised. In battle they might be mistaken for male warriors. They might be concealed in hoplite gear, or look like male archers and the like, clad in the skin-tight outfits that suited archery, where obstructive clothing was a hazard on foot and horse. Ancient confusions are reflected in our own difficulties in being sure that Amazons painted on vases are not in fact young males. Even where the painter has added a male name, the modern scholar may be led astray by the image of a feminine lad.[52] In fact we may wonder whether the artist is blurring distinctions on purpose, or prefers the viewer to decide. Ancient writers relish such confusions, which formed part of a wider taste for strategic errors and deceptions in war. Often enough they write of Amazon bodies discovered among the dead in surprise and consternation. To strip corpses after battle was a familiar practice, from Homer onwards. However, the stripping of dead Amazons gave a sexual twist to the routine – revelation, shock, prurience, and a sense of necrophilia. The pale body of the dead Amazon contrasted starkly with bodies of sunburnt males – an exceptional specimen, alluring to the male gaze and perhaps more besides. Already in Herodotus the stripping of Amazons inspires a plan to breed.[53] We are not told much about the archaic *Aethiopis'* treatment of Penthesilea's death, but her body was surely stripped. A much later version expresses the impact when Achilles removed only her helmet. The men around him were plunged into thoughts of sex, while Achilles was overwhelmed with a disturbing passion.[54] We see enough of that in Exekias' famous treatment of the scene in the sixth century BC.[55] The full power of Amazons comes to light as their armour and clothes are removed. They wield not only the weapons of the battlefield – they could deploy too the arms of Aphrodite, their father's lover. Myth made them devotees of Artemis, but the rival goddesses are never far apart.

---

[52] Barringer 2004 takes a painted Toxaris to be female on such grounds, though she knows the name is always male.
[53] Hdt. 4.111.   [54] Quintus of Smyrna, 1.891–922; Borowski 2021.
[55] Brilliantly discussed by Moignard 2015, ch. 3.

The wounded Amazon featured too in male desire for Amazon bodies.[56] The Amazon challenge had been met – conquest in every sense. Images of dying Amazons were necrophilia in the making, complete with claims to heroism for male and female alike. At the same time, the Amazon fulfilled her destiny – violent death in beautiful youth. The wound – the penetration of her body – could only carry an erotic charge, especially in a Greek culture which expressed military victory over men in sexual terms, too.[57] Their usual virginity had been ended, as their very lives – pierced by male partners in war, sanctioned on the field of battle, where – arguably – the maiden should never have ventured in any case. Meanwhile, images of dying Amazons also address their manner of death – like men, like women, or something rarer. As foreigners, dying Amazons shared much with other dying barbarians – notably the warrior Gauls, seen at their best in death.[58] Different ways of life opened doors to different ways of death. Amazons must die both as individuals and as a people with a challenging lifestyle. In that sense, the dying Amazon was a metonymy for her people's demise.

Body modification never features in tales of stripped Amazons, where there is silence too on tattoos – for Amazons had none, despite modern writers' quest for tattooed Amazons. Occasional notions of breast removal or reduction are always aired at a general level, but no individual Amazon ever appears with the results of such a practice, either in texts or in art.[59] These notions arise from a sense that the female body might usefully be

[56] Bol 1998.   [57] Davidson 2000.   [58] Braund 2022.
[59] Cf. Cohen 1997.

modified to enable an Amazon lifestyle. In essence, this was a claim that female biology was naturally unsuited to warfare, even at a distance. And there is discouragement here to young women who might find such a lifestyle attractive. Some Greek men clearly saw the breast as obstructing the use of weapons and/or limiting the potential strength of the arm and shoulder. At Sinope, women posing as soldiers, and sporting kitchen equipment as weapons to fool the enemy, were instructed not to throw anything, on the grounds that their action would reveal their female identity.[60] These were everyday females of the city, as the story goes. However, modern athletics demonstrate the basic nonsense in claims that breasts need reduction or removal. Training was enough, while archers and javelineers might employ the chest guards used by modern archers, irrespective of gender – much better than high-risk surgery in childhood![61]

Amazons neither needed nor endured body modification. Again and again, they appear as young women who are the same as their Greek counterparts in biological terms, except that they represent especially strong, trained, and alluring examples of womanhood – the offspring of a god, after all. They carry weapons, but these are weapons considered appropriate for women, even a closeted Greek woman. The Amazons mattered in Greek culture precisely because these exceptional women resembled the real women of Greece biologically – physically and probably psychologically, too – we hear very little about any difference between Amazon minds and the minds of everyday Greek women, except such inferences as can be drawn

[60] Braund 2010.   [61] See p. 65 on motherhood.

61

from their respective lifestyles. And biology may trump lifestyle. It is intriguing that archaic vase-painters gave a white colour to female flesh, with no regard to distinction between the closeted women of Greek culture and the outdoor women of the Amazons, whose skin should hardly be so pale.

3

Sex and Motherhood

～

In the male imaginations of ancient Greece, Amazons are sexy. It helped that their freedom from male control/ protection made them available – if dangerous. Their clothes enhance that sexuality and sense of availability – flimsy and revealing, skin-tight, or even trousers, not the loose drapery that usually concealed Greek girls. And Amazons did not wear veils in public, as grander Greek ladies might.[1] Amazons can protect themselves, of course, but that might also be attractive to the ancient Greek male, the aspiring hero. Their fleeting lives are stuck in this stage of life, on the threshold of marriage. They are seldom children and never aged. Exceptionally, Greek women might be similar. The mythical Atalanta of Arcadia exemplifies the type, as a string of fine young men risk and lose their lives in the hope of winning her hand. And let us not forget that Amazons tend also to be clever, with the brains that *hetaerae* deployed for success with men – often enough Thracian females, like the famous Rhodope. We have seen that Thracian women were sassy, perhaps all the more appealing to men when set beside the rather dreary ideal of Greek womanhood. Amid such attitudes there was a short distance between battle and bed. We must remember that Amazons were overwhelmingly a myth of men. Male drinking-parties

[1] Llewellyn-Jones 2003.

63

routinely featured their images, as on the pottery that has survived, portraying an exotic allure and alluding to challenges overcome by the likes of Heracles and Theseus, their heroes. With these images came flesh-and-blood females, no less available for male consumption and entertainment of every kind. It was not only public buildings and Amazon battles that occupied the men of Athens and elsewhere.

In *Lysistrata*, Aristophanes has his men revel in the sexuality of women – riding on horseback like Amazons, and so riding on them, straddled in sex on top of their man. They reference an actual painting of an Amazon astride a horse – sober enough, one might think. The men say:

> Woman is especially good with horses, and bestriding them,
> And she won't slip off at the gallop. Look at the Amazons,
> That Mikon painted – mounted up and grappling with the men.
>
> (Ar. *Lys.* 677–9)

As the men confront the rebellious Greek women in this scene, they wish to throw off their clothes. Nudity will make them heroic in subduing these uppity females, and also ready to complete their conquest through sex. Amazons are very rare in Aristophanic comedy,[2] but here Aristophanes has his men express in all vigour the sense that troublesome females need to be bedded. Typically enough, his carnivalesque comedy takes full advantage of the idea that horsewomen are very proficient riders and keep their saddles – whether mounted astride

---

[2] This is the only time they are named in his extant plays, probably alluding to Mikon's painting in the Stoa Poikile: p. 205. On Amazon names in this play, see p. 154.

a horse or astride a man. A few years after the bawdy humour of *Lysistrata*, in the formal context of his *Funeral Oration* the orator Lysias tones down much the same view, referring to Athens' handling of the Amazon army that had come to lay siege to the city – facing real men (Athenians), Amazons discovered their female natures.[3] His gentler formulation helps to illustrate how the rampant urges of Aristophanes' men might be channelled into the sober sculpture of a grand public building, or a funeral monument of the wealthy. From fourth-century Athens we have a rather neglected example, part of a larger scene that has not survived (Plate 14). A Greek warrior stands naked, but in battle – his shield and fine helmet (part of a hoplite's armour, usually) highlight his heroic nudity as he takes on Amazons in their flimsy dresses. The eroticism is palpable, and heroic – the scene evokes multiple responses that might commemorate the dead and show the prospects of immortal fame. The riotous comedy of Aristophanes has shown Athenian men responding to Amazon images in overtly sexual ways, even taking inspiration from painting that seems not to aspire to be pornography much or at all.

Meanwhile, sex might mean marriage and motherhood. While Amazon sex might avoid complications, Amazon marriage and motherhood were fraught with problems. Already, deep in the archaic period, there was a powerful sexual element in Achilles' killing of the Amazon Queen Penthesilea, in text and art. Exekias managed to express that in his most famous painting, on a vase deposited in a burial at Vulci in Etruria (Plate 12). We saw the strong

---

[3] So Lysias, quoted p. 48.

sexual dimension as the armoured warrior pierced the sprawling Amazon with his spear, fixing his captivated gaze on the face and eyes of his now-defenceless opponent. While poets wrote of his sudden love, the many-sided sexual passion in their poses is no less clear than the one-sided nature of their physical duel.

In the fifth century we start to meet the notion that Amazons must kill an enemy in battle before sex. The law is often mentioned thereafter with a variety of different details – how many enemies? was sex otherwise illegal or was it only marriage? and what of cohabitation? These details matter much less, however, than the association of sex and battle – again. The law is also singular, for otherwise we hear almost nothing of the laws under which Amazons lived. Clearly, the bed–battle association had a special importance for Greeks.[4] Any law tended to suggest an orderly society, as did the existence of Amazon queens, but theirs was a barbarity in this particular measure. This legislation foregrounded the two issues in Amazon myth that mattered most to Greek men – battle and bed. Some might also see a motivation in this law – these women must fight and fight well precisely in order to have sex and the families which might seem more 'natural' female desires. Since Amazon blood is also a recurrent theme, some might also have noted that under this law it would be the male enemy who would shed first blood in putting an end to Amazon virginity, not the virgin herself. Only a few Greeks might reflect on the value of such a law – selecting for battle-qualities in reproduction, but also placing an unwelcome limit on

---

[4] The law might feature in the Theseus story, see Chapter 8.

numbers of children. Finally, we should note that even Amazons maintained some place for Aphrodite, who will have demanded a measure of respect even from the adherents of Artemis.

We have seen how myth about Amazons left many a question unanswered in its focus on key issues. Until the late fourth century BC, at least, Amazons were an *ethnos* – a people – without an ethnography. They were a people whose ways were largely unexplored and uncharted. The nearest we get to earlier Greek concern with such themes is a short section of a medical text in the Hippocratic tradition, dated around 425, like the *Histories* of Herodotus. But this was no ethnography. Rather it signals the existence of lost tales which the author had read or at least heard. We glimpse ethnography, perhaps, but the focus is very much on how Amazon tales – marked as myth – might have a bearing on medical matters in actual experience and practice. We see inchoate concern with the means by which female rule could have persisted among Amazons, specifically through attention to joints in children. It is in that context that we glimpse the mutilation of male babies (awful, but rational too) and the work they might do in later life in a state run by women. Shocking enough, but we must set this in the context of the abuse and abandonment of infants (especially females) that was almost routine in the ancient Greek world, together with the appalling rates of infant mortality with which the ancients had to cope.

For the Hippocratic *On Joints* includes a story that Amazon mothers deliberately cripple their male babies – though without commitment to belief in the notion. The Amazon mothers did so – supposedly – with a view to the future. Their purpose was to hinder adult males, who might otherwise take over the state. The disabled males were given sedentary tasks, which also lacked prestige. Cruelty is unusual in accounts of Amazons at this date. But this is not mindless brutality. Nor is it rage against men. Rather this is a way – albeit horrendous – to secure female power in the Amazon state. There were few other options, all of which arise in later accounts – male babies might be given away, abandoned, or simply killed. However, the idea that mothers might routinely kill their male babies was particularly hard for Greek society to digest, so that we find it only late – not in Hellanicus (c. 400 BC) as often claimed.[5] Of marginal relevance too is a phrase attributed to the archaic poet Mimnermus of Smyrna, which is – much later – put in the mouth of a joshing Amazon in Scythia, 'the lame mate best' – apparently a proverb, of no special relevance to Amazons.[6] We are not told that Mimnermus wrote about Amazons.[7] But the Hippocratic text is clear as far as it goes:

Some tell mythical tales that the Amazons dislocate the limbs of their own babies of the male sex as soon as they are born – some dislocate the knees, others the hips, so that – as if – the males would become lame and not plot against the females. They use them in handicrafts, for working leather or bronze or another seated occupation. If this is true at all, I do not know, but I do

---

[5] It is especially regrettable, therefore, that the practice has been inserted into Hellanicus' writings by modern scholars. They have misread a Byzantine text (Tzetzes), which mentions both Hellanicus and Amazon infanticide, but does not attribute the latter to the former.

[6] She is named Antianeira: Pausanias, *Collection of Attic Names*, 149 seems the earliest reference, around the second century AD.

[7] On lameness and tyrants, Ogden 1997.

know that such would be the outcome if someone were dis-
located as a baby.

(*On Joints* 53)[8]

The author's primary concern is medical – dislocation of
joints in babies and its consequences. Amazons seem only to
sugar the pill for readers – something of a Hippocratic
habit.[9] While our author considers the supposed Amazon
practice to be medically plausible, he shows scant interest in
its truth or fiction otherwise. However, by mentioning
accounts of Amazon abuse of male babies as a strategy to
maintain female dominance in their society, this medical
text gives a valuable warning that the wilder fantasies of later
times already had some precedents by the end of the fifth
century BC. We are left to wonder what else these mythical
accounts had to say, for example about sex and reproduction. Are we to imagine that the disabled workers were also
used for sex by the dominant women? Certainly, there were
stories enough about powerful women using men for sex –
Omphale or Semiramis, for example.[10] Elsewhere in the
Black Sea Greeks told similar tales of Scythians, whose
stories sometimes re-emerge in accounts of Amazons. In
this instance, we must observe that Herodotus writes that
Scythians blinded their slaves and put them to sedentary
work with milk. When Scythian males leave on long campaign their women have sex with these slaves. When the
Scythian warriors eventually come home they are faced with
a servile army. Briefly, the abandoned Scythian women had

---

[8] Compare the blinded slaves of the Scythians at Hdt. 4.2, whose
drudgery does not require movement.

[9] Cf. Galen 28.148 on Hippocratic discussion of women and
ambidexterity.

[10] Pembroke 1967.

taken an Amazonian path, we might say, as far as could be from the Homeric role model of ever-patient Penelope. However, the returning Scythian warriors soon put an end to that, relieving Greek male anxiety that their women might have sex with slaves and take over.

The whole idea of motherhood was very awkward in Amazon myth. Insofar as Amazons were regularly imagined as nubile virgins, caught at the stage of transition to womanhood, they would cease to be Amazons as soon as they moved across this threshold in life. Myth had dealt with this in a neat nexus of ideas that made reproduction irrelevant. They were born from outside in a supernatural way – daughters of Ares. Their mothers were nymphs, not Amazons. Soon they would die and their people would become extinct. There was no need for reproduction, while laws might be imagined to obstruct it under normal circumstances.

How could Amazon mothers bring up boys – in their own society or anywhere? Only girls were brought up in a more normal way, albeit in militarism. One author 'explains' that Amazons retained one breast for rearing children,[11] though some modern writers have declared – unwisely – that even damage to one breast was a rejection of motherhood. Possibly there had been some such talk before Alexander, but we do not hear it. By and large, these ravings were inspired by the supposed discovery of living Amazons in newly explored parts of the world. However, only the gullible treated them as more than absurdities. More serious souls (and probably Alexander himself) met these tales with amusement or irritation.

[11] Apollodorus 2.5.9.

Around AD 25 the Greek geographer Strabo complained bitterly that improved knowledge of the wider world should have had the opposite effect and quashed all notions of Amazons – old myths and more recent claims together. To Strabo's annoyance, the long-dead Amazons had been brought back to life and were being equipped with sensational ethnography by Diodorus Siculus and his like – with or without some claim to truth. However, his angle on Amazons is not entirely that. For him the more fundamental problem is the implausibility of the whole conception of an all-female state creating an empire and forging on as far as Athens. The old myths were already absurd, but widely supported, while tales around Alexander were a virulent accretion, which was at least a minority concern. 'As to where Amazons are now, few give a view – untested and unbelievable.'[12] Strabo's huge *Geography* incorporates a good deal about Amazons, even so. Evidently, he felt the pressure of tradition to include much that was worthless in his personal view. He could maintain an authorial distance by ascribing a great deal to the accounts of others. But he gives no quarter at all to the lurid nonsense created after Alexander's supposed Amazon adventures – these tales were both unsupported by tradition and absurd in themselves.

In fact, there had long been a problem regarding the children of Amazons. Very few such children are ever mentioned as individuals. Of these, only one has a measure of clear success, a daughter of Penthesilea's nurse, who establishes a queenly line at Caulonia in southern Italy – an exceptional case in an exceptional location,

[12] Str. 11.5.4.

with its own local traditions no doubt. And our first mention of her comes after Alexander.[13] A Byzantine tradition attributes a son to Penthesilea, too.[14] Bizarrely, modern writers tend to name his father as Achilles. Before their duel, one supposes. But our minimal sources do not in fact identify him or anyone else as the father – someone less renowned than the Amazon, we must imagine. At any rate, Penthesilea's son featured in a tale which brought him to Syria. There, he may figure – with the local goddess Derceto (alias Atargatis at times) – as the father of Semiramis. This granddaughter of an Amazon queen grows to become the Graeco-Roman archetype of unchecked female rule and domination. To link Semiramis to Penthesilea made a lot of sense, but it is most unclear when such a connection had first been made among Greeks. The Amazon's son is named as Cayster, also the name of the river that flows from Mt Tmolus near Sardis down to the sea by Ephesus, with multiple evocations of Artemis and Amazons.[15] Perhaps there was a place for Penthesilea's son there, but a significant tale of that kind should have received attention before late antiquity, where its origins more probably lie.[16]

Late antiquity also provides the story of another Amazon's son, again with a riverine connection – a young man called Tanais. He is the son of the Amazon Lysippe ('Horse-looser'), otherwise unknown.[17] His father was a King Berossus, whose name turns thoughts to Syria, where Cayster's story also headed. Whereas the

---

[13] Further p. 134.   [14] Scholiast on *Iliad* 2.461d.   [15] See p. 182.
[16] Etym. Magnum s.v. Kaystros seems to suggest the idea that the river takes its name from that lad.
[17] Ps.-Plut. *On Rivers*, 14.

latter had a child, however, youthful Tanais earned Aphrodite's anger through his revulsion from women and a contempt for marriage. In response, Aphrodite inflicted upon Tanais an overwhelming passion to have sex with his Amazon mother. The appalled youth committed suicide, by leaping into a great river. This had been called the river Amazon, because Amazons bathed in its waters. Now its name was changed to the river Tanais, after the wretched lad – the modern Don. The story survives in a set of similarly extreme tales about rivers, which is hard to date, but is usually located late and in the novelistic tradition. That is probably right, but we know that Aphrodite Ourania, the goddess of Ascalon, was indeed important at historical Tanais, and it remains possible that the story was told there in some form, part of an accumulation of Amazon stories around the area and its Sauromatians.[18] We are left to wonder whether a similar story was told of Cayster – had he also thrown himself into the river that bore his name? Certainly, his story entailed a lot of death – his daughter had been left to die by her mother, and the mother herself – Derceto – had attempted suicide in a lake near Ascalon, where she had been turned into a goddess.[19]

These boys of Amazon mothers were disastrous in matters of sex and marriage, albeit in their different ways. At Caulonia, the child was a daughter (with a line of daughters thereafter), possibly suggesting that the specific problem was male children, especially as the grand-daughter Semiramis was also a success in her way – the

---

[18] See Chapter 6.

[19] Diod. 2.4 gives a relatively early version, but Cayster is not named, nor is Amazon parentage indicated.

most famous woman ever known, as Diodorus Siculus saw her. Inherited characteristics apart, how would an Amazon mother relate to a son? While we are told almost nothing about Amazons and their daughters, they might be thought more attuned to each other perhaps. At any rate, these late stories of problematic young men raise the case, aired long before in classical Athens, of Hippolytus, by far the best-known son of an Amazon. A century or so thereafter, the issue of Amazon sex and parenthood would again be raised around Alexander and the (much-derided) claims of his sexual encounter with an Amazon queen somewhere in the distant east. And that would return the discussion, with additional force, to the strange desires of Achilles and perhaps Penthesilea too, as she died, pierced by his conquering spear.

Amazon's Son: The Tragedy of Hippolytus

The only son of an Amazon that we know from classical Greek culture is Hippolytus – a myth of course, like his mother and father, the Athenian King Theseus. He is best known from a tragedy that Euripides wrote about him, the *Hippolytus* of 428 BC – in fact, Euripides' second play on the tragic youth (the first is lost).[20] Amazons had become newly topical in the Athens of the day. While the play's themes were revisited by Euripides in other tragedies, we should note that the recollection of Amazons in *Hippolytus* had a special resonance in the years after 431, when – like the Amazons – Spartan forces besieged Athens at the outset of the Peloponnesian War. The great siege of the

---

[20] The first is lost: see Wright 2019.

74

city had been that of the Amazons. Moreover, Theseus had led Athenian resistance to them, with Hippolytus' Amazon mother fighting at his side. She died battling for the city and her family, killed at a gate where she was duly monumentalised. Her tomb became an Athenian landmark. We have seen the importance of the event in Athenian culture.[21] Theseus' Amazon was usually named Hippolyte at Athens,[22] so that the youth's name evokes her and the equine passions of Amazons – it means 'Looser of horses'. In the play, we are reminded of the Amazon love of horses,[23] which the youth inherited. At the play's end, he would die because of his horses, appropriately enough for vengeful Aphrodite. Spooked, they crash his beloved chariot. Almost two decades later, as we have seen, Aristophanes would have bawdy fun with a very different take on Amazons and horses, in the *Lysistrata* of 411 – shortly after the Spartans had renewed and intensified their siege.

As Euripides' play begins, Hippolytus' mother is already dead, but her role remains significant even so. She is identified in the play by her ethnicity, not a personal name. She is called simply 'the Amazon' – four times over. A foreign mother was no problem in early Athens, whether real or imagined, Greek or non-Greek. The rich and powerful favoured such matches, which opened ways to wealth and opportunities in the wider world. For example, the great statesman and general Cimon was the son of a Thracian princess,

---

[21] p. 54.

[22] Simonides of Ceos (alias Cea, died c. 468 BC) also called her Hippolyte, according to Ps.-Apollod. *Epit.* 1.16.

[23] *Hipp.* 307, 581.

Hegesipyle. Since Cimon made so much of Theseus, these Thracian women might even seem a connection – Amazons were Thracians, after all. All well and good, but an Amazon in the palace?

Theseus' Amazon was blameless in herself. Snatched from Themiscyra, she had done all she could in her new life at Athens – in death a civic heroine and model of loyalty. In the play, Theseus had clearly recognised his paternity of her son, but there had been no formal marriage – the confused Hippolytus blames his problems on his bastard status.[24] After all, Theseus had not kept him close, but sent him to the palace of Pittheus in Troezen – Hippolytus was Theseus' son, but not quite an insider. Meanwhile, his Amazon mother might expect criticism, for she had brought war upon Athens, if unwittingly. It was for that reason that Helen found resentment at Troy, albeit in rather different circumstances. However, we find instead a focus on the Amazon's goodness – a subtle personality. As a later tradition held, she had gone out of her way to prevent conflict between Theseus and one of his friends who had himself developed a passion for her, during the long voyage back from the Black Sea to Athens. Again we find Greeks with a desire for sex with Amazons, and a range of Amazon ways to handle that intelligently.[25] Clearly, it would be hard for an Amazon to become a lady of Athens, a massive transition by any account. An Athenian vase (now in Japan) shows her taking instruction on the transition. She sits demurely enough in her Amazon outfit, while Theseus (in his favourite hat) explains his expectations. Another

[24] *Hipp.* 1083; cf. 309, 962.
[25] Plut. *Thes.* 26 attributed such tales to Hellenistic writers, and some earlier sense of this is possible.

young woman – in Greek attire – is at hand to illustrate the new style and maybe assist. Her eyes meet the Amazon's rather nervous gaze.

Was such a transition possible? The Amazon's death soon made the question redundant. But it remained to see how an Amazon's son might behave – what had he taken from his remarkable mother? There were no examples to call upon. However, the play shows the son as a most unusual fellow, who contrasts sharply with his amorous father. For Hippolytus shows no interest in sex and marriage – he rejects the works of Aphrodite (alias Kypris) and devotes himself wholly to her great rival, Artemis. The goddess Aphrodite shows her fury at the outset of the play:

> Mighty among mortals and famed,
> Goddess, I am called Kypris, as in heaven too.
> Of those who in the bounds of Pontus and Atlantic
> Dwell, and see the light of sun,
> I support those that respect my powers.
> But I bring down any who despise me.
> For in the race of gods too there is this –
> They rejoice when honoured by mankind.
> I shall soon show the truth of these words.
> For Theseus' boy, Amazon offspring,
> Hippolytus, ward of holy Pittheus,
> Alone of citizens of this Troezenian land,
> Says that I am the worst of deities.
> He shuns and spurns the marriage-bed.
> But Phoebus' sister, Artemis, daughter of Zeus,
> He honours and holds the greatest of deities.
> He roves the green woods, with the virgin always.
> With swift hounds he empties the land of prey,

In company greater than mortal.
I am not envious. Why should I be?
For his sins against me, I shall punish
Hippolytus today. Most of that
I set up long since – easy for me.
When he came from Pittheus' halls
To the rites of the sacred mysteries,
To Pandion's land, his father's noble wife
Saw – Phaedra, her heart seized by
Terrible desire, my scheme.
Before she came to this Troezenian land,
By the rock of Pallas Athena she established
A viewpoint of this land, a temple of Kypris,
Loving a foreign lover.
In future they shall name this foundation
'The Goddess-by-Hippolytus'.

(Eur. *Hippolytus*, 1–33)

The goddess has been disrespected and has grounds for anger, but there is a disturbing petulance about her summary of the situation here, expressing her emotional tendencies perhaps. She seems to sneer at Hippolytus' Amazon mother, for Amazons were devotees of Artemis as well. Despite her claims, there is a palpable jealousy in her words, heavily laced with menace. But she is not concerned with causes. The Athenian audience is left to consider how much of his behaviour arises from Amazon roots. For no other explanation seems available in the play. Hippolytus is a male version of an Amazon, insofar as he shuns the usual path out of adolescence to marriage, maturity, and reproduction. Aphrodite adds a special twist in devising an appropriate punishment – as with the women of Lemnos. This sexless youth responded badly to the advances of his father's wife, the hapless Phaedra. She panicked and accused him of raping her, with deadly consequences for both of them. Humans have no protection against divine power, while Aphrodite's machinations are at least as deadly as any thunderbolt of Zeus. As Aphrodite had boasted in the prologue, all this was easy for her. Meanwhile, the irony of her schemes (sexless youth as rapist, his Artemis-related horses as the agents of his death) adds a particular nasty twist, as the goddess incorporates mockery into her chosen punishment of Hippolytus. Beyond the play, Hippolytus may be returned to life by the healing-god Asclepius – an idea already current in Euripides' day.[26]

Euripides' Aphrodite has a lot to say about geography, with her earthly realm stretching to the eastern Pontus, the Black Sea.[27] More important in the play, however, is the interaction between Athens (indeed, the very acropolis, 'Pandion's rock') and Troezen in the Argolid, across the Saronic Gulf. Amazons were strongly represented in the Argolid, and on the fabric of public buildings there, though we have little understanding of their Argive context.[28] Local myths offered a range of Amazon connections. The Argive princess Io encountered Amazons in her travels and travails around the Black Sea. The Amazonian Danaids (descendants of Io) ultimately returned to Argos from North Africa.[29] We know that the Argive hero Bellerophon was commemorated in Asclepius' temple at Epidaurus, where his conquest of Amazons may have featured. Hippolytus was

<hr>

[26] Cinesias fr. 774, Campbell; later authors may take him to Aricia in Italy: Ovid, *Fasti* 6.735; Paus. 2.27.4; cf. 31.4.
[27] A regular conception: cf. Plato, *Phaedo* 109b.   [28] Pfaff 2003.
[29] See pp. 100, 128 on Aeschylus' *Suppliants* and *Prometheus Bound*.

returned to life there, it seems. In antiquity an inscription recorded his grateful dedication of twenty horses to the god.[30] The western pediment of the temple included a mounted Amazon – damaged, but still sexy enough in her very short dress, riding bareback and booted on a powerful horse (Plate 15).[31] Was she Hippolytus' mother? Or perhaps an opponent of Bellerophon? Scholars tend to identify her as Penthesilea, who might appear on horseback, and to see her killing Machaon, a son of Asclepius, as later told. A fifth-century vase, now in Brisbane, may show her fleeting success and hint at her imminent demise, too.[32] However, even if a son's death at Amazon hands was a subject for his father's temple, there is a problematic and (as far as we know) older tradition that Machaon was killed by Eurypylus, son of Telephus.[33] Much is speculation, and it would be safer to suppose a more commonplace theme (featuring Heracles, perhaps), but an Amazon would be at home with Asclepius insofar as he was Apollo's son. And there were other Amazon associations in the Argolid too, most importantly traditions that Theseus had defeated invading Amazons there around Troezen.[34]

From Theseus to Cadmus: The Amazon Sphinx

By around 300 BC an Amazon wife was brought into the story of Cadmus of Thebes, as we know from the author and compiler Palaephatus. His work is a collection of

---

[30] Paus. 2.27.   [31] Rolley 1999, 203–4; cf. Arafat 1995.
[32] The so-called Naples krater, R. D. Milns Antiquities Museum 87.208, where the principal Greek warrior is taken to be Theseus.
[33] Paus. 3.26.9–10, citing the Little Iliad and practice at Pergamum.
[34] Further, Paus. 2.31–2.

rationalising versions of well-known myths – in this case, the Sphinx, a female monster that killed travellers in Boeotia, to the north of Athens. Palaephatus turns her into an Amazon, the alienated wife of Cadmus:

Cadmus – with an Amazon wife, called Sphinx, came to Thebes, killed Dracon, and took over his property and realm – then also Dracon's sister, called Harmonia. When Sphinx saw that he was going to marry the other woman, she persuaded many of the citizens to join her, and seized most of his money and took the swift dog that he had brought with him . . .

(Palaephatus, *On Incredible Things* 4)[35]

She headed into the mountains with this following and staged ambushes with the success to be expected from an Amazon. Oedipus finally defeated her by night. We cannot be sure about the traction of this version of the myth, but we know that Boeotia had its own Amazon traditions, including even a river Thermodon. Given the importance of Heracles in Thebes and Boeotia more generally, as well as the Amazon march on Athens through Boeotia, there was ample scope for Boeotian conceptions of Amazon myth. Palaephatus' quirky tale need be no part of that, but the idea of his Amazon wife sharpens an abiding question about the possibility of any connection between his usual wife named Harmonia and the nymph Harmonia who was mother of the Amazons, located on the plain of Themiscyra. We may wonder what was said about that in Boeotia, and whether Cadmus' activities in Colchis might have entailed Themiscyra in local minds. Meanwhile Boeotian Pindar had already associated Amazons with civil disorder.[36] At any rate,

---

[35] In general, Hayes 2014.
[36] *Olympian Ode* 12.16 makes *stasis* itself *antianeira*.

Sphinx the Amazon illustrates again how Amazon tales constitute a warning to men of the consequences of mistreating their womenfolk – part of that broader theme across Greek culture. We may bracket this Sphinx with the – similarly isolated – story that Theseus' Amazon rose up against him on much the same grounds. Nor was this the prerogative only of Amazons – we may compare Euripides' Medea and other tragic females. We may suppose that Sphinx the Amazon had been brought from the eastern Black Sea by her Greek lover, as had Medea.[37]

---

[37] On Cadmus and Colchis, see Braund 1994, ch. 1. In Pindar, see his fr. 172.

4

A Duel of Death and Desire

Penthesilea vs. Achilles

≈

We find Amazons in our earliest Greek texts and art of historical times, from around 700 or so. Probably our first Amazon image appears on the 'Tiryns shield' – a painted terracotta roundel. It was found in fragments on the citadel of Tiryns, above the plain of Argos. Reconstructed (Plate 16), it shows female warriors (right: the larger clearly with breasts) getting the worse of battle with male warriors (left). The principal male has grasped the larger female by the top of her helmet – a grip repeated in later art, involving Amazons and others. In his right hand, he has raised his sword for the kill. We may have Achilles and Penthesilea, the Amazon queen who fought and died for Troy, as many have thought.[1] The back of the roundel is also painted. It shows a centaur – possibly Chiron, Achilles' teacher. We shall see that Achilles' Amazon duel was popular enough in art and text from archaic times onwards – a key part of the Trojan War and the beginning of the end for the mighty Achilles.

Already, Amazons were understood to be part of a lost age – the bygone world of heroes – Heracles, the Argonauts, Troy, and very much more besides. In this imagined prehistory, gods and goddesses strode the earth, involved in derring-do, and meeting challenges to their Olympian authority. For ancient Greeks, this was a formative past. It

---

[1] Langdon 2002, discussing other identifications.

shaped, explained, and made sense of the world around them – the source of their traditions and practices. Amazons were part of that distant past, at the beginning of culture for Greeks. They were creations of the supernatural, specifically the daughters of the war-god Ares. As such, they were a challenge faced and overcome by archetypal heroes – tough in battle and at least as hard to resist in bed. Their female power showed a possible alternative to women's domesticity, so that Greek males must put an end to them or risk revolutionary change. They could be killed, but they were better tamed and brought into proper society under male control. In that sense, they have much in common with other kinds of challenge to good order – the rapist Giants, rampant Centaurs, and uncontrolled females from Helen to her sister Clytaemnestra. In the art and texts of Greek culture, Amazons and their like would be recalled repeatedly as assertions of the social order. They had challenged that order and been stopped forever. And yet, within their catastrophic stories, there was also much to admire – intelligence, courage, subtlety, and wisdom beyond their martial skills. In defeat they had made a massive contribution to the real world of Greek culture. Their society had been extinguished by heroes (and the divine Olympians, inevitably in charge), but, at the same time, their stories and examples lived on in ways that maintained a sense of challenge for real Greeks. Amazons belonged to prehistory – at least until Alexander seemed to find some more – but echoed loudly through the social and material fabric of Greek reality, from archaic times into the Roman empire and beyond.

The earliest Greek literature was all poetry: epic tales of heroes on spectacular expeditions into danger – the Greek assault on Troy, the voyage of the Argonauts to fetch the

Golden Fleece from the world's end at the farthest coast of the Black Sea. Amazons featured in these tales, and in other epic adventures too. The Amazon homeland was at this wild frontier, by the Caucasus, where Zeus had nailed up Prometheus for giving fire to mankind.[2] Amazons were right for epic – early, powerful, and close to the divine. We see them several times in Homer's *Iliad* – buried at Troy, slaughtered in Lycia (south-west Turkey) and taking on a huge army in Phrygia (north-west Turkey). Their adventures took them far from their homeland – as far as Athens, Africa, and the western Mediterranean.

Homer, Heroes, and Greek Youth

In the *Iliad* Amazons are first named by Priam – Troy's aged king. He recalls an episode of his youth for Helen as together they look out from the city walls upon the massive Greek army. He thinks back to a huge army in Phrygia, where he had been in the ranks 'on the day the Amazons came, matches for men'.[3] That was the biggest army he had seen in his long life, until these Greeks arrived at his gates. Size is the issue, but we glimpse here too the obscure story of Acmon and the Amazons.[4] The Amazon army must also have been huge, though Priam does not mention that. Already, Amazons are a known quantity. The poem's audience is expected to recognise them. For there is no explanation of their identity, only an epithet – *antianeirai*. The

[2] Some ancient critics later made Amazons out of the Alizones at *Iliad* 2.856–7, for no good reason: see Strabo 12.3.22–4.
[3] *Iliad* 3.189, an Amazon attack; cf. schol. *Iliad* 3.189. In general, Borowski 2021.
[4] On Acmon at Themiscyra, see pp. 172–73.

Greek word shows that they are female, while its meaning is clear: 'matches for men'. The word implies no hostility to men, but asserts their capacity to stand against men, whether in battle or in other ways. The audience must know enough to understand this passing allusion. Some knew that Amazons would later come to fight for Troy and Priam, aware or not of the old king's past.

Amazons occur again a little later, killed by the Greek hero Bellerophon in Lycia. Once more, however, much is left for the audience to do. The poet recounts three successes of the hero in Lycia. First, killing the monstrous (female) Chimaera, second defeating the doughty Solymi, and third killing Amazons: 'third he cut down Amazons, matches for men'.[5] As with Priam, the formulation could hardly be more spare – the audience should know about them. By contrast, the Chimaera is described at some length – a fire-breathing monster – and the obscure Solymi are tagged as especially warlike men – Bellerophon's hardest battle. The Amazons were tough, but not as tough as the Solymi, it would seem. Meanwhile, Homer's two passages show Amazons to north and south of western Asia Minor – not so much an inconsistency as an early indication that Amazons can appear far and wide, and will continue to do so. They are not nomads, but they like to go on campaigns. Both passages highlight gender, not only through the epithet *antianeirai*, but also through the wider context, for in both the Amazons follow warriors who are specified as men – Phrygian and Solymian, as well as the fine Greek men upon whom Priam and Helen gaze. The Amazons bring female violence into the frame, while the female monster – the Chimaera – leaves no doubt

[5] *Iliad* 6.189.

86

that the female might indeed be deadlier than the male –
until Bellerophon kills her. The hero must deal with male
and female threats, as they come. However, there was an
abiding question about the hero's killing of women, which
might seem inglorious. For Greek tales were told of male
armies abandoning the fight rather than be forced to battle
with women who had taken up arms against them.[6] The
epithet *antianeirai* gave judgment that Amazons were worthy
opponents – matches for men.

Bellerophon's Amazon victory echoed down the centuries, sanctified by the authority of the *Iliad*. The hero
was especially important at Corinth. So when in 464
a Corinthian youth enjoyed victory at the great games of
Olympia, thoughts of Bellerophon were to be expected –
the city's hero revived through the prowess of its victorious athlete. The poet Pindar was commissioned to write
a poem to honour the youth – a song that was sung in
celebration in the city. Of course, Amazons were recalled:

> And once on Pegasus, striking
> From the chill folds of the upper air,
> He slew the Amazons'
> Archer female army,
> fire-breath Chimaera, and Solymi.
> (Pindar, *Olympian Odes* 13.86–90)

Amazons were matches for men, as Homer insisted. But not
for a hero like Bellerophon, whose flying horse allowed him
to kill these deadly archer-women. This was brute force, but
also strategy, for on his trusty steed the hero could tackle
a force that could keep most opponents at a safe distance

---

[6] See Chapter 2.

through their archery. The hero would strike from on high, an impossible target. The youth was left to dream of conquering Amazons and the rest. While celebrating the fact that – in a sense – he had done so at Olympia, at the games created for Zeus by the most famous of Amazon-slayers – Heracles.[7] Pindar's ode of victory demonstrates the relevance of Homer's Amazons and their heroic conqueror to the real-world culture of Corinth and its young men in the fifth century. The youth would never see an Amazon in the flesh, and probably knew that very well. But he would face challenges that were broadly comparable, as he had done at Olympia. He might very well have to go to war in grim and gory reality. He would also have to deal with women – probably not archers, but dangerous enough perhaps, in their own ways. As Greeks travelled and settled around the Mediterranean and Black Sea, they not only took Amazon tales with them, but would encounter foreigners, male and female. In the early stages of colonial settlement, we know that male settlers tended to find their women from local populations, so that a Corinthian lad, for example, might find himself married to a non-Greek female. For Amazons were about love as much as war – about women as much as women warriors. Corinthian men who gathered in their gymnasia and symposia understood that, while the city's potters and painters satisfied the demand for appropriate vessels and images – among our earliest Amazon images.[8]

Beyond Corinth, the conquest of Amazon was a theme relevant to a host of Greek cities. On Aegina, for example, Pindar had brought the theme into another victory ode about a decade earlier, for a youth of the island. While we see

---

[7] Chapter 5.   [8] *LIMC* Amazones, 1; cf. Henderson 1994.

Amazons on the fabric of Aegina's public buildings, Pindar's song recalled the specific success of an earlier son of the island – the hero Telamon, father of Ajax and uncle of Achilles. He defeated the bronze-bowed Amazons, writes Pindar, 'and man-taming fear never took the edge off his wits'.[9] The honorand knew something of that – he was a pancratiast-boxer – a Telamon of sorts. As at Corinth, Pindar's poetry illustrates the significance of beating Amazons, which he brought into other work too.[10] Another ode for a youth of Aegina takes us to Apollo, foreseeing the fall of Troy. He leaves the city and heads north by way of 'the fine-horsed Amazons and the Danube'.[11] Their mention in this context turns thoughts to Penthesilea, killed in the closing stages of the Trojan War, and to Achilles her killer. For Achilles' family had its beginnings on Aegina. At the island's main harbour, a major temple of Apollo displayed images of Amazons, as his temples often did from archaic times.

Myrrhine's Trojan Tomb

The tomb of Myrrhine lay outside Troy. Hector marshalled the city's forces there:

> There is a steep hill before the city
> On the plain, with a road around on either side,
> Men call it Batieia,
> But immortals 'the tomb of leaping Myrrhine',
> There then, Trojans and allies were set apart.
>
> (*Iliad* 2.811–15)

---

[9] *Nem.* 3.36–40.
[10] Pindar fr. 173: Telamon on Heracles' expedition for the belt.
[11] Pindar, *Olympian Odes* 8.46–7.

Myrrhine was an Amazon, no doubt the great queen who died long before the Trojan War – surely in battle, as ever. Her 'leaping' marks her prowess – fast and furious in action, jumping into the enemy, as acted out in the Amazon war dance.[12] Her tomb was a landmark, redolent of energy and battle – Amazon tombs were powerful medicine. A Byzantine commentator reveals some of her Trojan tale. She had become the wife of Dardanus, Troy's founder. Her story is interwoven with tales of a local princess, Batieia or Bateia.[13] Amazons are often in foundation-stories, as at Troy, it seems. She may have died fighting for her man's new city, as Theseus' Amazon would do at Athens, and receive her own landmark-tomb there.

Towards the end of the Trojan War another Amazon queen would come to fight for Troy – Penthesilea. She too would be given a tomb there, after Achilles killed her. That story was told in an epic, known as the *Aethiopis*, attributed to a Milesian called Arctinus. The five-book poem began with her arrival at Troy after Priam had buried Hector. Queen Penthesilea receives attention not seen among Amazons of the *Iliad*. However, the poem is lost.[14] We have only a later summary, by a certain Proclus. He outlines Penthesilea's tale at the outset:

Amazon Penthesilea comes to the Trojans, to be their ally – daughter of Ares, Thracian woman born. Achilles kills her, fighting at her best, and the Trojans bury her. And Achilles

---

[12] Aelian, *NA* 12.9. Myrrhine's horses: Strabo 12.8.6, 13.3.6.
[13] Eustathius, *Comm. Iliad* 551, with Dardanus' Samothracian journey. Note Myrrhine there: p. 130.
[14] Davies 2001 surveys this and other epics, oddly sure that Amazons are 'un-Homeric'.

does away with Thersites, for rebuking him and accusing him of
love for Penthesilea. So strife occurs among the Achaeans
around the killing of Thersites.

(Proclus, *Chrestomathie* 175–81)

Thersites' tongue had got him a beating in the *Iliad*, but
Achilles was so enraged by his remarks that he killed him
on the spot.[15] The summary is oddly full on Thersites'
jeer – his tongue was again the problem, not anything he
did.[16] He had touched a nerve in mocking Achilles. He
had spent much of the *Iliad* fuming over his loss of another
woman at its outset, Trojan Briseis. Now he was in love
with his victim, Penthesilea. At the very moment he killed
her, he was captivated by her beauty and allure – the
beginning of his own demise. A duel with a woman –
even a Penthesilea – left scope for a jeer, but Thersites'
focus was probably on Achilles' evident passion for the
queen, and the special care he took for her body. Achilles
wanted the live queen, not her dead body – only a late
commentator suggests that someone had claimed even
that, perhaps Thersites.[17] The hero and the queen had
defeated each other, and both would be dead soon
enough. The supercharged duel attracted artists and
authors from archaic times onwards.

[15] Marks 2005.

[16] Much later some commentators said he had gouged out the queen's
eye(s), as they tried to understand Lycophron's challenging words on
her death (esp. lines 999–1000). However, such gouging is otherwise
unknown, and the words are better taken (as by Tzetzes' comments on
these lines) to mean that Achilles had struck her eye, but her gaze had
struck him, which would cause him to kill Thersites for his nasty
remarks on the matter.

[17] Hardly the *Aethiopis*, a grand epic. The only clear suggestion of sex with
her corpse is in schol. Soph. *Phil.* 445, possibly arising from Thersites'
remarks.

At Olympia the renowned fifth-century painter Panaenus depicted Achilles and the queen among the paintings that covered screens around the cult-statue of Zeus, Achilles' forefather. Its tender scene showed Achilles supporting the queen as she breathed her last.[18] Half a century or so earlier, an archaic Athenian vase shows Achilles carrying her body over his shoulder, evidently taking it to the Trojans for burial, as the *Aethiopis* told. Her body has not been stripped, as would be usual, though she has lost her helmet (Plate 17) – we see her eyes closed and her white face peaceful in death, while her hands hang lifeless. A smaller warrior crosses Achilles' path, turned to stare at the body. He is surely Thersites, poised to jeer.[19] Penthesilea became (after Myrrhine) the second Amazon queen buried at Troy. She had escaped the brutality meted out to Hector's body. For Achilles loved her, and hated Hector. How the *Aethiopis* handled her burial is unknown, but later epic had Penthesilea buried beside Priam's father – Laomedon, whose Troy was sacked by Heracles, as was the city of the Amazons at Themiscyra. Pindar had linked the events for his victor on Aegina and elsewhere. Penthesilea's dead companions were buried on the plain.[20]

Quintus' version shows Penthesilea rampaging across the battlefield,[21] killing Greek warriors as she goes. As the summary has it, 'fighting at her best' – her *aristeia*. Full of misplaced optimism she hurls two spears – one at Achilles,

[18] Paus. 5.11.4–6.
[19] Achilles and Penthesilea are not named: *ABV* 362.33, 355.
[20] Quintus of Smyrna 1.802–3.
[21] Around AD 400, perhaps. Cf. Blok 1995, 195–210, where Apollodorus offers little.

the other at nearby Ajax. Neither causes harm, and Ajax goes away, uninterested in her. Achilles soon kills her. He had no qualms about killing a woman – she boasts of her blood from Ares. Achilles denounces her foolish ambition in tackling him. But when he sees her properly, without her helmet, he is overwhelmed with passion. She would have made an outstanding wife, but he has killed her. Meanwhile the Greeks around the scene turn their thoughts to their far-off wives in their beds at home. At this point, Thersites provokes an Achilles disturbed by his feelings for the queen. Thersites rebukes him for being obsessed with women, and so not properly a hero. Achilles hits him so hard that he knocks his teeth out and kills him, which gives rise to the tensions mentioned in the summary. In broad terms Quintus had followed the *Aethiopis* on Penthesilea's story, and perhaps also in detail.

Exekias' vase-painting of the duel sets a standard for archaic art, but no vase was much known in its day. Exekias provides an outstanding version of a scene that was familiar, reproduced in different forms on vases and elsewhere. Artists were at liberty to follow their fancies, albeit with some concern for the market as well as their own predilections.[22] Penthesilea's duel with Achilles could be shown in many ways, so that we cannot always be sure that we should see them. For example, a long-limbed Penthesilea (as usually identified: Plate 11)[23] is shown as an archer on a large jar, dated around 500. Certainly she is an Amazon, but is she Penthesilea? Her thigh is pierced by the long spear of a heroically nude (but

---

[22] Further, e.g. Lowenstam 1993, with bibliography.
[23] Problematic: e.g. Muth 2008, 712.

helmeted) Achilles, who leans over her reclined and scantily clad body. His wide-eyed gaze stares down at her, while her eyes are closed.[24] Her bow is held away from her body – it stands out and does not form any barrier between them. Achilles' opponent is shown with a spear by Exekias and other artists. The clash of Greek spear and Amazon bow offers rich symbolism and helps a striking image, so that we find it elsewhere too, notably with a (very damaged) vase of about 480, attributed to the so-called Pan Painter. There a winged Victory brings a garland to the winner, Achilles.[25] Perhaps that does not fit the literary tradition very well, but such a pairing can only evoke Penthesilea and Achilles, whatever may have been the painter's intention. The so-called Penthesilea Painter shows Amazon defeat in a scene from which his modern name is derived (Plate 18). Its crowded image shows a downed Amazon reaching up to a large Greek: they could well be Penthesilea and Achilles, but they are not named. If there was a duel, it is over. The Amazon may be dying, holding on to the Greek and gazing up at him, appealingly. A dead Amazon lies to their right, while a Greek warrior wields a sword to their left – possibly Thersites.[26] In Exekias' painting, Achilles' gaze devours the queen, downed and wounded at the end of his spear – helpless and dying as blood spurts from her lower neck at Achilles' spear-point.[27] His gaze dominates the scene, a glimpse of the humanity inside armour that makes him otherwise look like a killing machine. His physical vulnerability was his heel, but his gimlet eye

---

[24] *ARV²* 209. 169: Padgett 2017, 42. The identification of the pair is usual, though not confirmed by inscriptions on the vessel.
[25] *ARV²* 550.3.   [26] E.g. Robertson 1992, 161.   [27] Moignard 2015.

was both a weapon and a window to his soul. The queen herself has an open-faced helmet and wears a dress, with some leopard-like fur. Quintus, at least, would make much of her big-cat spirit for leaping and killing. The idea may already be in the *Aethiopis*, for there was something of that in Homer's leaping Amazon Myrrhine.

Sex is everywhere in this violent clash between these fine physical specimens of male and female. Penthesilea had demonstrated that she was a match for men, but no-one was a match for Achilles in battle. Her sexual appeal to the hero would bring her much more success. The story suggests what Quintus (and perhaps already the *Aethiopis*) had made explicit – she should have stayed away from the battlefield, and perhaps dealt with the hero on other terms. For Greek heroes often had a weakness for women, and the works of Aphrodite. When Priam speaks of Amazons to Helen in the *Iliad*, he speaks of deadly women to another deadly woman. For Helen had brought war to Troy, with Aphrodite.[28] Beautiful Helen was no Amazon warrior, but Amazons were Helens of a kind – much desired for sex and breeding. At least one vase-painter exploited the fact that both Helen and an Amazon queen were abducted by womanising Theseus.[29] A famous painting at fifth-century Delphi bracketed Helen and Penthesilea. There Helen's seducer Paris tries to catch the queen – who snubs him.[30] The duel of Achilles and Penthesilea echoes across the centuries in a much broader conversation about the relationships between men and women, love and war, sex and violence.[31] Meanwhile, a Byzantine poet of the twelfth

[28] Eur. *Helen* 198; 238; Morales 2016.
[29] *ARV*[2] 1620, about 500; Bundrick 2019, 21.   [30] Paus. 10.31.8.
[31] Fantuzzi 2012.

century captures Penthesilea's twin strengths with the striking description of her shield. It showed Penthesilea herself, with Ares and Eros at odds on either side of her – a dilemma for herself, her opponents, and others.[32] Meanwhile, we should note the trouble for which – not unlike Helen – Penthesilea can be held responsible. Her female allure had led quickly to murder and disruption, by Achilles' agency. Women were not for the battlefield, said Achilles, even if glory could be wrung from the death of a Penthesilea.[33]

These epic Amazons may be failures in a sense, but they are treated with honour. These women warriors are not monsters, and have no place in the monster-rich *Odyssey*. They are cultured in heroic battle and evidently play by its rules. Like the Trojans, they are not Greeks, but they seem so similar that their 'barbarism' can fade away into the background, while Amazon queens enjoy special status in any case. These epic Amazons may threaten to create female dominance, but they always lose before too long – more attractive than repellent. Myrrhine seems to have exemplified in epic the taming of Amazons that we shall find again in Greek culture. As Achilles' story suggests, Amazons might be still more dangerous when they put away their weapons and became women of more familiar ways.

Thracian Women: From Otrera to Phidalea

Proclus' summary identifies Penthesilea as Thracian by ethnicity, naming her parents as Ares (as always with Amazon queens) and a certain Otrera. Her mother's

---

[32] Tzetzes, esp. 6–71. [33] E.g. Sen. *Troades* 236; Quintus 4.178.

name highlights her daughter's fighting energy, for it means 'dynamic', 'fearless', and on occasion 'brave'.[34] Amazons are characterised by the repeated use of a few names for key figures, especially queens – though very many names were used for other Amazons, many being painters' fancy. This repetition brings uncertainty – for example, whether we should understand Penthesilea's mother to be the Queen Otrera who built a stone temple for Ares on his rock in the Black Sea (together with a Queen Antiope, who may or may not be Theseus' Amazon).[35] In Italy, we shall see that all the Amazon rulers of Clete were themselves called Clete, as was the first Amazon queen there. The name means 'Invited', a fine name for her story.[36] The name Hippolyte recurs for a range of leading Amazons. Small wonder that an Otrera is attested also as the name of Ares' daughter.[37] While Penthesilea's mother bore a name fit for an Amazon, she might be a nymph, like Harmonia, given as the mother of all Amazons. Ares favoured sex with nymphs, not Amazons. Meanwhile, the paucity of names for key Amazons seems to suggest a Greek tendency to treat them as all the same, without individual personalities. Penthesilea is the only queen to bear her name, with its evocations of grief (Greek, *penthos*) for enemies as well as friends.[38] However, even in the duel with Achilles, we find her in archaic images sometimes named Andromache

---

[34] E.g. Hom. *Od.* 1.109; schol. on Lycophron 997.
[35] Ap. Rhod. 2.370ff.   [36] Cf. Hom. *Od.* 17.386.
[37] Hyginus, *Fab.* 163, a Roman list; cf. ibid. 30, where another is mother of the Hippolyte killed by Heracles. For idiosyncratic claims on an Otrera at Ephesus, ibid. 223, 225.
[38] *ARV²* 1066.10 (475–450) need not be the queen.

('Man-fight'). It is no coincidence that this was also the name of the wife of Hector, whom she succeeded as Troy's champion. Hector's wife had a military awareness unusual among women.[39] Whether she was ever an Amazon in pre-Homeric epic may be doubted, but her name certainly evokes a female warrior.[40] Meanwhile, the emergence of Penthesilea as a standard name may indicate the impact of the *Aethiopis*.[41]

Later texts suggest that Penthesilea used an axe, at least as her secondary weapon. For painters, the axe suited archers, while it was a favourite Amazon weapon in any case.[42] A vase-painting attributed to Polygnotus shows her (named) facing Achilles with a large axe.[43] Some even said she invented the battle-axe.[44] A Roman poet opines that Achilles had better die by her axe than by unworthy Paris' arrow.[45] We may wonder whether she wielded an axe in the *Aethiopis*. In Quintus' version, she was bringing her axe into play as she lost consciousness.[46] Clearly, there was ample scope for artistic choice from early days: an archaic Athenian vase shows the pair duelling on horseback, both named.[47] By Roman times it was claimed that Penthesilea was the last of the major Amazon queens, so that her death also marks a decline that defines the Amazon story.[48] As so often, we are shown finality and

---

[39] *Iliad* 6.433–9; cf. 8.185–90 (horses).
[40] On her warrior talent, see Tsagalis 2008.
[41] Andromache was named in archaic art.   [42] E.g. *ABV* 367.95.
[43] *ARV*² 1030.35, c. 475–425.   [44] Plin. *NH* 7.201.
[45] Ovid, *Met.* 12.611–12; cf. Aeschylus, *Eum.* 624–8.   [46] 1.587.
[47] *ABV* 321.10. Her horse often features in paintings, while Quintus' poem made much of it, too.
[48] Diod. 2.46.

death. At the centre of the story Achilles ponders his lost opportunity – a future with Penthesilea. But where is her response? Of course, in the throes of death, she was hardly able to respond, but Greeks who heard the story and viewed the images might imagine an alternative outcome, where the couple lived happily ever after. Under different circumstances, might this Amazon queen have taken the path of Theseus' Amazon? Myrrhine may have done so at Troy long before. However, Amazons were more about death than life, and Achilles was set on his own path to early death. Inescapably, therefore, theirs was a relationship of moments, which artists strove to capture for viewers to muse on life, love, and death, with all the potential poignancy that might be wrung from this moment of heroic bonding (see Plates 19 and 20).

Proclus' summary informs us that Penthesilea was Thracian. From archaic times onwards, Greeks thought that the language of Amazons was Thracian.[49] After all, Thrace was the earthly home of their father Ares, the war-god. For Greeks considered Thracians to be a people with a liking for war, as they not only fought Greeks but served with Greek armies.[50] Gender roles among Thracians also seemed unusual. Plato, for example, contrasts the indoors life of Greek women with the agricultural and herding work demanded of women in Thrace.[51] Like Amazons, Thracians were farmers – not nomads – and yet had a strong association with horses, illustrated by the flesh-eating mares of Thracian Diomedes, Heracles' Eighth Labour.[52] Thracian women also had a reputation as killers

---

[49] Schol. Ap. Rhod. 2.946, citing Hecataeus, *FGrH* 1 F34.
[50] E.g. Hom. *Od.* 8.361.   [51] *Laws* 805d–e.   [52] E.g. Tsiafakis 2000.

of males, most famously Orpheus, while the axe figured prominently in Thracian tales, wielded by men and women alike.[53] Moreover, as with the Amazons, 'Queen Artemis' had a special importance among Thracian deities, as attested for Greeks even at Delos.[54] How and why the Thracian Amazons had migrated eastwards to Themiscyra is nowhere explained, though we find an allusion to their move amid the jumbled geography of the Aeschylean *Prometheus Bound* around 440.[55] We have seen Pindar's verses on Apollo's journey from Troy northwards over Amazons and the Danube.[56]

Remarkably, however, Amazons are rare in the civic traditions of Thrace, in sharp contrast with their various stories in the cities of Asia Minor, Greece, and elsewhere. The only exception may be Apollonia Pontica, the city of Amazon-friendly Apollo, where recent archaeology probably shows Amazons on the temple of Apollo there. A local Amazon tale is likely enough, and might entail nearby Salmydessus, which the *Prometheus Bound* seems to associate with Amazons (above).[57] However, if some mark was imagined of their expedition to Theseus' Athens, for example, we hear nothing of it. Amazons have been claimed on some Greek coins of Thrace – civic and royal – but in fact there are none. Similarly, wall paintings in the grand Thracian tombs actually show no Amazons, though sometimes claimed there.[58] We would expect

---

[53] Cohen 2000; Braund 2021; Chapter 2, above.   [54] Hdt. 4.33.

[55] Aesch. *PV* 725, setting them by Salmydessus 'stepmother of ships'. The work has survived with the plays of Aeschylus, but is widely thought to belong to another playwright.

[56] Xanthus must be the river Scamander at Troy: *Iliad* 20.74.

[57] Virgil later moves Thermodon to Thrace: *Aen.* 11.659–63.

[58] Manetta forthcoming.

them for many reasons – the importance of Heracles in Thrace, Thracian involvement with Athens and its mythical past, and the Thracian identity of Amazons. However, we find them only at the Thracian versions of the Greek symposia – not only on imported vases, but also on the fine metalware which wealthy Thracians particularly enjoyed (Plate 21). It seems that Thracians shared the Greek liking for Amazons in festive contexts, amid tales of heroism and such,[59] but were not attracted to their wider significance, for example in death, construction, and creativity. As Greeks liked to stress, Thracian taste was more boisterous and excessive than philosophical, while the Greeks of Thrace had no strong reason to respond to the Amazons' Thracian ethnicity. While Amazons came from Thrace, their major stories had no strong Thracian dimension, whether for Thracians or Greeks.

Thracian Phidalea and Her Snakes at Byzantium

Phidalea's story is almost an exception to regional neglect of Amazons, but she was not specifically an Amazon – any more than Mysian Hiera, who was said to have led female cavalry into battle on the opposite side of the Hellespont.[60] This Amazonian female of Thrace appears in the local traditions of Byzantium. We first hear of her very late, in Christian Byzantium, but she belongs to the city's origins, and may well be early enough. She was important to its citizens. The removal of her statue caused an earthquake,

[59] Marazov 2013.
[60] Late in texts, her Attalid link won her a place on the Great Altar at Hellenistic Pergamum: Philostratus, *Heroicus*, 23.27.

they said, which could only be steadied by a saint's intervention. Her name evokes the snakes (Greek, *ophidia*) that are
key to her story. She had married the founder of Byzantium,
Byzas from Megara.[61] She was vital to the foundation. Her
father – Barbysius – had been ruler and guardian of the
earliest settlement on the site of Byzantium, an emporium
for seaborne trade. His name echoes the key river Barbyses,
a heroic figure in local tradition.[62] On his deathbed he told
her to build a defensive wall to protect the developing
settlement from the hinterland – a wall from the Horn to
the sea.[63] Her name was linked to a string of buildings and
landmarks around ancient Byzantium. For example, she had
built Aphrodite's temple on the city's acropolis, while Byzas
built another for Artemis. The rival goddesses had both
been honoured by the ruling couple.[64] In the sixth century
AD, Stephanus of Byzantium – who knew his own city –
writes:

There is also Women's Harbour in the area called Phidalea ...
They say that it was there that the wife of Byzas, Phidalea and
the other women chased those who attacked the city under
Stroibos, Byzas' brother, while the male citizens were absent,

---

[61] On Byzas' foundation, see Robu 2014; Russell 2012. Dion. Byz. gives us
a very different Phidalea, commemorated by an offshore rock by
Women's Harbour, where she lived out her days and was buried after
Poseidon saved her from suicide by drowning after unmarried sex with
Byzas (Dion. Byz. 60, of uncertain Roman imperial date, perhaps second
century AD).

[62] The modern Kağıthane Suyu, flowing into the Golden Horn. Malalas
13.7; Chron. Paschale 464. On the river as a hero, see Dion, Byz.
Anaplus, 24, with further mythology.

[63] Cf. Mango 1985, esp. 13–14 on early fortifications, impatient of local
belief.

[64] Malalas 12.20.

and that she defeated them after chasing them as far as the harbour, thus giving it its name . . .[65]

The harbour is attested centuries earlier as Women's Harbour, which may take Phidalea earlier too.[66] Her initiative in the absence of men echoes several early tales of Greek women in war – Telesilla and others – and her Thracian ethnicity raises also the spectre of Amazons, as do her building activities. However, it was her resistance to the onslaught of another foe that made her entirely extraordinary. A late (sixth-century AD) writer of the city tells us:

When victorious Byzas was driving the enemy into Thrace, Odryses, king of the Scythians, crossed the Danube, advanced to the very walls of Byzantium, and laid siege to those inside the city. Against him was the remarkable Phidalea, wife of Byzas, unperturbed by the size of this hostile force. Using her woman's hand, she fought back, outwitting the barbarian with the help of serpents. For she gathered the snakes of the city, and kept them in one place. Appearing suddenly to the enemy she launched the creatures against them, like arrows or javelins. And inflicting very many casualties in this way, she saved the city. This is the ancient reason why snakes caught in the city are not to be killed, on the grounds that they had been benefactors.

(Hesychius Illustris *Hist. Constantinople*, 18)

Again, Phidalea goes into action in the absence of her husband with the city's army. Her enemies are Scythians. Their king is named Odryses – usually the ethnic term for an Odrysian Thracian. The place where snakes were collected no doubt bore an appropriate name to recall the event, perhaps the area which Stephanus calls Phidalea. The snakes recall the poisoned missiles attributed to peoples

---

[65] Steph. Byz., s.v. Gynaikopolis.   [66] Plin. *NH* 4.46: cf. Dion. Byz. 60.

of the north. However, Byzantine tolerance for snakes also caused a chain of problems in the city – finally sorted out by the wonder-worker Apollonius of Tyana in the second century AD.[67] As a battling and resourceful woman of Thrace, Phidalea has much of the Amazon about her, close to the supernatural. In late texts Amazons are associated with reptiles in notions about Sauromatians.[68] Most important, the Amazonian Phidalea – Thracian born – uses her talents for war in defence of the Greek city of her husband. In that, she resembles Amazons who have been domesticated into Greek culture, most notably Theseus' Amazon, with whom we have already compared Myrrhine at Troy – and, if things had been different, Achilles' wife, Penthesilea.

[67] On snakes, see Hesychius 23–25, with Chapter 6, below; on Glycon, see Lucian, *Alexander the False Prophet*, with Ogden 2013.
[68] Chapter 6.

5

Heracles' Amazon Labour

Delphi, Olympia, and Colonial Worlds

~

Archaic colonialism took Greek culture far and wide – from Gibraltar to Syria and the far coasts of the Black Sea. Amazons, embedded in archaic culture, were carried along. The scramble for a better life in distant parts was largely a free-for-all, but the more successful colonies also established further colonies in their orbits – small empires like those of Massilia (modern Marseilles) in the west, and Sinope in the Black Sea. Colonies also developed their own local cults and traditions – continuity from their old home-lands and new tales and practices to suit their new environ-ments. This expanding Greek world retained connections, however, with the great panhellenic centres, where all Greeks could hope to participate in festivals, contests, and games in honour of the main Greek gods and goddesses. These great cult-centres offered shared celebration and competition that brought a measure of connectedness to Greeks. Delphi and Olympia were the most important of these centres, made ever more wealthy by colonial expan-sion. Amazons already connected the many and various Greek states in shared stories, while their fundamental foreignness and distant locations exemplified Greek experience – challenges and opportunities – that might be imagined at the colonial frontiers. Particularly so, when we recall that Greek settlers were largely male and took their women from local populations, whether by force, diplomacy, or exchange. At the same time, Amazons were disrupters of tradition – agents of change – wanted and unwanted – and were themselves creators of new communities, colonists of a kind and with the supernatural aura that was often claimed for settlement. In this chapter, we shall explore the opaque story of Amazons in Africa and the western Mediterranean, in the context of Delphi and Olympia. Their eastern and more northerly activities demand separate treatment, in the next chapter. However, we begin with Heracles, the pre-eminent roving hero of Greeks. His Labours took him far and wide – in many ways a role model for the Greek youth. In his wild way, he championed what Greeks considered civilised order around a world in which there had been various kinds of deviance.

Ravaging Themiscyra

Heracles' so-called Ninth Labour was a mission to the south-eastern Black Sea. As all the Labours, it was not of his choosing. The gods had placed him in the hands of King Eurystheus in Argos. This tyrant was to test him repeatedly, through a series of deadly and apparently impossible missions. With one success after another, Heracles was elevated to divinity in his own right – that started to become clear soon after his conquest of the Amazons, during his Tenth Labour, as he brought back to Argos the wondrous cattle of Geryon from distant Spain.

Each Labour was a different challenge. The early Labours tend to show our hero slaughtering monsters – most famously the great lion of Nemea (his first). He would sport its great skin on his head and shoulders (and often down to his waist and beyond), as if absorbing its strength – and also perhaps its savagery. For Heracles was a notably animalian hero, a force of primitive nature directed towards civilisation. Appropriately, his characteristic weapon was a huge length of wood – the mighty club, though he used a bow and sword too. There is an unresolved tension between his uncultured violence and the cultured world that he creates by destroying a series of monsters in his early Labours. However, not all his Labours involved dead monsters – not even all the early ones. His Third Labour had him pursue a special deer – the Ceryneian hind. The chase started in southern Greece, like all the early Labours, but took him as far as the mythical Hyperboreans, who lived a blessed life on the imagined shores of a balmy Baltic. However, there was nothing particularly monstrous about the hapless deer.[1] King Eurystheus had noted its golden horns. He also knew it was sacred to Artemis. Brute violence would not meet this challenge, though Heracles needed the stamina to chase the hind for a year. To kill Artemis' favourite was a great risk, and so (unusually) he brought the deer back alive to Argos. The speedy creature had been outrun and outwitted by a hero who now showed brains as well as brawn – with a talent for diplomacy, so that Artemis (with and without Apollo) accepted that Eurystheus was to blame for the abuse of her animal. As later with the golden apples of the Hesperides (the Eleventh Labour), the hero had managed restraint and diplomacy. To that extent, his violence could be harnessed to reason.

---

[1] See Aston 2021, esp. 63 for possible monstrosity.

With that in mind we better understand his Amazon mission. For that was not simple violence, while the Amazons were not monsters. We may note that the very many Amazon names that feature in Heracles' mission are all more-or-less Greek – Greeks did not give their own names to monsters. As with the hind and the apples, Heracles had been sent to the Amazons for gold. He would also join the Argo in quest of the Golden Fleece from Colchis, just along the coast from the Amazons – except that he left that expedition long before it had reached these parts. There is an Argonautic flavour to his Amazon mission. For both endeavours were directed to the same corner of the world, and each had as its objective not simply gold, but gold that was talismanic, charged with ruling power from the gods, as we shall see.[2] And heroes like Achilles' father, Peleus, joined him on both Black Sea quests. It was even said – exceptionally – that all the Argonauts joined Heracles against the Amazons,[3] though mighty Heracles rarely needed much help or even a ship for such missions.[4] Gold was thought to lie at the edges of the earth – a spur to colonialism, no doubt.[5] But this was very special gold.

For the specific objective of Heracles' mission to the Amazons was the golden belt of their queen, usually named Hippolyte. The slaughter of Amazons was not

[2] On the talismanic Fleece, Braund 1994.
[3] For participants, see Gantz 1993, 224–5, 397–400. Pindar fr. 172 notes these twin deeds of the 'god-like' Peleus. Cf. schol. Pindar, *Nem.* 3.64b for Telamon killing Melanippe, and Hellanicus' claim that all the Argonauts went on the Amazon mission (*FGrH.* 4.F106).
[4] Schol. Ap. Rhod. 2.777–9. His charioteer and nephew Iolaus was often on hand, e.g. Eur. *Her.* 408; *Hcld.* 215–17.
[5] Hdt. 3.116.

his task or desire. Amazons were favourites of Artemis. This was not a mission to destroy them and gain the wrath of the goddess, though the queen might not give up her belt without a fight. Peaceful agreement was better and entirely possible, as Heracles later managed in obtaining the golden apples of the Hesperides – shining nymphs of the far west. It might help or hinder success that the Amazon mission was charged with sexuality. For to remove a woman's belt was to begin undressing her for sex, as painters sometimes showed in marital scenes.[6] Heracles might have sex with the Amazon queen to get her belt, with no violence necessarily involved – a tactic he used elsewhere, with the snake-woman of Hylaea in the north-western Black Sea.[7]

At the same time, such a belt – a *zoster* – might be a battle-belt, holding weapons and the like. Such belts could be plated, bejewelled, and very valuable. A minor scandal of Roman imperialism in the Black Sea was the theft of the belt of Mithridates VI Eupator after his suicide in 63 BC. This belt was valued at 400 talents, not much less than the annual income of the Athenian empire at the height of its power.[8] Already in Homer's *Iliad* mighty men went into battle with belts covered with precious metal – a *zoster* that was both valuable and of practical use.[9] In the fifth century such a belt was displayed at Mycenae as the belt that Heracles had brought from the

---

[6] Sutton 1997–8, 30.
[7] Hdt. 4.8–10, getting his horses back from the mysterious snake-woman of Hylaea. More generally, Blondell 2005.
[8] Specified as a sword-belt: Plut. *Pomp.* 42.3.
[9] E.g. Homer, *Iliad* 4.132–5, the belt of Menelaus.

Amazons.[10] Possibly it was kept in a temple of Artemis there – some compensation for the demise of her Amazon favourites. The belt had moved from myth to a material reality, still charged with power. Such objects might be claimed in many places, like the statue of the Taurians' Artemis, brought to Greece by Orestes.[11] In the Crimean city of Chersonesus (modern Sevastopol) the citizens swore an oath to 'preserve the belt'. Most likely this was Leto's belt, but it might be Heracles' Amazon trophy, especially as he was particularly important in this colony of Heraclea Pontica.[12]

Eurystheus' daughter, Admete, had sparked Heracles' mission, though perhaps not in all versions of the tale. The princess desired the great golden belt of the Amazon queen. Her name – 'Untamed' – had an Amazon flavour, evoking even Artemis.[13] Later, on Samos – with its own Amazon myth[14] – she became a wild virgin.[15] With the talismanic belt, perhaps she had hoped to succeed her tyrannical father in Argos. Meanwhile, the Amazon queen bore a name that would not be out of place among Greeks. She is Hippolyte in later texts, but archaic pottery shows her named as Andromache, roughly 'Man-battle'. Amazonian enough, perhaps, but this too was Greek, and a name also borne by Hector's saintly wife at Troy.[16]

---

[10] Euripides, *Heracles* 418 – perhaps from a shaft grave there.
[11] Paus. 3.16. [12] Braund 2018. [13] Soph. *Electra* 1239.
[14] At Panaima, where Dionysus spilled much Amazon blood: Plut. *Mor.* 303e–f.
[15] Admete on Samos: Athen. *Deipn.* 15. 671f–674a, quoting Menodotus, c. 200 BC.
[16] On Heracles and Amazons on early Greek pottery, see Stafford 2013, 41; Bothmer 1957; Muth 2008. See also Ibycus on names, p. 131.

On arrival among the Amazons, Heracles tried to get the belt by asking the queen to give it to him. However, a promising start went sour. Heracles was set upon and forced to violence. The ensuing melee became the story of the mission. The supermale and his gang of heroes overcome the best of fighting females. They not only take the belt, but put an end to the extraordinary Amazon society at Themiscyra – unwillingly or not. This was the ultimate enforcement of male-led order. The fighting could have only one ending, and it did not last long. From the viewpoint of real Greek youths – alone or in the company of their friends – Heracles and his companions demonstrated heroism on this far-off mission across the dangerous Black Sea. This was success against serious warriors – women or not – and yet females, whose attitude needed correction in the cause of culture and justice. In any case, as the myth makes clear, Heracles had not set out to fight the Amazons – just to get the belt, as Eurystheus had ordered. Of course, the battle also had enormous visual appeal – a favourite theme in art from at least 600 BC onwards.[17] The mighty Heracles – with lion skin and club or other weapon – made a stunning contrast with his young female opponents, whether armed and armoured or more bare-fleshed (Plate 22; cf. Plate 13).

Throughout, we are not far from the nexus of ideas (and artistic opportunity) that surrounds Achilles' duel with Penthesilea – and probably all such Amazonomachies where Greek men invariably have the better of it. The duelling pair – with Achilles' thunderstruck gaze – brings to the fore an aspect less obvious in the mass scenes

[17] E.g. *LIMC* Amazones no. 1.

around Heracles. The Amazons have not only the weapons of war, but also the weapons of desire, as their bodies silently declare to the viewer. Both scenes, and both stories support a traditional outlook, that Amazons would do better to wield the weapons of desire against Greek males. Aphrodite would serve their cause better than Artemis or Ares in such circumstances – a conclusion convenient for powerful men. On occasion, in fact, we find the Amazon queen deploying her outstanding desirability – attested rather late, but surely current earlier:

Heracles opened the belt of the Amazon, who was unmanning him and thought she would conquer him with beauty. But having been with her, he showed that he would never be defeated by beauty, and would not remain far from his lands for the sake of a woman – not ever.

(Dio Chrys. 8.32, c. AD 100)[18]

It would take more than sex to overcome Heracles. Heroism demanded resistance to weapons of every kind, including the manipulation of male desire.[19]

Images of heroism (sexual, military, and more) filled the meeting-places of men – the symposia and gymnasia around which Greek everyday life was centred for men. They would also be deposited in burials, satisfying the living and confirming the heroic ambitions of the dead. Meanwhile, would-be heroes might also think that sexual desire might work for them too. Jason's exploits illustrate the effect of male desirability, as Theseus, Odysseus, and the rest – including Heracles. One version of Heracles' expedition claimed that it was lust for Theseus that caused

[18] Probably also earlier, and not only in comedy.
[19] Cf. Muth 2008, 334, 717, including Theseus.

an Amazon to betray Themiscyra to the Greeks. The treacherous female who betrays her land was a common theme, as Medea in Colchis. In this case the female traitor betrays her fellow females for love of a man. Presumably she was the Amazon who returned to Athens and fought and died loyally for Athens and her man.[20] Meanwhile, some even insisted that Heracles' negotiations had got him the belt – that he had captured the queen's sister, Melanippe, and exchanged her for the belt.[21] Clearly, across the Greek world, over space and time, very many tales were told about this famous expedition. Our main problem with the several versions of the tale is that its popularity in archaic art is not matched by accounts in the archaic texts that have survived.[22]

However, the idea that Heracles used diplomacy as well as violence tends to recur in different forms. As in Achilles' case, killing women was problematic for a hero – there was scant glory for the mighty Heracles in slaughtering even Amazons – except of necessity. Vase images can even show the Amazon queen holding her belt out for Heracles to take.[23] Diplomacy was certainly possible with Amazons – at Athens Theseus had exchanged oaths with them to end their great siege of the city.[24] Seldom do we have any explanation for the breakdown of discussions. In Roman times, at least, we are told that a vengeful Hera intervened.

[20] On her treachery, see Pausanias, 1.2.1, from Theseus' own Troezen. On her name(s) and loyalty, see Chapter 8. There is scant reason to insert her in Euripides' *Heraclidae*, despite later Hyginus, *Fab.* 30.

[21] Ap. Rhod. *Argon.* 2.966–9.

[22] The verses on Telamon in schol. Pind. *Nem.* 3.64b might be from Hesiod.

[23] Schauenburg 1960; *LIMC* 1, 1981, 586; Shapiro 1983.

[24] Plut. *Thes.* 27.

She embodied marriage as the wife of wayward Zeus – Heracles was the result of one of his many amours. In sum she was hostile to the Amazon lifestyle, and had long wished to kill Heracles. Accordingly, the goddess appeared at Themiscyra in the form of an Amazon.[25] She spread the rumour that Heracles was abducting the queen. Tricked, the Amazons went to war against Heracles – brave and foolishly optimistic. Hera, the embodiment of traditional marriage, makes a striking Amazon. But in myth opposites tend to coalesce, as we see with Artemis and Aphrodite often enough. We may note the cult of Artemis at the great temple of Hera at Argos, with its (wrecked) Amazon sculptures.[26]

The various versions of Heracles' Amazon mission had a consistent enough set of ideas at their core. Given their significance for Greeks, Heracles' destruction of Amazon society at Themiscyra was treated widely across Greek culture. It was also a beginning – the consequent Amazon diaspora sparked new foundations, new cults, and more. Accordingly, Heracles' mission overshadowed tales of other expeditions to sack Themiscyra, rooted in specific local traditions. By far the most important of these are Athenian tales of Theseus. We cannot hope to follow the archaic interplay of these versions, for we lack data.[27] Through the fifth century, however, Athenians managed to retain Heracles' mission, while also tracing the end of the Amazons to their own victory over Amazon imperialism directed against Theseus' inchoate city.[28] Athenians' tales always mattered beyond Athens, not only by reason of

---

[25] Apollodorus 2.5.9.   [26] Pfaff 2013, and below on Hera in Italy.
[27] Boardman 1982 offers extended speculation.   [28] Chapter 8.

their power and widespread presence through the classical period, but also because Athens remained a principal hub and showcase for Greek culture in general. In all these tales a male protagonist destroyed Amazon society, alone or with other men – Heracles, Theseus, Telamon, and no doubt many others – including Dionysus and Bellerophon away from Themiscyra around Samos and Lycia. Men might die in the process, though only Sthenelus receives much attention, buried on the southern coast of the Black Sea by Heracles.[29] However, women too were responsible for the sack of Themiscyra – and not only the overconfident Amazons themselves. Admete had identified the Amazon belt as Heracles' objective. The goddess Hera had undermined Heracles' attempt to negotiate – no friend of him or the Amazons. But Admete and Hera appear only with Apollodorus' account, written at the time of the Roman empire, and we cannot assume their involvement in earlier versions. However, while there is scant sign of sympathy for Amazons among Greek females at any time, Heracles' Amazon mission is overwhelmingly a celebration of male conquest over female resistance in every sense.

Panhellenic Centres: Delphi and Olympia

The sack of Themiscyra was a special example of a more familiar event – Greeks knew what to expect if a city was sacked. The sack of Troy was the paradigm, but grim reality was part of ancient experience, too. Practice varied

---

[29] Ap. Rhod. 2.911 brings a ghostly Sthenelus from his tomb to gaze upon the Argonauts.

in reality, but the people of a sacked city who could not be sold into slavery could anticipate execution, while rape and looting were sure to occur.[30] At Themiscyra we are spared the ghastly details, while the absence of men made its sack unusual in any case. We hear a little of Amazon women being handed out when the booty was divided. Trophies were routinely taken, too – some to be dedicated in sanctuaries. From the Amazons of Themiscyra, Heracles took not only the famous belt, but also the queen's battle-axe, which would become a talisman of power in Lydia and Caria.[31] He also brought a great tapestry from Themiscyra to Greece, where he deposited it at Delphi – a very appropriate place for it.

For Delphi belonged to Apollo, while Artemis also had a stake there. They were twins, after all. Already in the sixth century we see them as a pair of archers fighting the Giants on a lavish treasury, built around 525 by the islanders of Siphnos. It may also show battling Amazons, but damage makes certainty impossible.[32] Artemis might suffice to bring Amazons to Delphi, but Apollo had his own links to them, and not only because of his archery. While literary texts only mention Apollo among Amazons on occasion,[33] Amazons were shown prominently on a series of Greek temples from the late sixth century onwards. At Eretria Theseus was shown carrying his Amazon on the temple of Apollo Daphnephorus (Plate 23), as at Apollo's temple at

[30] E.g. Haft 1990; Gaca 2014.   [31] pp. 190–91.
[32] On treasuries, Neer 2001.
[33] Notably Pindar, *Olympian* 8.46–8, for an Aeginetan victor. Cf. Paus. 3.25.2 on ancient cults of Artemis Astrateia and Apollo Amazonius in Laconia. The cult statues were said to be Amazon dedications. Amazons are uncommon in pre-Roman Sparta: see also Palagia 1994.

the main harbour of Aegina. In the Cyclades there were perhaps Amazons on the late temple of Pythian Apollo at Carthaea on the island of Cea, where the nearby temple of Athena has provided marble remnants of Amazonomachy from much the same time in the late sixth century. From that same temple we also have damaged terracotta figures of Theseus and his Amazon, which evidently stood above the south pediment of the temple, while below them, the pediment itself is taken to have shown Athena.[34] Modern restoration shows Theseus and his Amazon standing above Athena on the roof, identified by name: the Amazon is here named Antiope.[35] Rather as Eretria, the island enjoyed close relations with nearby Athens. Recently, another archaic Amazon frieze (in terracotta) has been discovered in Bulgaria, at Apollonia Pontica, decorating the temple of Apollo the Healer on the offshore island of St Kirik.[36] A bit later, there was also the extraordinary temple of Apollo the Helper high in the hills at Bassae in the western Peloponnese, erected around 420 BC. We are told that its architect was Ictinus, who had been one of the architects of the Parthenon in Athens.[37] This temple boasted a frieze inside its walls, showing Heracles, with club and lion skin, defeating Amazons in battle. Amazons were at home with

[34] She is the reason why the temple is ascribed to the goddess. It might belong to another deity, though epigraphic evidence confirms that its neighbour is a temple of Pythian Apollo.

[35] See Angliker 2022, with bibliography. The inscribed names are cut in archaic letters, though they are located (on the usual restoration) very awkwardly for viewers from below.

[36] See the careful study of Stoyanova and Damyanov 2021, with well-illustrated Stoyanova 2022 in detail. They are more likely Amazons than Thracian warriors. I am grateful to Daniela Stoyanova for discussion of these figures.

[37] Paus. 8.41.7–9 (second century AD).

Apollo, and so at home in Delphi, as we shall see. Sadly, the fabric of Delphi has been severely damaged. Accordingly, we have little idea about the decoration of Apollo's temple in its different forms there. However, we may assume sculpture throughout its history, while our list of Amazons on Apollo's temples gives reason at least to suspect that his temple at Delphi also bore Amazons.

In this context, Heracles' dedication of an Amazon tapestry at Delphi was appropriate enough. We see it only through Euripides' *Ion*, a tragedy centred upon a temple servant at Delphi – the son of Apollo and a princess of early Athens – Creusa, daughter of King Erechtheus. Ion (the first of the Ionians) had grown up in the temple, not knowing the identity of his parents. During the play, Ion creates a gigantic tent in which the people of Delphi will all come to feast. At this point, Euripides brings Amazons. For the tent is fashioned around a great tapestry of the heavens which – we are told here – had been brought back from the Amazons by Heracles. Nowhere else do we hear of this trophy, though a dedication at Delphi was appropriate, if only to appease its twin deities. However, Euripides makes much of the tapestry, with a detailed account of the astronomical scene it displayed:

> He took sacred textiles from the treasuries and
> Made a shady covering, wondrous for mortals to see.
> First he set out a wing of weaving for a roof,
> a dedication of the son of Zeus, Heracles –
> Amazons' booty he brought for the deity.
> Woven thereon were scenes with lettering:
> Heaven gathering stars in the upper air's circle;
> Horses drove to final flame the
> Sun, drawing on the shining light of Evening;

And black-robed Night a yoke-drawn
Chariot dashed, and met the stars in sight.
Pleiad fared through upper air's middle course,
And Orion with his sword, and above
Bear turning golden-tailed on pole, and
Full-moon's circle launched its javelin on high,
Month's divider, and Hyades, sailors'
Clearest sign, and light-bringing
Dawn, chasing the stars. And on the walls
He fitted other weavings of barbarians –
Well-oared ships against Greek vessels
And man-beasts, and riding after
Deer and savage lions in hunts.

(Euripides, Ion 1141–62)

The tapestry ceiling of Ion's massive tent was astronomy for
Amazons. We see Bear – Artemis' favourite, key to her
myths and cults. And Artemis may be the Moon, in her
own name or as Hecate,[38] evoking female biology.[39] Here
the Moon hurls a javelin – standard weapon of Amazons.
The Hyades were daughters of Erechtheus, as Ion's mother.
Their myth of self-sacrifice showed that the death of young
women could bring victory (here, over King Eurystheus) in
ways other than simple combat. Horses are prominent, too,
together with Uranus (Heaven) and Night, always female.
The Pleiades were made daughters of an (unnamed)
Amazon queen by Callimachus.[40] They had been granted
a place among the stars so that they might escape the rapist
Orion, who still follows them across the sky.[41] Orion and his

---

[38] Ní-Mheallaigh 2020, 13–14.
[39] See pp. 193–94 on Amazons at Hecate's Lagina in Caria.
[40] So schol. Theocritus 13.25–28a.
[41] Hesiod, *Works* 618–20; Pindar, *Nem.* 2.17.

phallic sword recall the tales around his relationship with Artemis and her entourage. He had hunted with Artemis, but taken a sexual interest in her – until her brother intervened. Orion also raped Oupis, her follower – a name of Artemis herself on occasion. His punishment was a place in the firmament.[42] Oupis had come from the Hyperboreans, who lived beyond the far north in a warm paradise where Apollo liked to rest and Heracles had ventured.[43] Her evocation here contributes to the northward sense of this picture of the heavens, with Day and Night standing for east and west. This was an astronomical vision appropriate to the Amazons of Themiscyra, as were the hunting scenes that Ion also used – also non-Greek work, perhaps Amazonian.

The poet has avoided awkward questions, by never quite saying that the Amazons had made the astronomical tapestry. Astronomy raised no great issues, for Amazons were architects and builders, well connected with the great forces of the universe – as with Apollo, Artemis, and Ares. However, textile-work was the most traditional of female occupations among Greeks. The making of tapestry did not sit comfortably with the Amazon lifestyle. In Herodotus' Sauromatian tale, the shipwrecked Amazons had played on that when they persuaded their Scythian boyfriends that they must create a new people – far from the woolworking women of Scythia closeted in their wagons. They claimed that they could never get on with such women – an argument that was conclusive. Evidently these Scythian women were homebirds, but the tapestry suggests that these Amazons were overstating

---

[42] E.g. Homer, *Od.* 5.124, implying Apollo's intervention: cf. Pseudo-Hyginus, *Astronomica* 2.34; Hesiod, fr. 4.

[43] Gagné 2021, esp. 352.

their case. Amazons could weave tapestries too. For we can hardly suppose that they had taken this very Amazonian tapestry from elsewhere.[44]

The Amazon tapestry, the microcosm created by Ion's tent, and above all the rite of festival transported the people of Delphi to a new world and cosmos, full of Artemis and Apollo, far away from Greece – and yet still in Delphi. We may recall the mystic Aristeas of Proconnesus, who travelled far and wide in spirit 'taken by Phoebus'.[45] Such was the power of this unwitting son of Apollo. Meanwhile, Amazons evoked a central theme of the play – family dysfunction, with a misguided mother (Athenian Creusa) plotting to kill Ion – who would be revealed in due course as her own son. There is much more than casual exoticism to Euripides' use of the Amazon tapestry, especially when we consider also the Athenian (and more broadly Ionian) history with Amazons. Euripides had used Amazon parental issues before, in his *Hippolytus*.[46] Some fifteen years before *Ion* Euripides had brought the Amazons – and probably their textiles (his play has not survived well) – into his *Children of Heracles*, where once again parentage had been central. There had also been some (less specific) astronomy, with regard to the notion that Heracles had held up the heavens for Atlas, with further ramifications.[47]

The *Ion* was a play primarily for an Athenian audience, and it seems to suggest that Athenians had a rather

---

[44] Later, see Diod. 2.45 with Bosak-Schroeder 2020, 63–4.
[45] Hdt. 4.13.   [46] pp. 78–79.
[47] Atlas fathered the Pleiades on an Amazon queen in a work of Callimachus, we are told, though their mother is usually given as a daughter of Ocean: see schol. on Theocritus 13, 25–28a, where she is not named.

proprietorial attitude to the all-Greek site at Delphi in the fifth century. Certainly, they were among the Greeks who built grand treasure-houses there. Their impressive treasury was built by around 490 BC, decorated with sculptured slabs which showed the deeds of Heracles and those of Theseus. Again, however, we are frustrated by poor survival. The top corners of the building were evidently decorated with mounted Amazons, while Heracles and Theseus (Plate 1) were each shown in action against various opponents, including Amazons.[48] The co-existence of the two tales on an Athenian public building, erected at significant collective expense, shows that the democracy was well able to accommodate both heroes, singly and together, as later across the buildings that were raised in Athens itself.[49]

Of special interest among other treasuries is one built by the Greek colonial city at Massilia, now Marseilles. The building is firmly archaic, erected in the later sixth century, before the Athenian treasury. It bore an Amazonomachy, which seems to have centred upon Heracles.[50] Its sixth-century date undermines further the much-repeated claim that the Persian Wars explain images on the subsequent Athenian treasury.[51] The Amazon mission was popular in sculpture, as well as vase-painting. In nearby Boeotia Heracles probably featured again with the surviving Amazon (and others) on the damaged pediment of a temple at Copae – perhaps of Demeter Tauropolus.[52]

[48] Emerson 2018, 66; Gensheimer 2017, esp. 12 n. 73 listing the metopes.
[49] So too Euripides, *Heraclidae* 217. Cf. Jones 2019. On the treasury, Arafat 2013, esp. 83–4.
[50] See Hermary 2020; cf. Persson 1921, esp. 322–3.
[51] Gensheimer 2017, seemingly unaware of Arafat 2013.
[52] Copae: Hansen and Nielsen 2004, 443–4; the cult might have a Black Sea link, through the Tauri.

Heracles was important in Boeotia, treated as a great local hero there. His Amazon mission helps to explain the various Amazons there, complete with a Boeotian river, Thermodon.[53]

However, the Greeks of Massilia surely chose and approved the themes and images of their showpiece treasury. These Greeks of the far west were clearly concerned to have Amazons on their costly building at prestigious Delphi. Local myth at Massilia told how Heracles had passed through their lands on his way from Spain to Italy with the cattle of Geryon. Moreover, Artemis of Ephesus had been key to the city's foundation. It remained bound to the goddess, who had joined in the Phocaean settlement there. The goddess had protected and guided the whole endeavour – and a grateful city would duly carry her cult to various further settlements around the western Mediterranean. Crucially, Amazons had played an important role in the creation of the cult itself at Ephesus, being first at its altar and dancing in arms for Artemis. She had offered them protection too, after Dionysus and also Heracles had all but destroyed them.[54] In building a treasury at Delphi, the people of Massilia can only have been very aware of their own cult of Artemis, its role in their foundation, and the Amazons who were at the root of all that. Their choice of Amazons for the decoration was far more than a matter of fashion and aesthetics, though such considerations will also have played some part in their decision-making.

The likelihood of Amazons on Apollo's temple at Delphi becomes ever stronger as we look around the little that is left of the site. We also happen to know from

[53] p. 169.   [54] See Chapter 5.

literary evidence that there were other Amazons on show there too. For among the famous frescoes by Apollo's temple (inside the so-called Lesche of the Cnidians) there was the remarkable encounter of the Amazon queen, Penthesilea, and the playboy prince of Troy, Paris. Its artist was Polygnotus, who worked in the middle decades of the fifth century: we shall meet his work again at Athens, where he also painted Amazons. Pausanias describes the painting at Delphi, long since destroyed:

Paris – as yet beardless – is clapping his hands like a slob. It is as though he were calling Penthesilea to come to him. She too is depicted, looking at Paris, and yet tossing her head in disdain and contempt. You can see that Penthesilea is a maiden, with a Scythian-style bow, and a leopard's skin on her shoulders.

(Pausanias 10.31.8)

We should not be surprised that some in antiquity speculated on the possible interaction between the Trojan lover and the Amazon queen who bedazzled Achilles with her rare beauty.[55] Helen might have lost her heart to boyish Paris, but the Amazon queen will have nothing to do with him – fellow archer or not. The queen means business in the last days of Troy. This and other scenes no doubt inspired many a conversation among the people of Delphi and visitors who gathered in this building. For this was designedly a special place for meeting and relaxation – talking and perhaps enjoying performers of tales. It was also primarily male space, inevitably. The painter and his

---

[55] Cf. Dictys 4.2, where Paris persuades the queen to help by giving her gold and silver. Twists on the earlier versions are not uncommon among such imperial Greek writers as him. By late antiquity, the queen might be killed not by Achilles, but by his son, Neoptolemus (Dares, *Fall of Troy* 36).

commissioners knew that when they chose their subject and its treatment.[56] We surely admire the queen, but in the men's-club atmosphere of the Lesche we may also be amused by silly Paris' approach to this fine and dangerous female. In any event, as so often, there is no hint of barbarism in the conduct of the Amazon, rather by contrast with the absurd Trojan. Wiser viewers would reflect – especially in this context of the end of Troy – on the events to follow the vignette. For the queen would be killed by Achilles, and he would in his turn be killed by Paris. As often with Amazons, sexuality and death tend to merge. Apollo himself will make Paris' success possible.[57]

At Olympia Heracles was still more important than at Delphi – with Zeus and Hera presiding. Heracles was made founder of the Olympic games – again a role model for Greek youths in his physical prowess. Indeed, our earliest expression of Heracles' canonical Twelve Labours comes from Olympia, where they featured on sculpted slabs to the front and rear of the great temple of Zeus – Heracles' father – built around 475–450 BC.[58] Pausanias describes the metope-slab which showed Heracles 'taking the belt off the Amazon' – the victor stripping the belt from her dead body. Beside this striking scene was his seizure of the hind with the golden horns – two quests for gold, as we noted.[59] In broad terms, Olympia offered a more extensive version of what we saw at Delphi, with its own local traditions and tendencies. At both sites Amazons featured on dedications, notably on grip-bands from shields that showed battling

[56] Bremmer 2015.   [57] Blok 1995, 148.   [58] Stafford 2011, 24.
[59] Paus. 5.10.9.

Amazons and were dedicated to the gods in archaic times, at Delphi and Olympia alike.[60]

Inside Zeus' great temple was the huge gold and ivory statue of Zeus himself – enthroned, the master of the universe. The work of Pheidias, this seated statue was reckoned another wonder of the world. Here there were more Amazons. They were incorporated amid the extensive decoration of Zeus's bejewelled throne – arranged along cross-struts between its legs. Pausanias counted twenty-nine figures with Heracles and his companions (here including Theseus) battling the Amazons – a striking image, albeit one among others, including Heracles taking the weight of the heavens from Atlas, and more besides.[61] One of the screens around the statue was painted with the duel of Achilles and Penthesilea.[62]

Rather as at Delphi, it is especially Heracles who brings Amazons to the fore at the great all-Greek cult-centre – with and without Theseus. However, Heracles had done so much else, while Zeus was not known for direct dealings with Amazons – his granddaughters through Ares. Hera, however, presents a more complex set of issues. As the champion of regular marriage, she was no friend of Amazons, as we have seen. And yet, rather as Artemis had a role in childbirth, so Hera consorted with what might seem her opposite. At Hera's festival at Olympia there were prenuptial athletic contests. Young women competed there – with a bared breast. To that extent, these strong girls recalled Amazons – not in marble, but in flesh and blood, ripe for marriage. We have no information about the myth

---

[60] *LIMC* Amazones, nos. 170–4 (173 from Delphi). Heracles, Stafford 2011, 18.
[61] Paus. 5.11.4. [62] Paus. 5.11.5.

behind these performances, but scholars have often thought of Amazons – rather as did Aeschylus' king of Argos when he saw the Danaids (below). We have seen that Hera's temple at Argos displayed Amazons. After all, Hera the wife and mother had passed through adolescence too, as illustrated by the Arcadian temple of Hera the Girl.[63] However, for all that, it was especially at Delphi that Amazons mattered.

Out of Africa

Amazons had their homeland in the south-eastern Black Sea region – at least until Greeks displaced and destroyed them. But their cultural importance meant that they were also in demand elsewhere, especially as Greeks of the periphery constructed their own local traditions.[64] Amazons not only campaigned in strange regions, but had even lived there, it was claimed. Particularly striking are some lines of Aeschylus from mid fifth-century Athens. The playwright conjures up a remarkable vision of females roving North Africa on camels. The play is set in Greece, where the king of Argos struggles to identify a group of strange women who have come to his land and announced themselves as Argives, his subjects:

> Incredible tales you give me to hear, foreign women,
> How we have here Argive blood.
> For you look more like Libyan
> Women – not from here at all.
> Nile would more nurture such a plant.

[63] Paus. 8.22.2; Serwint 1993. On female athletics in general, see Tsouvala 2021.

[64] Repeated modern notions that Amazon homelands moved with Greek expansion are at odds with most of our evidence.

There's a Cypriot stamp in these females,
Like the types stamped by craftsmen.
Such women I hear of – nomad riders
Wandering the land on camels,
Neighbours to the Ethiopians.
And manless, carnivore Amazons
I'd sooner have thought you, had you bows.
But I would like to know more,
How your bloodline seed is Argive.

(Aeschylus, *Suppliants* 277–90)

We are reminded that the Greek world includes North Africa. In Argos the king is struck by the appearance of Danaus' daughters, who have indeed come from south of the Mediterranean, despite their Argive origins – granddaughters of Io of Argos. He sees that they are not the indoor women of Argos, but more like African camel-women. They would look like Amazons, if armed with bows. The play was for Athenians, whose extensive imperialism and mythology embraced both Egypt and Amazons – who are notably tough here.[65] However, although Africa and Amazons are mentioned together, it is not clear that African Amazons are envisaged in these lines. Aeschylus directs the audience to the Danaids' killing of their unwanted bridegrooms, sons of Aegyptus. The wise king has observed much of their story, perhaps over-stating his confusion. The Danaids were in fact both Argive and Amazonian enough. We may recall that the Danaids' grandmother, Io, had even visited the Amazons of the Black Sea in a play attributed to Aeschylus.[66] In principle,

---

[65] Sunburnt and fierce, but there is nothing here of cannibalism as sometimes claimed: p. 151.
[66] Aesch. *PV* 723.

we may be confident that Amazon tales were woven among the Greeks of North Africa – no less committed to Artemis, Apollo, and Ares than Greeks elsewhere. More problematic, however, is the extent to which such local tales were connected with the fantastical myth that we have from Diodorus Siculus. Even he is careful to distance himself from notions of a great Amazon city called Chersonesus ('Peninsula') on a large and bounteous island (called Hespera, 'West') in the huge Lake Tritonis, located towards the Atlantic and the people of Atlantis.[67] Simple fiction in large part, but it can include genuine local traditions, too, so that some link to the local myths of North Africa cannot be ruled out. The ruminations of Aeschylus' Argive king are not so far from tales of the North African interior and female power around Lake Tritonis, such as we find in Herodotus and indeed at Argos.[68]

Greek myths were certainly developed in Africa, as elsewhere. The Argonauts reached Cyrenaica and mysterious Lake Tritonis.[69] The world of heroes and Amazons spanned the continents. Diodorus writes of early Amazons under the mighty Queen Myrrhine.[70] Their vast army ranged across Libya, Egypt, Arabia, Syria, Cilicia, and beyond, founding cities and making a treaty with Horus, son of Egyptian Isis – a gigantic concoction. These Amazons too were ultimately destroyed by a Heracles bent on Gibraltar – with a massive earthquake, Gorgons, and more. The Amazons themselves were adapted to their environment, using as armour the skins of the snakes for which Africa was renowned.

[67] As Tyrrell 1984.
[68] Further, Paus. 2.21.5–6, with Hernández 2010; Calame 2003.
[69] Hdt. 4.179.   [70] Diod. 3.52–5, with Muntz 2017, esp. 109.

Among Greeks of Africa and the western Mediterranean, this may have looked less bizarre. However, without corroboration we cannot be sure which parts of all this may represent more widely held Greek traditions.[71] Uncertainty reigns. For example, there is every reason to think that Myrrhine's exploits were well received on Lemnos, but we can only guess what was said on neighbouring Samothrace, where – as Diodorus' account relates – the Amazon queen founded the cult of the Mother of the Gods there and even named the island.[72] It is worth recalling that on Lesbos, not so far away, coins show a local tradition of Amazon foundation at Mytilene, which Diodorus says was founded by Myrrhine and named after her sister.[73] This was the native city of the only source that Diodorus names on these matters – Dionysius Scytobrachion, who wrote about a hundred years before him and worked in North Africa – at Alexandria under the patronage of the Ptolemies, where queens had a special place.[74] Clearly Amazons were linked to civic foundations both in victory and in defeat, or some mixture of the two. However, as usual with Amazons, it is their demise that tends to attract most attention in ancient thought, writing, and art.

Amazons in Italy

Among the Greeks of the west, too, a commitment to Heracles brought Amazons to the fore. His Amazon mission

---

[71] The coinage of Cilician Soli, for example: p. 180.   [72] Diod. 3.55.7.
[73] See Bodenstedt 1977, with the survey of Fabbri 2022.
[74] On Scytobrachion, Alexander and his city, Rusten *BNJ* 32; cf. Nesselrath 2005 on utopianism and Atlantis.

was not his most prominent Labour there – that was the Tenth, the cattle of Geryon – as treated by the major archaic poet of the region, Stesichorus.[75] Heracles' pursuit of the Amazon belt was not so fundamental to the culture of the region, but it featured too in word and art. Our earliest indications of Amazons in the traditions of the region come from remnants of archaic poetry, composed by Ibycus. He came from Rhegium at the toe of Italy, and evidently followed western Greek traditions on Amazons. For that reason ancient commentators thought his version of the Amazon mission unusual.[76] His name for the Amazon queen was not the usual Hippolyte, but Oiolyke ('Lone she-wolf'), while other unidentified authors used the name Deilyke ('Deadly she-wolf'). A wolf, not a horse – but even this fierce name is Greek enough.[77] Exceptionally, he also made the Amazon queen the daughter of Briareus, the hundred-handed Giant important in the west – a rare hint of monstrosity among Amazons. Briareus was buried beneath the volcanic Mt Etna in Sicily, where eruptions were explained as his movements.[78] In western Greek art, we see the theme on a sculptured slab of a great temple at Selinus in Sicily – Temple E, built c. 450 (Plate 24). There Heracles is about to kill an Amazon. He has grabbed her head, and stands on her foot – no doubt the Amazon queen.[79] Clearly, negotiation had been abandoned, for

[75] See Finglass and Kelly 2015, largely concerned with literary matters.
[76] Schol. Ap. Rhod. 2.777–9. On South Italian vases, see Schauenburg 1960.
[77] Cf. Ap. Rhod. 2.956, a man named Deileon, 'deadly lion'. On wolves, p. 169.
[78] Callimachus, *Hymn to Delos* 141–3.
[79] The metopes have a male-female theme on this temple of Hera or Aphrodite: Spawforth 2006, 131.

whatever reason. The sculpture commemorated the hero's success in violence. However, we should bear in mind a fine image on a Campanian vase, now held in the University of Manchester's museum, dating from c. 400 BC or a bit later. For this depicts Heracles' encounter with the Amazon queen in a very different way (Plate 25). There we see the queen holding out her belt for the hero to take. The viewer is left to recall or reimagine their agreement, or indeed to reflect that soon all would go wrong and the hero would kill the queen. We see her horse and a suggestion of her court. And we observe her statuesque presence, at least as impressive as Heracles'. This is very much an Amazon queen – impressive, powerful, and attractive. Even without her fine fox-fur hat she seems here to be rather taller than the mighty Heracles, whose male companion is smaller still.

There was also scope for comedy around Heracles' quest for the belt, probably centred on Heracles' passionate ways and Amazon attractions. Around 450, as the temple was erected, a Greek comedian of Syracuse wrote a play entitled 'Heracles in Quest of the Belt'. The comedian was Epicharmus, a star of local Greek culture. Most of the play is lost, but we know that it included humour about the gigantic beetles of Etna. They were part of the deep past there, symbols of the land,[80] and probably clashed with Heracles. In Sicily they may have preferred to think that Heracles had acquired the Amazon belt somewhere far

---

[80] De Callataÿ 2010 on the coin of c. 465 (produced for the city of Etna, modern Catania), where a small image of a beetle appears in the obverse design. Suggested identification obscures its evocations. Epicharmus perhaps made the beetles dung-beetles, as being more comic and appropriate to his theme in another play, the *Rock-Rolling Sisyphus*.

closer than Themiscyra.[81] The fact that another Sicilian comedian wrote a play called 'Amazons' further confirms local interest, at least.[82]

Greek colonisation was a process of interaction with local populations. Amazons and Heracles were part of that interaction, for it was not only on imported Greek vases that Amazons appeared. In the Spartan colony at Tarentum, Amazons were especially prominent in funerary art – the city of Heracles and Apollo.[83] To the north, Etruscan culture shows Amazons enough, decorating the cinerary urns from Praeneste. There was also a remarkable painted sarcophagus near Tarquinia (the 'Amazon Sarcophagus', dated towards 300 BC). For all its gaudy colours and local detail, we find on this sarcophagus a familiar set of contests between well-armoured men and young women hardly covered by flimsy dresses. This Amazon battle occupies all four sides of the sarcophagus, while Actaeon the hunter appears too, another evocation of Artemis.[84] The deceased is identified – a woman with a firmly Etruscan name, Ramtha Huzcnai. Interpretation is contested, but the collocation of Greek and Etruscan is evident.[85] Amazons were part of a wide-ranging cultural exchange from archaic times onwards. We can only

[81] Epicharmus fr. 65 KA, preserved by a late commentator on Aristophanes' *Peace*, in which the comic hero rides a great dung-beetle: schol. Ar. *Peace* 73.

[82] Deinolochus, contemporary of Epicharmus.

[83] Carter 1975; Lippolis 1994, 109–27.

[84] Warden 2009; cf. Riva 2022.

[85] Carpino 2016, esp. 417 on Heracles (Etruscan Hercle) fighting an Amazon on a fourth-century mirror; also 424: further Etruscan sarcophagi with Amazonomachies (male deceased). See Wiseman 1993; Van der Meer 1995; 2004; Wiseman 2004, esp. 108–9.

reflect on the thinking of those who chose to deposit vases with Amazons in burials at Vulci and elsewhere. Clearly, Amazons – especially in battle – were integrated into funerary ideology and practice locally.[86]

A Hellenistic poem treats the goddess Roma – the militaristic deity of the Roman state – as a sister of the Amazons. She and the Amazons were Ares' only daughters, though he had very many sons.[87] Subsequently we see Amazons at home in imperial Rome, both Greek and Italian – and indeed Roman. Virgil and other Roman writers take their Amazons not only from Greece, but also from an Italian–Greek cultural mix that we can only grasp in general terms. In the *Aeneid* Virgil portrays an Italian Amazon, the warrior Camilla,[88] preceded not only by the ruling queen of a rising Carthage – Dido – but also by the reliefs on her temple of Juno (Hera) there. The last of these shows Penthesilea herself.[89] Much might be said of this interplay of Italy, Troy, Greece, and Africa around Amazons, and its own historical context under the emperor Augustus.[90] Most important here, however, is the story of another Amazon – Clete. She has no direct connection with Heracles, but links rather to Achilles' duel with Penthesilea. Clete was a servant of the Amazon queen, shipwrecked in southern Italy. We have her story primarily from another Ptolemaic author – the poet Lycophron, whose work is learned and obscure. These are the prophetic ravings of Cassandra, the Trojan princess:

> And others will take the steep Tylesian
> Hills and sea-washed Linus' craggy cape,

[86] Further, Bundrick 2019.   [87] Bowra 1957.
[88] *Aen.* 11.648, a poem much discussed by Borowski 2021
[89] E.g. Lowenstam 1993.   [90] Henderson 1994.

134

The land plots of the Amazon,
Submitting to the yoke of a slave woman,
Servant of Otrere's bronze-capped daughter,
Whom a wave will lead to a foreign land, a wanderer.
While breathing her last, her stricken eye.
Doom for the ape-faced Aetolian,
Will cut him down by deadly timber.
Crotoniates sacked the city,
Destroying the Amazon's fearless daughter,
Clete, mistress of the homeland of her name.

(Lycophron 993–1004)

Three Amazons are indicated in this difficult verse. First, 'Otrere's daughter' is Penthesilea, with allusion to her death. A second Amazon is Clete, servant of the mighty queen. She had taken ship, while her mistress died at the hands of Achilles.[91] Shipwreck followed. She somehow became ruler of her new land in southern Italy, where the sea had brought her. Possibly she had married the ruler there, who had then died and left her as queen.[92] The third Amazon is also Clete, for the shipwrecked Clete had established a dynasty of queens who would all bear this name.

Much of the story is opaque, but it clearly belongs to south Italian traditions around Tarentum, the famous temple of Hera Lacinia (on a cape of this coast), and the maiden-centred myths of the western (or Epizephyrian) Locrians. Ancient commentators indicate that the first Clete herself founded a city (also called Clete) and ruled the area, where her throne passed through a female line. Lycophron says that the city and its last queen were ended by neighbouring Croton. However, the first Clete also had

---

[91] An ancient commentator suggests she was seeking her mistress.
[92] For sources, Moscati-Castelnuovo 1999.

a son, Caulon, who founded the city of Caulonia on this coast east of Rhegium, looking across to Sicily.[93] Was he another Hippolytus?[94] Or did this Amazon tale of the western Greeks allow the Amazons (perhaps with a favourable Hera) to have sons without catastrophe?

Around AD 77, when the elder Pliny sought to describe the southern coastline of Italy, he saw it not as a boot-sole, but as an inverted Amazon shield. Its crescent coastline, he explains, was framed by the outer horns of the 'shield' – the Lacinian promontory (the toe) on the west and Leucopetra on the east (the heel). As with the bow-shaped coastline of the Black Sea, it was easy to see in this physical geography (as also in Clete's shipwreck) the work of supernatural forces, such as were seen to have located Italy as a whole in an ideal place for empire.[95] While Clete's story tends to the western horn, we are also told of a city named Amazonia on the eastern side, among the Messapians.[96] Clete's story shows that Amazon traditions across the region were not all about Heracles, though much revolved around him in Italy as elsewhere – at Tarentum and nearby Messapian Amazonia, whose Boeotian-Euboean connections seem to link with the various Amazons and the river Thermodon there.[97]

---

[93] Servius, on *Aeneid* 3.553: he knew a fuller tradition; cf. also on 3.552.
[94] See Chapter 8.
[95] Pliny, *NH* 3.43; cf. 4.86 on the bow (also Amazonian). On possible Greek predecessors, Amm. Marc. 22.8,10.
[96] Steph. Byz. s.v. Amazones.
[97] E.g. Steph. Byz. s.v. Messapion; and s.v. Boeotia (once named Messapia).

6

Shipwreck and Reptiles
The Queens of Southern Russia

~

The defeat of Amazons was not so much an end as a beginning – of new communities, cults, structures, and customs. And what rose from the ashes of Amazon destruction – an individual Amazon death or their collective end – was usually more normative, so that an aberrant and failed Amazon lifestyle was effectively transformed from all-female idiosyncrasy into a new reality, less challenging to familiar Greek ideas and practices. In that way Amazon demise was often the beginning of Greek civic and cultural history, as well as the history of non-Greeks – so-called 'barbarians'. For Greeks imagined that Amazons (themselves barbarians) sparked important transformations among non-Greeks too, or (as often in Asia Minor) among peoples and settlements which were not simply Greek. Amazons were early – at the beginning of things. Their society and achievements – however strange and fleeting – seemed to offer explanations, among Greeks and non-Greeks alike. Moreover, the destruction of Amazons (with and without their imperial ambitions) fragmented and spread their possible influence well beyond their homeland in Themiscyra. Disaster and diaspora enabled their contribution to human society from past to present.

It was the Amazon diaspora from Themiscyra that created Amazonian customs in southern Russia, east of the river Don (the ancient river Tanais). The idea was well established by the late fifth century, when Herodotus told the origin-tale of a non-Greek people there – the Sauromatians. The story goes that they were the descendants of Amazon castaways and youths of the Scythians who lived west of the Don. He made no claim to direct knowledge of this area, and was clearly drawing upon earlier writers, perhaps very early ones. For in a survey of early stories of the region, we find these Sauromatians bracketed with peoples of early fantasy – the Hyperboreans in a north so high that its climate is Mediterranean, and the one-eyed Arimaspians, who battle griffins for gold.[1] Amazons may have featured there early, too. Herodotus was at least dubious about these tales, while maintaining respect for them.[2] There is scant reason to suppose that he believed the literal truth of the Amazon story he relates.

However, it is Herodotus who provides our first taste of the story, which continued to be told in the centuries that followed, albeit with variants. In fact, within this story, Herodotus provides our earliest prose account of Amazons in action, and at some length. That is all the more remarkable, since he otherwise chose to give Amazons a wide berth. They receive almost no attention in his wide-ranging *Histories*, despite the various exploits claimed for them by others by his day. Amazons should have had a place in his very first paragraph, which traced the abductions of women between Europe and Asia. Where, for example, was Theseus' abduction of his Amazon wife-to-be? And there

---

[1] Strabo 11.2.6, perhaps from Aristeas, on whom Braund 2024.
[2] Further, Gagné 2021.

is no word either of the extensive empire that Amazons were said to have created in Asia Minor, though our author finds space for a puzzling period of supposed Scythian rule there. Herodotus holds forth on Sauromatian origins not because of any Amazon interest, but as part of his tour de force on the Persians' invasion of the northern lands of the Black Sea region – an abject failure that is a prequel to their failed invasion of another apparent pushover, Greece itself. He tells how, as Persians advanced northwards, the Scythians looked for allies and a strategy for resistance. They gathered delegates from motley neighbours – some (the werewolf Neuri, the cannibal Maneaters) more outlandish than others. The Sauromatians sent delegates too. Herodotus offers a few words on each of these peoples, but says most about those with a connection to Greek culture. This is the context for the origin-story of the Sauromatians, wherein it was Greek agency that brought Amazons into play. Earlier Greek texts on the story might help to account for our author's unusual willingness to find space for Amazons at all.

The great value of his account is the vision it provides of Amazons' resilience and resourcefulness at their lowest ebb. We often glimpse these qualities elsewhere, but Herodotus' story brings them to the fore. Amazon mastery of language and manipulative persuasion drives the whole account. The narrative illustrates how military skills and physical courage were part of a much more developed Greek image of Amazons as powerful and independent in more subtle ways too. Their courage was intelligent, not simply brutish. Their physique was not only for battle but was also good in male eyes for bed and reproduction. Their very freedom was an erotic opportunity, which they might not be shy to take. All this is especially significant in an account provided by an author whose taste for Amazons was limited.

This story of Sauromatian origins provides an exceptionally expansive description of Amazons in thought, word, and deed. And yet we must bear in mind too that these are Amazons in a state of desperate crisis and impending doom. Certainly, their responses to these troubles are admirable and effective, but it remains unclear how far their choices and behaviour would have taken the same path under more regular circumstances. These Amazon castaways were clever and adaptable enough to make the most of options that were few. Their Scythian counterparts tend to look far more Greek than elsewhere in Herodotus' long disquisition on them – an ethnography remarkable for its gory horrors. He hints at Greek admiration for aspects of their grim culture, but keeps a clear distance from most of that and touches the thorny question of whether these Black Sea peoples were rather dim.[3] Certainly, we see the Amazons run rings around them.

The Origin-Story

The story starts with shipwreck near the mouth of the Don.[4] Three Greek vessels were shipping them back from a raid on their homeland, Themiscyra.[5] The Amazons had managed to take over the ships and kill the Greeks. They were not ready for slavery, but they now had a different problem. They knew nothing of sailing. These were early

[3] Hdt. 4.46. On Greekness here, see Dewald 1981.   [4] Hdt. 4.110.
[5] Herodotus makes no attempt to locate this raid in the various stories of such expeditions.

times, when Greeks claimed such knowledge for themselves. Even coastal non-Greek peoples might be ignorant of ships, like Odysseus' Cyclopes and our hapless Amazons, both very early.[6] When Amazons attacked Athens, they took an extraordinary detour to east and north, so that they could get there by land, around the Black Sea and down through Thrace and Thessaly. There was no shame in such ignorance, but rather the opposite. For a moral question attended movement by sea, which seemed to bring unwelcome contacts, corrosive change, and a collapse of space and distance that threatened traditional values and lifestyles. Amazons might take a pride in ignorance of such practices, but not at this precise moment.

These Amazons were now at the mercy of wind and wave, which carried them north from the Black Sea into ancient Maeotis, the Sea of Azov. At last the ships were cast ashore at a place called The Bluffs by Greeks,[7] who had a trading post there. It is probably modern Taganrog, famous for its red cliffs, where pottery finds indicate an early Greek presence by about 600 BC.[8] No doubt the Greeks there valued their small claim to fame in an Amazon story. Even a trading post might want an identity and links to a broader past. Indeed, Kremnoi should not be underestimated. Herodotus presents it elsewhere as a rare Greek landmark on the sweeping steppe of the dominant Scythian grouping – the nomadic Royal Scythians, who regarded other Scythians as their slaves.[9] Elsewhere again he also seems to know of a sea route

---

[6] Clay 1980.   [7] In Greek, *Kremnoi*.   [8] Kopylov and Larenok 1994.
[9] Hdt. 4.20.

between Themiscyra and southern Russia near the junction of the Black Sea and the Sea of Azov – much of the Amazons' journey. Perhaps we should infer, as in many origin tales, the unfolding of a supernatural plan, whereby nature would take the Amazons to a region which would suit them.[10]

For, when the Amazons came to land, the first thing they saw was a herd of horses feeding on a grassy plain. Nothing could be better. Kremnoi had not yet been established and might have been awkward in any case. Excellent with horses, the Amazons were soon mounted and roving this new land, not so unlike the homeland from which they had been seized. Fearless and desperate, they raided the Royal Scythians, who proved to be more than a match for them. However, the Scythians, puzzled by these bold and unknown raiders, were astonished to discover that they were women. Some Amazons died in battle with the Scythians, and their dead bodies – stripped and inspected – showed the unlikely and unexpected truth. The Scythians' response is very telling, and crucial to our understanding of the significance of Amazons in ancient society. The Scythian elders – ever confident in their superiority – decided that the best way to deal with these warrior women was to have children by them. For inspection of the dead Amazons and experience of fighting them had demonstrated that these were fantastic breeding stock, an idea which resonates throughout Greek traditions on Amazons. Strong young women make strong sons: the idea recurs in different tales, but the outcomes often prove unpredictable and disappointing, as here. For,

---

[10] Hdt. 4.86.

while Scythian elders anticipated the benefits of children from these remarkable women, their confident optimism was misplaced, as in many other stories of Herodotus' *Histories*, including the disappointment of Persian kings defeated by the Greeks against all expectation.[11]

The Amazons had not been asked, of course, and when the Scythian elders set their plan in motion, things soon enough took a different turn. All started well enough. The Scythians had sent a band of their young men to track the Amazons without engaging them in battle. When Amazons wandered from the main group (in search of a convenient bush), a Scythian youth approached her – cautiously, no doubt. In this way, contact was made. Importantly, these Amazons were very happy to have sex with the Scythian youths. Greek girls were not expected to behave with such sexual freedom: Greek traditions are full of young women who hold back or flee from such advances, even when their suitors are gods. But Amazons lived by different rules. In any case, this was an exceptional situation, in which Amazons' options were limited, albeit couched within the familiar polarity of bed and battle. Amazons never show distaste for sex with men, though we sometimes meet the notion that they had a law that required them to kill before they had the right to sex. By and large Amazon traditions show a taste for men that contributed to the erotics of young men's lust for these challenging (but available) beauties. The modern quest for homosexual Amazons or the like has proved fruitless and ever more desperate, since it lacks any basis in ancient sources and runs counter to what these tell us.

---

[11] Braund 1998.

As the Amazons and Scythians paired up, the plan of the Scythian elders began to unravel. The Amazons had their own plan. By now they had started to learn the language of the youths,[12] so that conversation was possible. The youths were notably slower. The story required that, since the future Sauromatian language was like Scythian, not the Thracian spoken by Amazons. And yet we are also left with a sense of the Amazons' superior intelligence, all the more so when they persuaded their boyfriends that their future demanded a home away from Scythian society. They pointed out that their Amazon ways were hardly compatible with the quiet ladies of Scythia, who spent their days sitting in wagons, making clothes and the like.

The Scythian elders had not thought or cared about that, but the point was a good one. Nevertheless, it was also revolutionary in Greek terms. For in Greek society the young woman married into her husband's home not only metaphorically, but also physically. The Amazons did not seek to return to their own lands, but neither did they follow the expected path to their in-laws. The Scythian elders had not anticipated such upheaval, but Greek culture was familiar enough with Amazons and knew their revolutionary tendencies, already clear enough in their seizure of the ships, their raiding, and their sexual activity. The Greek audience of the story would be less surprised than its Scythian elders when the new couples took the inheritances of the youths and departed from Scythia by crossing the Don eastwards, and there creating an entire new people, the Sauromatians. While the Scythian elders had planned to develop their own people

---

[12] See Nolan 2021 for a language-centred analysis of the story.

Plate 1 Theseus and Amazon, as restored on the Athenian Treasury at Delphi c. 490 BC. Public domain.

Plate 2 Terracotta thigh-guard, decorated with arming Amazons, c. 500 BC. Photo: David Braund.

Plate 3 Silver coin (obverse) of the city of Cyme, located north of Ephesus on the coast of the eastern Aegean (Aeolis). It shows the city's Amazon founder, named Cyme. c. 150 BC. Photo by courtesy of CNG (www.cngcoins.com).

Plate 4 Bronze coin of Cyme (obverse), showing the goddess Artemis (holding torch?), as she clasps hands with an Amazon (probably Cyme). Second century BC. Photo by courtesy of CNG (www.cngcoins.com).

Plate 5 A hunting Amazon, mounted. Detail from a mosaic floor showing four Amazons attacking big cats, partly damaged. She has a resonant Amazon name, as her three companions seem also to have, Melanip(p)e, in Greek letters. This and other fine mosaics were unearthed recently in a substantial villa near modern Urfa in south-eastern Turkey (ancient Edessa). Style and lettering suggest a date around AD 500 or so. Photo: David Braund.

Plate 6 Statue of a wounded Amazon: Roman copy of a Greek
original taken to have stood in Artemis' sanctuary at Ephesus.
Public domain.

Plate 7 Attic red-figure vase. Theseus (named on the vase), supported by his Amazon (here named Antiope, left), fights an Amazon (Queen Molpadia?). Around 475–425 BC, perhaps painted by Polygnotus. Photo: © The Israel Museum, Jerusalem, by Yoram Lehmann.

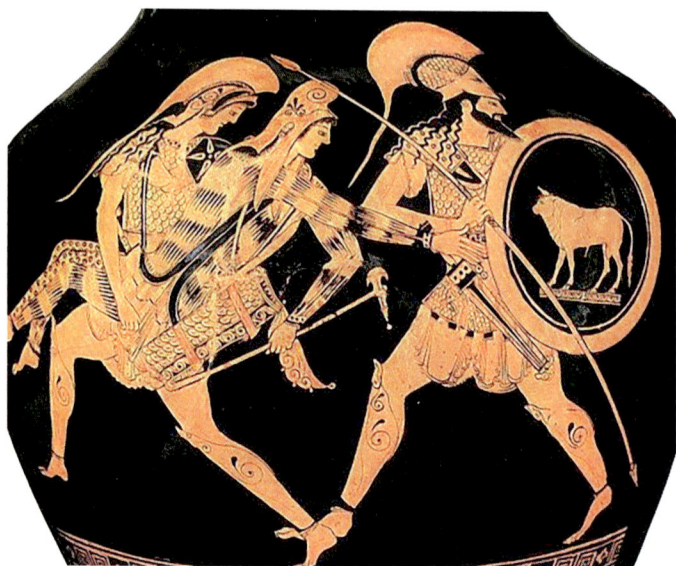

Plate 8 The so-called Croesus vase (side B). Attic red-figure.
Theseus (named) abducts Amazon (here named Antiope) from
Themiscyra, assisted by Pirithous (named). She retains her axe,
but does not use it. Painting attributed to Myson, around 500 B C.
Drawing.

Plate 9 Attic red-figure. A sorrowful Amazon leads a horse
away from a post, possibly a grave-marker. Her axe hangs loose
in her hand. Around 450 BC. Photo: Archaeological Museum,
Ferrara. Courtesy of Ministry of Culture – Photographic
Archive Regional Directorate of Museums of Emilia-Romagna.
The rights holder prohibits the further reproduction or dupli-
cation by any means.

Plate 10a Attic black-figure. Heracles (dressed in the Scythian style outfit of an archer) fights an Amazon who wields an enormous example of the familiar *pelta*, the crescent shield of light infantry in Thrace and elsewhere. She tries to protect a fallen Amazon. Around 525 BC. Photo by courtesy of Penn Museum, University of Pennsylvania.

Plate 10b Interior view of a *pelta* shield, probably held by Penthesilea. From the temple of Apollo Smintheus, decorated in marble with scenes of the Trojan War and life of Achilles (cf. Homer *Iliad* 1.39; Strabo 13.1.46). Around 150–125 BC. Photo: David Braund.

Plate 11 Attic red-figure, the shoulder of a water jar. Male warrior drives his spear into a long-limbed Amazon, armed with bow. Plausibly identified as Achilles' defeat of Penthesilea. Around 500 BC. Public domain.

Plate 12 Attic black-figure, made by Exekias (signed) and taken to be painted by him. Machine-like Achilles (named) kills fallen Penthesilea (named), hardly dressed for battle. Dated around 575–525 BC. Photo: David Braund.

Plate 13 Attic red-figure kantharos (wine cup). Heracles putting Amazons to the sword. Dated around 500–450 BC. Public domain.

Plate 14 Marble section of a battle scene, showing Greeks fighting Amazons, apparently in duelling pairs. Probably decoration surviving from a tomb. Here the Greek male is nude, but sports a helmet and substantial shield. The Amazons are lightly clad, but have shields here and weapons which have not survived. Found in Attica, dated to the fourth century B C. Photo: David Braund.

Plate 15 Marble image of a mounted Amazon, very lightly dressed. It survives from the decoration on the temple of Asclepius at Epidaurus, where it is thought central to a battle of Greeks and Amazons on the west pediment. The Amazon is usually identified as Penthesilea. Dated to the early fourth century BC. Photo: David Braund.

Plate 16 Central scene on the so-called Tiryns shield,
a terracotta roundel found in a pit on the site of ancient Tiryns.
A helmeted figure holds a sword on high, grasping an
opponent's hair, ready to strike. Identifications are problematic,
but the image is often interpreted as the killing of an Amazon,
possibly Achilles and Penthesilea. Dated around 700 BC, among
our earliest Amazon images. Public domain.

Plate 17 Attic black-figure, scene from the Trojan War. Achilles carries the lifeless body of Penthesilea (with white flesh) across the battlefield, after killing her. Her eyes are closed. A passing figure turns towards him, probably the insulting Thersites, whom he will soon also kill in response. Dated to last years of sixth century BC. Photo: David Braund.

Plate 18 Attic red-figure cup, decorated interior, usually taken to show Achilles putting Penthesilea to the sword as she gazes up at him. The smaller warrior to the left is probably Thersites, whose mouth is open: he seems to speak to Achilles. Dated to the first half of the fifth century BC. Public domain.

Plate 19 Campanian ware. Helmeted Achilles holds the body of Penthesilea, in her Amazon gear, with her horse in the background. Dated to the fourth century BC. Photo: Museum of University College Dublin.

Plate 20 Large marble plaque from the Roman imperial cult-complex at Aphrodisias in Caria. Achilles supports dying Penthesilea, as her great axe slips from her right hand. Dated to the first century AD. Photo: David Braund.

Plate 2 1 Gilded silver dish from Bulgarian Thrace, featuring Amazons in combat. Dated to the fourth century BC. From an uncertain context, most probably a burial. Photo: Ivan Marazov.

Plate 22 Attic black-figure. Heracles tackles a group of
Amazons, who combine hoplite helmets, shields, cuirasses, and
spears with bare limbs, shown in white. Dated around 530 BC.
Public domain.

Plate 23 Marble image from the west pediment of the temple of Apollo Daphnephorus at Eretria in Euboea. Theseus carries off his Amazon, abducting her from Themiscyra. Dated to the last decade or so of the sixth century BC. Photo: David Braund.

Plate 24 Marble image of Heracles, about to kill an axe-wielding Amazon. Decoration from a temple at Selinus in western Sicily (Temple E, probably of Hera). Dated to the middle of the fifth century BC. Public domain.

Plate 25 Campanian vase, southern Italy. A statuesque Amazon queen, holding a long spear vertically, offers her belt to a young and largely nude Heracles, leaning on his club. She sports a fox-fur hat and Thracian boots, while he has a wreath on his head. A young male stands behind him, largely nude. Her white horse grazes in the background. Dated to the fourth century BC. Photo: David Braund.

Plate 26 Upper portion of a marble cult-statue of Artemis at Ephesus, in the columnar form of Artemis that was usual there. For Artemis as archer-huntress, see the bronze coin from Cyme in Plate 4. Here the Ephesian goddess's clothing is covered with symbols. The protuberances on her chest are not part of her body, and are perhaps the honey of her bees (we know they were honey-coloured). Dated to Roman period. Photo: David Braund.

Plate 27 The so-called Kallithea Tomb (Athens), the burial monument of a family from the city of Istria, close to the south of the Danube delta on the western Black Sea coast. The head of the family was named Niceratus, and his family had grown wealthy in Athens. The tomb recalls the Mausoleum, and also had an Amazon frieze, of which parts have survived, visible towards the base. Dated to the later fourth century BC. Photo: David Braund.

Plate 28 Detail from the so-called Elgin Throne, from Athens. Theseus is killing an Amazon. Since the image of the Tyrannicides (shown on the other side of the chair) was copied from a famous monument in classical Athens, we must wonder whether this too reproduces such a statue. We know that Theseus killed the leader of the Amazon siege of the city (Queen Mopadia) and that this Amazon's death was monumentalised at Athens. Possibly the image here alludes to her monument. Both the Tyrannicides and Theseus' prior conquest of the Amazons were landmark events in the story of Athens and its democracy. Public domain.

Plates 29 **and** 30   Two marble slabs, brought up from the harbour of Athens at Piraeus. Both are Roman, probably copies of Greek originals. Many believe that these scenes reproduce scenes of Amazonomachy on the front of the shield held by the great statue of Athena in the Parthenon. Together they show Amazons attacking uphill, probably towards the Acropolis, with a wall representing Theseus' constructions of the new Athens. Photos: David Braund.

Plates 29 **and** 30 (cont.) Photos: David Braund.

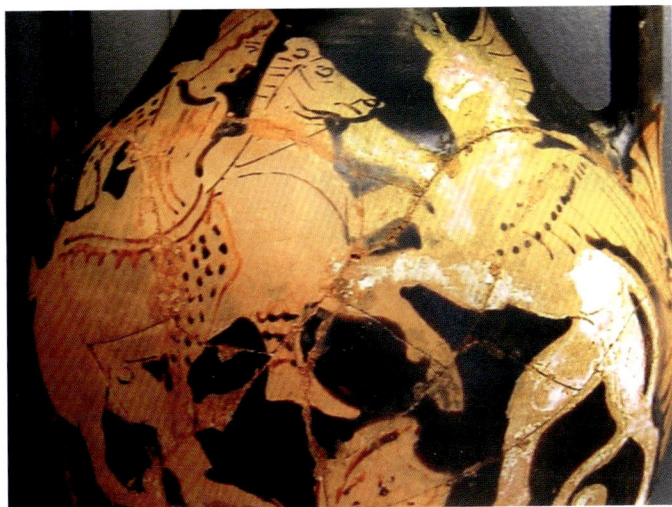

Plate 31 Attic red-figure vase (*pelike*), showing a mounted Amazon (sometimes claimed as an Arimaspian) battling a white griffin. So-called Kerch ware, fourth century BC. Photo: David Braund.

Plate 32 Gold platelet from the diadem (stylized *kalathos*, a wool-basket) worn by the deceased woman in Tomb 1, Bol'shaya Bliznitsa, Taman peninsula, South Russia. Dated to the fourth century BC. Photo: The State Hermitage Museum, St Petersburg © The State Hermitage Museum / Photo by Alexander Koksharov.

through the addition of Amazons, the new couples had made a fresh start elsewhere. The Scythians were thereby diminished, even if relations were broadly friendly with the Sauromatians, as in the meeting to create another plan – against the Persians.

The Naming of Amazons

The whole story served to explain how the women of the Sauromatians came to be so different in social position and habits from the women of Greece, Scythia, and elsewhere. The Sauromatian women are also given the marital restriction that we find among Amazons. Herodotus concludes:

> The women of the Sauromatians follow their old lifestyle, and go hunting on horseback, with their men and without them. And they go to war, dressed the same way as their men. In language, the Sauromatians have always spoken their own version of Scythian, since the Amazons had never learned it properly. As for marriages, their custom is not to permit a girl to marry before she has killed a man among their enemies, and some girls even die of old age without marrying, because they are unable to satisfy this rule.
>
> (Herodotus, *Histories*, 4.116–17)

These Sauromatian women are still Amazonian, it is claimed, though clearly they are not Amazons in Herodotus' account. They were wives and mothers – women who shared some of their menfolk's more violent occupations. Their supposed Amazon heritage does not mean that they have any political authority. They have hunting and warfare in common with men, we are told, but who is in charge of Sauromatian society? Who commands its army? Herodotus' silence suggests that the men

145

are routinely in charge. Similarly, the origin-story shows Amazons deploying their persuasive skills to bring the young Scythians to their way of thinking – the youths themselves actually take the decisions – or believe they do.

Herodotus makes clear that other Greek authors had written on the peoples of the north before him. On occasion he refers to them in praise or criticism. This origin-story was not his own confection, especially as his taste for Amazons was very limited. In fact, some decades later, Plato in his *Laws* brings Sauromatian women into his exploration of the significant advantages in bringing Greek women into the military, training girls along with the boys and giving them roles in the army of an ideal state.[13] He cites them as a real-world example of women who can do that, stressing also their numbers and consequent force – perhaps with a nod to Priam's remarks to Helen on the massive army that awaited the Amazons on the banks of the Sangarius in his youth.[14] At the same time, he nods also to the Amazons, as an Athenian author should, 'persuaded by the ancient myths'.[15] Plato's thinking was often extreme, designedly challenging. However, we have here a good example of the impact of ideas upon developing social thought, even where those ideas are rooted in myth and uncertain ethnography – likely from the influential Herodotus.

And yet there were other accounts, as we have seen. By chance a medical writer of the Hippocratic school almost brings Amazons and Sauromatians together for us, at around the same date. This unnamed writer takes a different angle:

In Europe there is a Scythian people, living around the Maeotis, different from the other peoples. They are called

[13] *Laws* 804e–806b.   [14] *Iliad* 3.189.   [15] *Laws* 804e.

'Sauromatians'. Their women ride horses, and launch arrows and javelins on horseback, and they battle with enemies until they are married. But they cannot leave their unmarried state until they have killed three of their enemies, and until then they do not cohabit or carry out the required sacrificial rites. She who takes a husband no longer goes riding, except when there is a need for full mobilisation. They do not have a right breast. For while they are still children, their mothers heat a bronze instrument made for the purpose and put it on the right breast and cauterise it, so that its development is halted and all strength and size is given to the right shoulder and arm.

(*Airs* 17)

Similarities with Herodotus' account are clear enough, but we should note the complete omission of Amazons from this medical version. They are visible only through an interpretative lens which focuses on the Amazonian practices mentioned. A medical writer had no need to explore origins and causes after the manner of a historian. His concern was real Sauromatians, not mythical Amazons. His omission of Amazons confirms again that serious writers of the fifth century BC drew a sharp distinction between the real women of their world – albeit distant – and the Amazons of legend.

At the same time, ethnographic details are rather different. The requirement to kill before marriage is extended from one to three kills, with extra flourish. Here the women cease riding and hunting upon marriage, whereas Herodotus suggests they did not. Most striking is the focus on cauterisation of the breast. Herodotus has no word about that, despite his own sustained interest in medical matters and, specifically, in the habits of the

Scythians in mutilating, skinning, and otherwise altering bodies and their remains. Herodotus even shows a concern with milk production in females, and in Scythia.[16]

For all their similarities, our two authors, with their different agendas, represent traditions that are significantly different in substance and detail. There were more voices besides, from which we hear much less. Hellanicus of Lesbos, for example, was a contemporary who somehow wrote of cauterising the breast, apparently among Amazons. The late antique confection of a learned commentator brings him into an etymological dispute on the name of the Amazons, though we should not assume that Hellanicus was even aware of such a debate:

Why are they called Amazons? Because they used to cut off the right breast, so that it would not impede archery. That is not true. For in that way they would kill. Hellanicus says – and Diodorus – that they cauterise the spot with iron before it has grown, so that it would not grow.[17]

Given his medical awareness, Herodotus may well have considered such breast-mutilation a nonsense. While Hellanicus made the obvious point that it would kill the patient, Herodotus will very likely have been aware of the danger and ineffectual results of cauterisation too, among real Sauromatians or imaginary Amazons. Consequently, if there had been some attempt already to find an etymology

---

[16] Hdt. 4.2, transferred to mares: further, on this gynaecology, see Thomas 2000.

[17] *FGrH* 4 F107, with Fowler 2013, 693 on the uncertain final clause of this text.

of the Amazon name in breast removal or reduction, he would not have been attracted to it. He was not against the study of names in itself. He notes the meaning of what he gives as the Scythian name for Amazons – Oiorpata, 'Men-killers' (Oior, 'men'; pata, 'killers'). How he 'knew' this remains unclear, while his research on Anacharsis does not encourage acceptance of his Scythian researches.[18] But etymology had a powerful appeal to ancient and mediaeval mentalities, where many a ludicrous example was taken seriously by some.

Centuries later, the naming of Amazons becomes more complicated. In the sixth century AD the grammarian Stephanus of Byzantium writes of 'Amazons by the Thermodon, whom they now call Sauromatian women (*Sauromatides*)'.[19] Evidently the late Greeks kept Amazons in their traditional location, but applied a name which touched more contemporary nightmares – the northern barbarians who were variously called Sarmatians (alias Sauromatians) and even Scythians. But this was a millennium or so after Herodotus and no more than a potential confusion for this study. Rather more interesting is a variant, first met in Stephanus' work, where Amazons may be called Sauropatides, he claims. This name looks like an amalgam of Sauromatides with Herodotus' supposed Scythian name for Amazons – Oiorpata. By these late times, Amazons had become a much darker theme, for reasons that are not entirely clear. The fading of local civic traditions, together with the rise of Christianity, seems to have left a space for horror-story fictions about Amazons that start to appear

---

[18] Hdt. 4.76.   [19] s.v. Amazones.

in the aftermath of Alexander's eastern campaigns. By the sixth century AD Amazons have become much more like the monsters that some scholars have attempted to find – without success – in the archaic and classical periods long before. Even Stephanus baulks at stories that these women crippled their male children, offering a tale of abandonment by their husbands – the Sarmatian men, fully occupied in the devastation of Europe. Their boys had grown and tried to displace their mothers, which forced the women to fight. The boys fled into the forest, where they met their end, and the women decided to hobble their sons in future to stop this happening again.

The Sauropatides, or 'female Lizard-treaders', are monstrous enough too. Stephanus reports that Amazons were given this name because they stamp on lizards and eat them. By the twelfth century they were also eating snakes and tortoises. Etymology had created an explanation for Amazons that had nothing to do with breasts – they did not eat a form of grain called *maza*,[20] either much or at all, an indication of savagery and poverty. Amazons were those 'without *maza*', wretched carnivores.[21] These later authors can contribute a great deal by preserving fragments and summaries of lost works from earlier times. However, they belong to a world very different from, say, classical Athens, and not only because of their Christian tendencies. Modern neglect of that gulf has

---

[20] A barley porridge: Schmitt-Pantel 2015, 225.

[21] So Eustathius, bishop of Thessaloniki, in his commentary on Dionysius Periegetes, 828, with his commentary on Homer's *Iliad*, 1.634 (adding tortoises, with an allusion to unspecified stories. The contemporary *Etymologicum Magnum* has much the same, s.v. Amazones).

caused immense confusion in the study of Amazons, which must be avoided at all costs.

As for reptiles, the name 'Sauromatian' might well turn Greek thoughts to lizards, since *sauro-* suggests 'lizard' in Greek. However, no ancient writer makes that connection until perhaps the second century AD. And then we have – at most – only an oblique hint, when Pausanias describes the reptilian appearance of Sauromatian armour dedicated at Athens. This scaly breastplate (made from slices of horses' hooves) was dedicated to the god Asclepius, who had much to do with snakes and their potential for health and sickness.[22] But there is nothing here about Amazons or the eating of reptiles. The best we can say about the occasional ancient concern with Amazon diet is that Greeks certainly had a tendency to name peoples after their food, while Aeschylus at least has Amazons as meat-eaters.[23] But that is a long way from the fantasies of mediaeval Byzantium, which are best set aside. So too the considerable range of other crackpot etymologies across the centuries, including notions that breasts might be involved in the naming of Amazons.[24]

Women in Charge

For Greeks, tales of Sauromatian ways involved a comparison which was seldom made explicit – with Greek norms, as well as occasional exceptions to them. Female

[22] Paus. 1.21.6.
[23] Aesch. *Suppliants* 287–9 (quoted pp. 127–28), with A. Bowie ad loc. There is no hint here that they eat meat raw, as sometimes claimed, but possibly that they do not eat bread much or at all.
[24] See pp. 148–49.

power among Sauromatians could be explained in terms of Amazon origins, while other aspects of Sauromatian society might point to the Scythian contribution, and the interaction of Scythian and Amazon might also be imagined, as with the Sauromatian language – Amazons had done well to learn Scythian quickly, but their shortcomings had produced a language that sounded like bad Scythian. However, the big issue for Greeks was the power of women in this society. The more theoretical thinkers perceived Sauromatian society within a tension between nature and culture. While Plato might ruminate on the practical advantages for a state in training girls to fight (albeit with the long-distance weapons that seemed to suit them), he had also to face questions about what was natural for women to do – were such military roles for women appropriate on that measure? The Sauromatian example might be taken to demonstrate that such roles were indeed natural, especially insofar as these barbarians might seem closer to nature than cultured Greeks. Playfully, he wonders whether he should believe the 'old myth' of Amazons, as he calls it. We have come full circle from a story to explain Sauromatians in terms of Amazons to the validation of the Amazon myth by the historical Sauromatians, even if Plato stops short of making that case.

Neither Herodotus nor Plato say that women controlled Sauromatian society, but there is some hint of their power in both texts. Herodotus' account shows Amazons persuading their besotted boyfriends to abandon their homes and create a new people in a new land, whereas Greek norms assumed that the woman would join her husband's family on marriage. Plato addresses only military matters, but his context was a routine Greek assumption that military significance brought with it political status too. But what of overt female power, such as monarchical structures tended to create – mighty queens, for example, who feature elsewhere in Herodotus' *Histories*? Or there was Aristotle's view that, by and large, arguments from barbarian ways do not much count here – barbarian men and women alike are by nature servile, so hardly a model for Greeks.[25] As Plato's student, the brilliant Aristotle knew about Sauromatians, but he only concerns himself with the quality of their sheep and wool.[26] For him Sauromatian customs were of scant importance. No doubt he would include them in a wider phenomenon among warlike peoples, as he saw them – they tend to be under female domination. Clearly, we should not assume that Sauromatians or others ruled by women are ipso facto weak or militarily vulnerable. Aristotle shows substantial interest in the larger theme of female power (in the home as well as the state) as found among Greeks, famously observing its damaging impact among Spartans.[27] For him gynaecocracy brings a series of moral problems, including a lack of commitment to freedom and an excessive respect for material wealth, so that domestic gynaecocracy was in the interest of forms of male tyranny in a state.[28] He seems also to suggest a conflict between the rule of law and the rule of women – a constitution of custom among the Lycians.[29] Amid Aristotle's ponderings we begin to see that notions of gynaecocracy may have a complex hinterland.

However, the ideas and ideals of such thinkers seldom express the outlooks of Greeks in general. While Aristotle is

---

[25] E.g. *Politics* 1252a–b.   [26] *On the Generation of Animals*, 783a14.
[27] Further, Figueira 2010 on Sparta.   [28] Esp. *Politics* 1269b, 1313b.
[29] Aristotle, fr. 43.

more grounded than the quirky Plato, there is a palpable disconnect between their ivory-tower philosophising and the broad sweep of Greek culture. What Greeks have in common, however, is a concern (perhaps better, a shared anxiety) about the possible rule of women, especially if it might be located among Greeks. In general, Amazons and Sauromatians tended to spark such concerns. If we look at Athenian comedy, for example, we find not only Aristophanes' famous plays on the theme, but two plays of the next century actually entitled *Gynaecocracy*, though their paltry fragments do not tell us much.[30] While this comedy had fun with familiar comic stereotypes of women – drunkards, sex-mad, irresponsible – as with the theorists, comic treatments of female power show women through a peculiar lens. However, these plays do reveal the sustained concern with the theme. Moreover, as with Sauromatian tales, Amazon myth and non-Greek women figure in the mix. In Aristophanes' *Lysistrata*, for example, we have not only reference to Amazons and the Amazonian women of Lemnos,[31] but also key characters with names that evoke Amazons – not only Myrrhine, but also Lampito the Spartan,[32] and perhaps others, including Lysistrata herself.[33] We may wonder whether their tussle with Scythians in the play entails allusion to the Scythian–Amazon encounters of the Sauromatian story – especially

---

[30] By Alexis and Amphis, major playwrights of their day.

[31] Ar. *Lys.* 672–82, 296–305, both spoken by men.

[32] Cf. Justin 4.1 (Lampado the Amazon queen). The name may evoke the torches that figured prominently in the night-time rituals of Artemis and Hecate,

[33] A plausible Amazon name, though it seems not to be attested, while in any case the name was appropriate to the play in other ways besides. Further, Thonemann 2020.

as Aristophanes alludes to Herodotus elsewhere.[34] Aristophanes' mention of Amazonian Artemisia – the Carian queen of Herodotus' native Halicarnassus – seems also to evoke Herodotus' famous account of her actions at the battle of Salamis. There Herodotus' Persian king pronounced her – wryly in defeat – the best man he had (literally, 'My men have become women, and my women men').[35] Throughout the play, its men see themselves as opposing not only Lysistrata's specific attempt to stop the war, but also the prospect of de facto female rule thereafter. Of course, this is comedy, which permits explicit stress on the sexuality of this combat, with the men announcing that they must fight these Amazonian women in the nude to subdue them. At the same time, the play makes much of the women's attempt to use their sexual powers to control their men and so achieve political aims – not so far from the Amazons' manipulation of the Scythian youths.

Rule by women might be imagined in many ways, while a male sense of vulnerability to women in bed might be more disturbing and powerful than any female warrior. Mockery was one way to cope, for male and female alike. Meanwhile, we should note the encounter of a Scythian and an Artemisia in another of Aristophanes' plays, the *Thesmophoriazusae*, first staged in the same year as *Lysistrata*, 411 – a year of political revolution at Athens such as had not occurred for many decades. Here a Scythian public slave is central to the action, while Euripides the playwright is brought on stage in the guise of a female brothel-keeper named Artemisia. Allusion to Salamis is explicit in *Lysistrata*, and (though not explicit) is

[34] Nesselrath 2014.
[35] Ar. *Lys.* 677–80, where her name evokes Artemis too; cf. Hdt. 7.90, 8.87–8; Faraone 1997.

clear enough here too.[36] However, not only the famous naval victory, but also the power of women and gynaecocracy seem to have been to the fore in Aristophanes' works of 411.

Herodotus had already told of the self-confident Queen Tomyris, for example, in the first book of his *Histories*. She ruled the Massagetae, near the Caspian Sea – near the Sauromatians from a distant Greek perspective. They had bizarre social customs, he says, but their queen had both power and quality. It was she who put an end to the insatiable imperialism of the Persian King Cyrus – another defeat where Persians had expected easy victory. To teach him a final lesson on imperialist folly (a favourite theme of our author) she had his severed head dropped in a bucket of blood, to drink its fill.[37]

However, few queens impressed as much. Greeks found it easy to infer from eastern queens that the men of their regions were not properly masculine.[38] On occasion the supposed degeneracy of eastern men, in particular, was connected with the Amazon myth. Most clearly, Lysias thundered that Amazons had only been able to establish their eastern empire because the men there were inadequate – Amazons could not defeat the real men of Athens, who brought out the Amazons' femininity.[39] Myth had a lot to say on female rule, including the sexual domination of men. The most masculine of Greek heroes – Heracles himself – was punished by being enslaved to an eastern queen – Omphale, queen of the decadent Lydians.[40] The abilities of queens varied, as with kings,

---

[36] Ar. *Thesmo.* 1200–1, with valuable comment by S. D. Olson ad loc.
[37] Hdt. 1.212. [38] Hall 1993, with Gruen 2010. [39] Further pp. 48–49.
[40] In general, see Hazewindus 2019; cf. Bichler 2016 on east–west perceptions.

but female rule was always a kind of enslavement. A horror, for sure, but female domination sparked other responses too in the sexual psychologies of Greek men.

In the fourth century BC an unnamed geographer (we call him Pseudo-Scylax) provides our first mention of Sauromatians as a people *gynaikokratoumenon* – 'ruled by women'.[41] Surviving fragments of Ephorus may suggest he also embraced that idea in his extensive history – much read in antiquity. Ephorus had a special interest in Amazons, for he was a man of Cyme, which took pride in its foundation by an Amazon of that name.[42] While no ancient text offers much insight into what female rule meant in practice among Sauromatians, our clearest statement of its force suggests that Greeks imagined a female control that ran right through society, whether or not there was a queen. For Nicolaus of Damascus, a learned courtier of King Herod in Judaea, wrote that Sauromatians 'obey their women in all things as their female masters'.[43] He comes rather late in the tradition, and yet the fact that Sauromatians were singled out as ruled by women suggests that the phenomenon amongst them was more than a matter of queens, who might be

---

[41] Ps.-Scylax 70. The Greek is compressed, so that we might understand him to mean all the Sauromatians or only one of the peoples who might be included under that name. The first is more likely.

[42] Ephorus *FGrH* 70 F160a, where there is no strong reason to attribute the idea of female rule to Ephorus, mentioned in the previous sentence. Stephanus of Byzantium s.v. Amazones (*FGrH* 70 F60b) does not show that Ephorus identified Amazons and current Sauromatians: he is simply mentioned before the identification is made, whether or not he himself made this claim, which is hard to reconcile with his other statements on Amazons.

[43] Nicolaus Dam. fr. 122.

found or imagined elsewhere and have no prominence in what we hear of Sauromatians.

The City of the Axe and Other Tales

Herodotus' concern to give specific detail about the peoples of the north was not shared by most later writers or their readers. While he located the Sauromatians well inland, Greeks tended to want them by the coast – closer to Greeks – and to rename them as the 'Women-ruled' – the Sauromatians' principal characteristic. This path soon leads to a fiction that has fewer roots in Greek communal traditions, for example the Greek novel named *Calligone*, written under the Roman empire. A fragment of it has a Greek girl in Amazon disguise. She refers to bad news about Sauromatians that has upset her, so as not to blow her cover.[44] Like most of the ancient world, the Black Sea region was a locus for such fiction. There were also the *Stratagems* of Polyaenus, broadly contemporary and only a little more historical. This work is a compendium of military vignettes – a handful concerning brave women. They are largely about mental sharpness. Polyaenus gives two stories of heroines, each set near the Sauromatians. Neither heroine is tagged as an Amazon, but we see a region where women are in charge.

One heroine is Amage, described as a queen of Sarmatians, alias Sauromatians. Her name, like her story, is Amazonian enough. She was in charge of the Sauromatians, because her husband had become an alcoholic hedonist. She

---

[44] *P. Oxy.* 5355 and *PSI* 981; cf. López Martínez 2022, with bibliography; see p. 265.

had the confidence to warn the Scythian king off attacking the Greek city of Crimean Chersonesus. And when he replied with contempt, she sent an elite hit-squad to his palace. With surprise on their side, this small detachment killed the king and his closest associates. Amage then put his son on the Scythian throne, after he swore not to wage war on his neighbours, Greek and non-Greek. There was something of Herodotus' Tomyris in this Sauromatian queen.[45] Similar qualities were on show too in Polyaenus' second story from the region – that of Tirgatao. Again the heroine's name is evocative. It echoes a founding figure of Scythian mythology named by Herodotus.[46] Polyaenus describes her as a Maeotian – like the Sauromatians often, from the shores of the Sea of Azov, ancient Maeotis.

Tirgatao was no Amazon. She was married to a certain Hecataeus, ruler of the Sindians, a people east of the Crimea. His name looks Greek, as in fact does most of the little we know about Sindians.[47] Our author's treatment of the local geography suggests that he had no precise grasp of the details, but he mentions a real Bosporan ruler, Satyrus, which dates the events of the story around 400 BC – a few decades after Herodotus completed his *Histories*. It was Satyrus who gave Hecataeus a refuge after his removal as Sindian ruler, and it was Satyrus too who gave a daughter in marriage to Hecataeus so as to seal their alliance. But what of his current wife, Tirgatao? Satyrus demanded that she be

---

[45] Polyaenus 8.56; cf. *ILS* 986 on a Scythian king warned off Chersonesus by the Romans in the mid-first century AD.

[46] Polyaenus 8.55; Gardiner-Garden 1986; Tokhtas'yev 2006; Braund 2018.

[47] Braund 2018.

killed. Instead, Hecataeus imprisoned her, until she managed to escape and evade recapture.

By day she hid in a forest and by night she walked the hard and empty roads until she reached the Maeotian Ixomatae, where her family's palace lay. There she found that her father had died. So she moved in with the man who had succeeded him, raising an army of the Ixomatae and other warlike Maeotians. They overran the land of the Sindians, so that her two enemies both sued for peace. During negotiations they sent Metrodorus, Satyrus' son, as a hostage. The ethical Tirgatao was ready to keep her word, but the men were not. Satyrus persuaded two friends to seek asylum with her and work against her. When she had given them refuge, Satyrus demanded their return.

She repeatedly wrote back that she had guaranteed their safety, honouring the custom of refuge for suppliants. They, however, attacked her. While one of them got her discussing apparently serious matters, the other struck at her with his sword. But the sword broke on her belt, which took the blow. Her bodyguard seized the traitors, and tortured a confession that Satyrus was behind the plot. So Tirgatao again went to war, killing the hostage and filling the land with all the horrors of slaughter and pillage, until Satyrus died in despair. His son and successor, Gorgippos, ended the war by suing for peace in person, with splendid gifts.

Tirgatao was tough in mind and body, underestimated by Satyrus in particular. She was superior also in her ethics. Her belt is especially interesting, given her Amazonian capacities. We remember the talismanic power of an Amazon queen's belt, and should perhaps suppose supernatural forces at work in the unlikely failure of the would-be assassins. As we have seen, such a belt was also a powerful relic of divine birthing (and perhaps its avoidance too) in Greek cult and communal ideology, as in the civic oath at Crimean Chersonesus. It was the belt and all its powers that saved this Maeotian queen in this broader Sauromatian environment. Meanwhile, the fiction seems to have some historical connections. King Satyrus of the Bosporus was real enough. Moreover, a Hecataeus is attested in a verse inscription found in recent years among the Sindians. He seems to have been their ruler. The surviving portion reads:

> After a vow, Leucon son of Satyrus set up this statue
> For Phoebus Apollo, him in Labrys,
> Master of this city of the Labrytae – ruler of the Bosporus
> And Theodosia – who with fight and force drove out
> Octamasades from the land of the Sindians, son of Hecataeus
> The king of the Sindians, who committed his father . . .
> Rule . . . of this city . . . .[48]

The poem marks the promised dedication of a statue (of Apollo?) to Apollo after military victory. Leucon, Satyrus' heir, has rescued Hecataeus, ruler of the Sindians in the middle years of the fourth century. Polyaenus' story entails a similar cast in a similar location. In addition, we seem to have a city named after an Amazon axe, for that is very specifically what *labrys* means. At Halicarnassus the labrys was the axe of the Amazon queen, which Heracles had taken at the time of his sack of Themiscyra – later to pass it to Omphale.[49] Herodotus (of Halicarnassus) may well have

[48] *SEG* 52.740, only these lines survive. Amazonomachy has been claimed in sculpture from the area: see Savostina 2001.
[49] See pp. 190–91.

known the story. For he certainly thought he knew the length of a voyage from Themiscyra to the Sindians.[50] The name of the city, Labrys, suggests that it claimed foundation (and possession of the axe?) after the sack of Themiscyra. If so, this was presumably the axe of the Amazon queen, as claimed at Halicarnassus. The main deity at Labrys (the archaeological site known as Semibratneye, where the stone was found) may well have been Apollo. If that is right, the story there would resemble the tale of Sauromatian origins, to which Herodotus gave space – local peoples were his concern, not Greek cities of the region, which he largely omits altogether, as Labrys. There seems to be some tension between the Halicarnassian claim to the labrys and the civic traditions suggested by the name in south Russia, but such contestation was not unusual. And we know many other versions of such stories of foundation caused by Themiscyra's destruction.[51] Meanwhile, Apollo's preeminence at Labrys would accord well enough with a role for his twin sister Artemis, with her favoured Amazons.

Clearly, there were tales of Amazons around the Don and southwards to the Black Sea. Some involved Greek settlements, and constituted a form of prehistory, even foundation. There was also a sense of female liberation in Greek thought about this area and its natives. Its scope ranged from the limited freedoms suggested by Herodotus and Plato to the female rule imagined by Pseudo-Scylax and others – which (as Aristotle makes clear) was consistent enough with military power and men's warlike ways there. An Amazon diaspora across the sea from looted Themiscyra offered an explanation for the phenomenon, which may have had roots in actual social practices, as Herodotus suggests among the Sauromatae. It has often been observed that nomadism might enhance female roles, but that is not much help here. Scythians were nomadic enough, but their women are specifically inactive by Amazon standards, both in Herodotus' account and in the Greek medical tradition. Moreover, the Sindians and Maeotians were not nomadic, nor were the settlements at Kremni and Labrys-Semibratneye. It was the Sauromatians who were picked out as 'woman-ruled'.

Finally, a few words are needed on the interesting case of Hypsikrateia, much discussed and mangled by modern fantasists. She was among the wives of Mithridates VI Eupator, who built an empire around the Black Sea coasts about 100 BC. After three wars with Rome and considerable family treachery, he committed suicide in the Crimea in 63 BC. Hypsikrateia is mentioned as especially loyal to the king. Her origins and life are unknown beyond that key quality. However, she seems to be named in an inscription found underwater in what would be the land of the Sindians, at Phanagoria – an epitaph or part of a larger memorial. In her boundless love for Mithridates, we are told, she set aside queenly adornments and dressed as a Persian-style cavalryman, so as to share his tribulations more easily. She cut her hair short, rode horses, and accustomed herself to weapons – all to join her man in his final flight from the Romans to the Crimea by way of the eastern Black Sea coast. Her story survives in two moralising accounts of Mithridates' demise.[52] Hypsikrateia was a remarkably committed and resourceful woman, as the moralists describe her, but she

[52] Valerius Maximus 4.6.ext.2, on conjugal love.

was not much of an Amazon. She was a woman willing to go to any lengths to share her man's sufferings, becoming a cavalryman to ride off at his side.[53]

---

[53] Val. Max. 4.6.ext.2; Plut. *Pomp.* 33; *SEG* 56.934; Heinen 2012; Facella 2017, 115.

7

Amazon Cities in Asia

Themiscyra, Ephesus, and Halicarnassus

≈

Amazons were a people of Asia Minor, modern Turkey. Mostly we find them there, although they range widely – not only in mainland Greece, but extensively around the frontiers of Greek colonial settlement. In consequence, they recur in local traditions across the Greek world, especially in stories of foundation and the earliest history of cities and cults. While their own migrations help to explain their widespread contributions to Greek beginnings, they also bring a measure of coherence to the varied traditions of these scattered settlements, with connections to central Greek places, as to Athens and its Amazon experience under King Theseus. In ethnic terms Amazons are firmly Thracian – already in early epic. But they are strangely absent from traditions in Thrace. For they moved eastwards to the south-eastern coastland of the Black Sea – they were part of a larger Greek sense that Thracians spread as far as the Caucasus, so that the whole Black Sea can look distinctly Thracian.[1] The principal Amazon home lay on that distant coast, towards Colchis – where the Argonauts went for the Golden Fleece. There, the Amazons occupied the fertile plain of Themiscyra in earliest times, immediately east of the future Greek colony at Amisus, modern Samsun. They had three main settlements there, as myth

---

[1] Braund 2021.

has it. Most famous was Themiscyra itself on the river Thermodon. The town was named after an Amazon, it was said, and shared its name with the plain on which it stood.[2] Two further towns are seldom mentioned – Chadesia and Lycastus.[3] For most ancient writers it sufficed to refer to their homeland as Themiscyra – whether town, plain, or both. Similarly, ancient writers also spoke of the river Thermodon, where the Amazons bathed, with scant concern for the other waters of the plain. For most ancient writers – and their readers – that was detail enough.

On the Plain of Themiscyra

Amazon geography deals in exotic locations – real and yet distant enough to be imaginary. The actual plain was crossed by substantial rivers and rivulets. Together with the considerable rainfall in this corner of the Black Sea, the plain offered lush pastures for the horses that Amazons loved so much. We should be clear that Amazons were not nomads (a repeated fantasy of modern writers), so needed a homeland rich in grassland. The plain also made agriculture much easier than usual, which helped to account for the Amazons' ability to feed themselves. For Mediterranean farming was hard and heavy work. Greek women could and did handle much of that, even preferring such toil to the traditional domestic labours.[4] However, Amazons had also to find

---

[2] Schol. Ap. Rhod. 3.369–72a; Appian, *Mith.* 78.

[3] Pliny, *NH* 6.9, looking eastwards along the coast, locates Chadesia closest to Amisus, Themiscyra farthest away, and Lycastus between them.

[4] Notably on Lemnos.

time and energy for military training and practice. After all, theirs was a military state, broadly comparable with Sparta, where servile helots were set to this work. Amazons had to manage for themselves. The excellent environment of the plain helped to make sense of the Amazons' ability to survive there, while the abundant hunting to be had in neighbouring uplands to the south gave a plausible context not only to food supply, but also to Amazon hunting as a preparation for war. The geographer Strabo describes the wonders of the plain of Themiscyra and its environs, not far to the north of his own beloved homeland at Amaseia in Cappadocia. Millet and sorghum were always available on the plain, he says. This was the rarest of lands – a place where drought never destroyed the crops. No doubt Strabo was encouraged too by his adherence to one of the great ladies of his day, Queen Pythodoris, whose realms neighboured Themiscyra – though his remarks also suggest that the queen had little time for Amazons. She was famously devoted to her husband Archaelaus.[5]

Our earliest detail about the plain and its Amazon settlements comes in a fragment of Hecataeus' *Genealogies*, written about 500 BC at Miletus – an attempt at some early Amazon history.[6] He wrote that Chadesia and the settlement at Lycastus shared the plain with the town at Themiscyra. The Amazons had seized both from an early people there – the Leucosyrii, or White Syrians.[7] In fact,

---

[5] Strabo 12.3.30–1 on the wonders of her own realm.

[6] *FGrH* 1F 7a (Steph. Byz. s.v, Chadesia), with 1F 200. It is not wholly clear that Hecataeus means the river of that name: he may have had a settlement in mind, otherwise unattested by that name. See Fowler 2013, 2.199–200; Dan 2011, and further below.

[7] E.g. Pindar, frr. 172–3, Maehler (in Strabo 12.3.9).

the whole plain may well have been thought theirs until the Amazons arrived. Hecataeus probably identified three groups of Amazons according to their towns – Themiscyrans, Chadesians, and Lycastians. On his authority, it seems, Apollonius Rhodius sketched the situation, with all the display of learning that was fashionable in his day, around 300 BC.[8] For he presents the Amazons as three kindred 'tribes', each settled at one of the three towns on the plain – all under a single queen, and all the daughters of Ares and a nymph named Harmonia. The poet may suggest (he is opaque) that each of these three groups had a military speciality, with the Themiscyrans more heavily armed, the Chadesians as javelin-throwers, and the Lycastians as cavalry.[9] Details remain elusive. However, Hecataeus had good reason to strive. His own city – Miletus – had a strong interest in the Black Sea, where it had been establishing colonial settlements in large numbers through the archaic period. The plain of Themiscyra was obscure enough, but it was also a key location in the geography of Milesian settlement along this coast. We shall see, too, that the commitment to Amazons in the eastern Aegean gave a special significance to their far-off homeland on the Themiscyra plain.

The river Thermodon – a byword for Amazons – collected abundant streams from the mountains behind the coastal plain. However, its wandering courses were only part of the irrigation there. Mighty in Amazon myth, the Thermodon was not the main river of the Amazon homeland. There was also the river Iris, whose delta dominated there, fed by the river Lycus. These rivers

[8] *FGrH* 1F 7b (schol. Ap. Rhod. 2.999).   [9] Ap. Rhod. 2.994–1000.

were no doubt laden with myths of their own, for Greeks
routinely created cults of river-gods and located mythical
events on riverbanks. The principle is beyond doubt, but
again details are elusive. There was a female divinity named
Iris (messenger of the Olympian gods in Homer and elsewhere), but Greeks considered all rivers and their deities to
be male, except the river Styx in the Underworld. The river
Lycus bears the Greek name for wolf – Amazons might
sport wolfish headgear as well as the Thracian hat of fox
fur, the *alopekis*. On occasion, Artemis herself might be
a she-wolf.[10] More locally we have mentioned the town
of Lycastus, while a tributary of the Lycus was named
Skylax, 'Cub'.[11] The Thermodon itself has a name suggesting warmth, but we are never told quite why – warm
outdoor bathing for the Amazons? It shared the name
with a minor river of Boeotia, where Thermodon himself –
the god of the Amazon river – appeared at the battle of
Chaeronea in 338 BC.[12]

Amazons enjoyed an agrarian paradise at Themiscyra,
with divine support never far away – Ares, Artemis, and
her twin brother, Apollo, himself patron of colonial foundations and more. Their small paradise was in tune with
their lifestyle. Their beloved horses could flourish there
in rich pastures. When Greeks imagined the splendid
Enetian horses in these parts, they might have the plain
especially in mind, complete with Amazons as human
fillies.[13] Greek art makes the connection by showing

---

[10] Porph. *Abst.* 4.16. A wolfish hat appears on Amisus' coins c. 87 BC.
[11] Str. 12.3.15. [12] See p. 201.
[13] Strabo 12.3.25, citing some authority. Note the appearance of Amazons
on the horse-rich Nesaean plain p. 241. On fillies in Alcman and
elsewhere, see Chapter 2. The equine nature of Amazons sharpens their

Amazons with reins as their belts.[14] Strabo's thoughts turned to the extraordinary fertility of the Nile delta.[15] Even the bees there were special, and particularly productive in quality honey even in winter, as Aristotle had noted.[16] Bees were close to Artemis, while the rarity of other sugar-sources in antiquity made honey important. However, possession of a paradise required the capacity to keep it against enemy attack. Those who held such lands were famously vulnerable to decline and military defeat by hungrier peoples.[17] The plain of Themiscyra both supported and demanded militarism. Meanwhile, the broader region was wild enough. To the east lay the Chalybes, for example, metalworkers and miners, who – like Amazons – could innovate in iron and steel.[18] The homeland of the Amazons was a bright spot in a corner of the world that was known for its grim darkness.

Greeks of Themiscyra

The first Greeks who came to Themiscyra were on missions to loot and destroy – at least in myth, in the prehistoric time of the Amazons. When real Greeks started to settle this rich land in archaic times and after, violence was best avoided, for diplomacy and cooperation were a surer recipe for colonial success. The Amazons seemed to have passed into myth and memorial, like the great Greek

similarity with Centaurs, usually male and still more equine: see DuBois 1982.

[14] Boardman 1980.
[15] Strabo 1.3.7 (cf. 2.5.24), probably encouraged by the old association of Egypt and the eastern Black Sea, as Hdt. 2.102–5.
[16] *Historia animalium* 554b.   [17] Hdt. 9.122.
[18] Encapsulated in scholia on Apollonius Rhodius 2.158–9.

heroes who had fought them – Heracles, Theseus, and the rest. Yet those epic tales of bygone adventure retained great power – here perhaps even more than in the Greek heartlands. For in the nameless obscurity of much of this colonial periphery, tales of Amazons and masculine heroes were rare beacons of Greek culture. Some of the greatest Greeks had come this way, and the colonial Greeks were no doubt especially proud of that past, which in many ways they had re-enacted through their own arrival and settlement. At Amisus – and so Themiscyra, its possession – an Athenian presence from c. 435 BC further enhanced the significance of Amazons, who were so important in Athenian tradition. Indeed, the extension of Athenian imperial interest in the whole Black Sea at that time must have brought Amazons still more to the fore in Athens and among Greeks of the entire area.[19] Myth merged with reality in this new Black Sea world, so that in the interior to the south, we hear of a mountain called Mt Amazon.[20]

A geographer of the fourth century BC describes the Greek settlement at Themiscyra as a 'Greek polis', suggesting a civic core and the lands around it – all in the hands of Greeks, and dominated by Amisus.[21] There was a pride in the Amazon past at Amisus, where an Amazon later appeared on civic coinage. Some no doubt traced the city's name to the Amazons, though no ancient source says so. At neighbouring Sinope there was an Amazon listed among the civic founders – she was named Sanape, giving rise to the name Sinope, some said.[22] Athenian

---

[19] Hansen and Nielsen 2004, 954.   [20] Pliny, *NH* 6.10; cf. 35.
[21] Pseudo-Scylax 89.   [22] pp. 175–76.

elements at Amisus – which was also named Piraeus after Athenian arrivals around 435 BC – will have been especially interested in the expedition of Theseus against the Amazons of Themiscyra – as also at Sinope. Their own voyages to the region had followed that expedition. They too were heroes, in the footsteps of their great king. When Myson painted Theseus abducting his Amazon (Plates 8 and 23), he was showing a scene from Themiscyra.[23] Themiscyra remained in the shadow of Amisus for centuries, but the Mithridatic Wars brought the Roman general Lucullus there in the late 70s BC. A new spotlight shone briefly on the Amazon past there, for Romans were very aware of myth in the region. When Lucullus attempted to capture Themiscyra by siege, bees and bears appeared to foil his army, they said. These creatures were the forces of Artemis, whose local cult may well have claimed renown from Amazons, devotees of the goddess.[24]

The plain of Themiscyra (or part of it) could also be named after a certain Doias, who belongs to Phrygian tradition – back westwards towards Thrace, whence the Amazons had come.[25] Probably the story was linked to the Grove of Acmon imagined beside the Thermodon, since Doias was Acmon's brother. By the third century BC (probably much earlier) this grove was identified as the place where Ares and Harmonia had sex and created

---

[23] Xenophon omitted Amisus from his self-serving *Anabasis* (Mattingly 1996), but the Athenian involvement there is beyond all doubt: Braund 2019.

[24] Appian, *Mithr.* 78 with Ballesteros-Pastor 2009.

[25] Doias was brother of Acmon and so uncle of the Mygdon named in the *Iliad* as at war with Amazons: see p. 85.

the Amazons.[26] In describing the moment, Apollonius Rhodius evidently tapped into a wealth of lost traditions, while getting his Argonauts past the Amazons before they had gathered their forces for battle. As usual, the Thermodon has a place in the tale.[27] The Argonauts could not tackle Amazons as well as the Colchians who had the Golden Fleece, while the multiple Greek destructions of Themiscyra in myth were also awkward to resolve. Apollonius' version of Heracles' sack of Themiscyra minimises the damage done – it is a negotiation, through which he obtains the queen's 'girdle' – a belt – as ransom for her captured sister, Melanippe ('Black Mare'). Amazons were builders too, so that repeated reconstruction might help to explain repeated Greek destruction. On the island of Ares, west of Amisus, two campaigning queens of the Amazons were credited with building a stone temple to Ares. Amazons had done much the same at Athens on the Hill of Ares, the Areopagus.[28] However, while Apollonius and others might evade inconsistency, the usual Greek view was that Heracles put an end to Themiscyra's Amazons, or (as Athenians might prefer) their defeat at Athens had caused their demise. And yet that was also the beginning of new Amazon tales, away from Themiscyra.

The destruction of Amazon power on the plain of Themiscyra caused an Amazon diaspora. Herodotus recounts the tale of captive Amazons, shipwrecked in southern Russia, who created the Sauromatians – a powerful, woman-led people.[29] He identifies their abductors as

---

[26] See schol. Ap. Rhod 2.992 (Pherecydes, 3F 15). It does not help that a variety of mythical figures bear the name Acmon ('Anvil' in Greek).

[27] See Bekker-Nielsen and Jensen 2015; Robert 1980.

[28] Ap. Rhod. 2.385–7, with p. 200 on Athens. [29] See Chapter 6.

Greeks, but he wisely avoids the awkward choice of a particular Greek expedition. Meanwhile other Amazons scattered across Asia Minor, and played key roles in the foundation and early history of certain cities and cults. Of course, foundation was usually a role for men – colonial traditions seldom include Greek women at an early stage. However, Amazons were close to key deities, especially the main god of colonial foundation – Artemis' twin, Apollo, whose archaic temples were often adorned with Amazon images. The creation of cities and cults always had a supernatural dimension, for which Amazons were well suited. Moreover, these were young women who would soon die, violently. Their deaths resembled blood sacrifice to initiate the new. Their world had ended, but not before their energy and creativity generated new cults and communities for Greek settlers and the like.[30] Indeed, the actions of human males in these matters are regularly accompanied at a supernatural level by female contributions – from goddesses, nymphs, and also Amazons, mortal females of divine parentage. In many a story of foundation there is an amalgamation of male and female actors which serves to bring the new community or cult into being. Amazons were a force for change – challenging, disruptive, and so creative. For there was a dreadful creativity in their fates, caught between girlhood and womanhood. We may compare the awful biography of Iphigenia (another devotee of Artemis), which echoes these themes and takes them beyond Amazons. Expecting marriage at Aulis, she had been sacrificed to Artemis – and yet saved by the goddess, whisked away to oversee the human sacrifices of the

[30] Dowden 1989; Russenberger 2015.

174

Taurians in the Black Sea, only to end her dark existence with cult at Brauron – the recipient of bloody rags left by women who had died in childbirth.[31]

Amazon Diasporas

Amazons had always travelled. Homer shows Amazon armies in very different places, while other accounts describe their ambitious expeditions around the Greek world and beyond. Their expedition from Themiscyra to Athens seems less remarkable when set in that context. Nevertheless, the sack of Themiscyra, however imagined, was the spur to tales of Amazon refugees – survivors in search of new opportunities because their towns and whole society had been wrecked by Greeks. Across Asia Minor, we find Amazons in Greek prehistory, acknowledged and celebrated in a range of cults and rituals. However, we often have minimal context for these practices, while only a few can be firmly linked to Heracles' unwitting creation of this Amazon diaspora.

Sinope's case illustrates the problem, all the more interestingly because the city lay close to the west of Amisus and Themiscyra. Sinope was one of the most important cities of the entire Black Sea. We have touched on its Amazon, Sanape. She had come as a refugee under unknown circumstances – possibly from Themiscyra. Her Thracian ethnicity is very clear. She was known by a Thracian word that declared her excessive consumption of wine, we are told. Thracian women – and men – had a reputation as heavy drinkers, so that Plato puzzled over

---

[31] Petsalis-Diomidis 2018, 461 for some context.

the relationship between warlike culture and drunkenness among northern peoples, including Thracian women.[32] She had married the king of the region – unusual for an Amazon, and probably a sign of her plight. She seems to have left him. Only these bare bones of her story survive, which do not explain why Sinope took her name. Perhaps she had fought for the city, as Theseus' Amazon had fought for Athens. Hecataeus was aware of the tradition c. 500 BC, but we have it largely from Andron of Teos, who wrote in the fourth century BC – his own city had founded Phanagoria, north across the sea from Sinope, and had a colony at Abdera in Thrace.[33] Around 100 BC we see an Amazon of Sinope flagged again in the *Periplus* of Pseudo-Scymnus, whose work was prepared for a king of nearby Bithynia. We may be sure that the Amazon was part of local tradition.

As often, information on relevant civic rituals is slight, but we have a glimpse already in Andron's day, when Sinope responded to a siege, it was said, by parading armed women on its walls:

When the people of Sinope found themselves dangerously short of men during their war against Datamas, they disguised and equipped the most physically suitable of their women to make them look as much as possible like men, giving them pitchers and similar bronze utensils in place of shields and helmets, and parading them on the wall where they were in fullest view of the

[32] Plato, *Laws* 804e–806b.
[33] *FGrH*1F 34, not the Abderan Hecataeus, notwithstanding the Teos–Abdera connection. The Milesian was the famous Hecataeus and needed no ethnic. He also showed considerable interest in non-Greek tongues: frr. 21, 272, 284, 322, 370. See in detail Braund 2010.

enemy. They were not allowed to throw anything however: a woman is recognisable a long way off by the way she throws. And care was taken, meanwhile, to prevent deserters from disclosing what was happening.

(Aeneas Tacticus, 40.4–5)

The story recalls many a ruse. However, at Sinope the Amazon tradition (perhaps in defence of the city) raises the suspicion that this ruse relates to Sanape's story. It resembles a celebration by its women – in procession with paraphernalia that brought women into male space, domesticity to war. This was an Amazon coast, where women at war (if only on show) raised the whole Amazon tradition, complete with its supernatural underpinning. We have seen how Artemis' bears and bees went into action in defence of Artemis' city against Lucullus.

At Ephesus, Artemis' strong ties to Amazons are still clearer (for Ephesian Artemis, see Plate 26).[34] The great temple of Ephesian Artemis dominated the landscape outside the city – often listed among the seven wonders of the ancient world. It is hard to overstate her importance in Greek religion, well beyond her city of Ephesus. Her cult-image is striking (Plate 26) – columnar and covered with symbols and protuberances (most likely honeycombs).[35] It contrasts sharply with forms of Artemis usual in Greek art – a youthful huntress. There was competition between Ephesian traditions about Artemis' birth (located nearby) and the other great centre of her cult, on the island of Delos, where her birth was more familiar to Greeks of the heartlands.[36] The Amazons featured with all forms of

---

[34] Further, Rogers 1991.   [35] Braund 2018.
[36] Tac. *Ann.* 3.61 reports Ephesian denial of their birth on Delos.

Artemis, but they had a special association with Ephesian Artemis and the beginnings of her cult. The details, however, were a matter of abiding disagreement. In the second century AD Pausanias responded to differences in traditions on the Ephesian cult which went back at least to Pindar, in the fifth century BC. Aware of a flurry of inconsistent tales, Pausanias writes:

It seems to me that Pindar did not learn everything about the goddess, for he says that this sanctuary was founded by the Amazons during their campaign against Athens and Theseus. It is true that these women from the Thermodon sacrificed to the Ephesian goddess, since they knew the sanctuary long before. They did so both on this occasion and when they had fled from Heracles. And earlier still some of them had fled from Dionysus, had come to the sanctuary as suppliants, and sacrificed there. But it was not Amazons who founded the sanctuary. It was Coresus, a native of the place, and Ephesus, who is considered a son of the river Cayster. The city of Ephesus took its name from him.[37]

He proceeds to report that Amazons also stayed in the area of Ephesia's sanctuary, to receive its protection. Pausanias came from western Asia Minor,[38] and addresses a key feature of the temple and its environs. The sanctuary was recognised as a place of asylum, where safe refuge could be found under the protection of the goddess.[39] Amazon refugees started that tradition (despite Pindar), seeking protection from the wrath of Dionysus,[40] and later from

---

[37] Paus. 7.2.7. Ephesians favoured Androclus as their founder: Habicht 1984.

[38] Habicht 1984. [39] Its scope changed across time: Fleischer 2002.

[40] Dionysus' defeat of Amazons was local, including Samos: Diod. 3.55. At Ephesus he pardoned them: Tac. *Ann.* 3.61.

Heracles. The Amazon diaspora was important across the area. For several other cities of western Asia Minor imagined fleeing Amazons and the like as principal figures in their foundation and early history – the causes of so much. Famous among these were Smyrna and Cyme, but there were settlements of all size, as well as smaller land-marks, such as fountains and other springs. The sheer number of these Amazon stories was considerable. However, there was also variety – tales were multiplied by the various versions of many such stories.

Beyond Pausanias, mighty Ephesus, for example, was said to take its name from the 'release' (Greek, *aphesis*) felt by Amazons who took refuge there. Amazon asylum could look like the beginning of the city on that view, with Artemis to the fore, especially as *aphesis* also meant the beginning of a race – the course of civic history there. A learned bishop of Byzantine times includes that version in his dazzling survey of such Amazon foundation-stories. He mentions the his-torian Arrian (his lost Bithynian study), but he also had other works which have not survived for us:

That the Amazons once upon a time held many places in Asia, even some springs show, with the same names as Amazons. And indeed cities – such as Ephesus itself, Anaia, Myrina, Aeolian Cyme. There is also an Elaea, a place by Nicomedia, named, according to Arrian, after an Amazon called Elaea. And on the Black Sea there is a placed named Thiba, spelt with an i, from the name of a dying Amazon, one of those destroyed by Heracles. Of those outstanding and more noteworthy, according to Arrian, are those named Tralla, Isocratea, Thiba, Palla, and others. And Smyrna, being an Amazon is also said herself to have taken possession of Ephesus – from her the part of Ephesus called Smyrna has its name. And they say that Ephesus itself was once called Smyrna . . .

They say that Ephesus is the main name, as there was a woman called Ephesus, from whom the city has its name – a handmaid of Artemis – and researchers say that her daughter was Amazo, from whom came the Amazons. And they say that the Amazons were pursued by Heracles (when Eurystheus ordered him to fetch the belt of Hippolyte) and took refuge at Artemis' altar and there gained salvation (*aphesē*), and that the place thereby became Ephesus through a letter-change of its name, Aphesus.[41]

The complexities can be overwhelming. The key point, however, is the scale of the Amazon presence in these civic traditions of Asia Minor. Much remains opaque – notably the way that Amazons took their name from Amazo, who is elsewhere an Amazon princess.[42] And these are far from all – we may notice Sinope's omission, for example. Nor was this only a matter of refugees. The extraordinary account of the imperialist campaigns of an early Amazon queen called Myrina[43] might seem to be simple fiction, without roots in civic traditions. But coins show that it actually does incorporate such traditions – with a possible Amazon presence at Soli in Cilicia (perhaps held responsible for its famous solecisms of language, as among the Sauromatians).[44] She certainly figured in the eastern Aegean, no doubt at the two cities that bear her name (one on Lemnos). There was also her elusive conquest of Lesbos, which seems to be marked on some coins of Mytilene.[45] Although we hear a lot about

[41] Eustathius of Thessaloniki (twelfth century), *Comm. on Dionys.* 828. On Arrian and Alexander's Amazons, see pp. 240–42.

[42] Steph. Byz. s.v. Ephesus says her mother was both queen and Artemis' temple-servant.

[43] Alias Myrine or Myrrhine: see p. 218 on Lemnos.

[44] It was the Amazons' version of Scythian language that created Sauromatian: see Nolan 2021 on linguistics, with Chapter 6.

[45] Ares on the obverse and what seems an Amazon on the reverse (Myrina).

Amazons in local traditions of Asia Minor, there were surely still more, for our data is clearly incomplete.

As for the sanctuary at Ephesus,[46] Amazons had a much wider role than Pausanias indicates. The Ptolemaic poet Callimachus (a contemporary of Apollonius Rhodius) writes not only of Amazon contributions to the early development of the sanctuary, but also of Amazon origins of ritual dancing there. It was Amazons who established the first cult-image of the goddess there, he says, a simple upright log of wood. We must recall the notably upright statue of the cult in historical time, taken to replicate the stiff stance of the initial oak trunk. It was the Amazons who first celebrated rites around this trunk, no doubt under the guiding hand of the goddess herself. And it was the Amazons' extensive dancing that marked the wide foundations of the extraordinary cult-centre to come, again as agents for the goddess. Callimachus not only stresses the key role of Amazons at the very beginning of this most important of sites, but also makes explicit the connection with rituals that have been performed there ever since:

For you also Amazons, enthusiasts for war,
Once in coastal Ephesus set an image
Beneath an oak trunk, and Hippo performed the rite.
And they, mistress Oupis,[47] danced a war dance around it,
First with shields, in armour, and again circling
Having arranged their dancing wide. And shrill pipes
Gave fine accompaniment to maintain the step . . .
. . . . And the sound ran

[46] On important archaeology there, see Østby 1993, esp. 174. On refuge in general, Sinn 1993. On the goddess, Braund 2018 with bibliography.
[47] Artemis.

To Sardis and the Berecynthian land. And they
Stamped their feet in time, and made their quivers sound.
Thereafter that wide foundation around the image
Was built, and the dawn will see nothing more divine,
And nothing more magnificent, easily surpassing even Delphi.
(Callimachus, *Hymn to Artemis*, 237–50, excerpted)

Here the raucous dancing of the Amazons was a female counterpart to other such dance, performed by warrior youths, similarly foundational – the dance of the Curetes along the coast in the grove of Ephesian Ortygia, where Leto had given birth to Artemis and Apollo.[48] Both dances were notably noisy, as befits a war dance. At Ephesian Ortygia the noise frightened off the jealous Hera, who might otherwise have destroyed Leto and her children. The noise of dancing Amazons had a function too, possibly also protection from Hera – again the theme of asylum at the sanctuary. Weapons-dances could be deafening, as here – feet stamping, quivers rattling, shields banging. Our poet stresses the volume of the Amazons' performance.[49] It was so very loud that its sound reached far inland to Sardis, which boasted its own great temple of the goddess, with Mt Tmolus behind. The Berecynthian mountain-range was in Phrygia – the home of noisy dances for Cybele, the Great Mother, and a loud kind of pipes.[50] We glimpse a network of cultic relationships, including Ephesian Artemis and her Amazons, where war and raucous dance in arms met motherhood and security, with young men and women to the fore – all at the interface of Greek and Anatolian religion in western

[48] Strabo 14.1.20. On the various Ortygias, Strabo, and early testimony for Ephesian rites, see *IEph* 1449, with Stephens 2015, 102.
[49] Bron 1996; Bremmer 2008.   [50] Munn 2006.

Asia Minor. Images of Cybele were familiar finds in Ephesian excavations, now displayed in the museum of nearby Selçuk.

Callimachus goes on to make an obscure allusion to the story of Hippo ('Mare'). Her name evokes many another Amazon name, most obviously as a short form of Hippolyte. In that sense she stands for all Amazons, even the most powerful of them, the queen herself. While Amazons, and Hippo in particular, may have established Artemis' cult, the goddess demanded to be in charge and demonstrated her colossal power by disciplining Hippo. We are not given details, but we are told that Hippo refused to dance, that is to perform the ritual that persisted into historical times, as Callimachus had it. Enraged by Hippo's disrespect, Artemis inflicted a vicious punishment, not specified for us. The goddess was very much in charge, and the Amazons were hers to guide, protect, punish, or destroy. Hippo's story exemplified the consequences of Amazon misbehaviour, so that Artemis' control of the Amazons within the culture of her sanctuary and its rites was made abundantly clear.

More broadly beyond the Amazons themselves, Hippo's suffering teaches other women to participate enthusiastically in Artemis' rites. Even Queen Hippo must obey Queen Oupis. An Amazon queen was no more than a servant to Artemis. We may recall Amazo's mother – a queen who was a servant at Artemis' sanctuary. While mortal rulers should always recognise the greater power of immortals, the Amazons were also refugees, so that no Amazon queen should refuse the goddess, whether through pride or for some other reason. While Heracles had smashed Amazon society at Themiscyra, it seems that Artemis not only protected remnants at Ephesus, but also brought them under control in her cult there, after the pounding they had taken from Heracles – tamed and domesticated under the goddess. They retained their weaponry, but for dance and in the goddess's service, safe in Artemis' sanctuary, where they were no longer a threat to wider society, in battle or through their example as independent young women. Amazo's story illustrates that new life, with her mother even finding a man to father her daughter under Artemis' auspices, as it seems. We may understand the Amazon dancing at Ephesus as enacting in ritual the taming of Amazons under the goddess's guiding strong hand. Hippo's refusal to dance was not only disrespectful sacrilege, but also a refusal to be tamed that could only end in disaster for her – a warning for any others who might be tempted to refuse to dance, whether Amazons or women in general.

Ephesian Artemis was so important that her rituals were well-known in classical Athens.[51] We find likely allusion to her Amazon stories even in Athenian vase-painting.[52] After all, the destruction of Amazons was a theme shared across the Aegean, inconsistencies not-withstanding. Meanwhile, of course, the sanctuary was of prime significance for the city of Ephesus itself. A vivid account has survived in a fictional love story from antiquity, describing festal processions of girls and boys from Ephesus to the sanctuary.[53] The great cult was enormously wealthy from archaic times. Greeks apart, King Croesus of Lydia had donated generously in the sixth century BC, as he had also done at Delphi, where

[51] In the comedy of Autocartes (see Aelian, *HA* 12.8, quoting from his *Tympanistai* fr.1 KA); cf. Ar. *Clouds* 598–9.
[52] Bron 1996, fig. 61.   [53] Xenophon of Ephesus, 1.2.

Artemis was prominent together with her twin, Apollo.[54] The so-called Croesus vase (Plate 8) shows Theseus' abduction of his Amazon on one side, and on the other side Croesus on his pyre, in despair. Interpretation is controversial, but the fall of the powerful (Amazon queen and Lydian king) is central to both scenes, while Ephesian traditions further bind Croesus and Amazons together around the sanctuary. Presumably Artemis' temple was decorated from the first with Amazons. Certainly, there were bronze statues of Amazons in classical times – some marble copies (as it seems) have survived from the Roman period.[55] These are wounded Amazons, damaged refugees, scantily dressed and designedly sexy in their vulnerable poses – with delicate wounds.[56] There were also flesh-and-blood 'Amazons' who served in the sanctuary, for in Roman times we find a girl named 'Amazon' at Ephesus, from a priestly family there. Her unusual name most likely arises from her office, as elsewhere too.[57]

While Amazon traditions were strong across Asia Minor, each community and cult supported stories that were local and specific to themselves – whether or not they connected with others – the flurry that we saw sketched by Bishop Eustathius. For example, an Amazon named Smyrna, who

[54] Braund 2018, with bibliography.
[55] Pliny *NH* 34.53 (cf. 5.155) has caused widespread belief in a group of five Amazons at the sanctuary, though he refers only to competition imagined between five bronze statues by famous sculptors, from the fifth century BC onwards: see Ridgway 1974 (with a stone Amazon from the theatre); Devambez 1976; Hölscher 1998; Weber 2008 (terracotta evidence); Blinkenberg Hartrup 2017.
[56] See Stewart 1995.
[57] *IEph* 941. The only direct parallel for the name in the imperial east is also a case (from Perge) where a regular name is given too: *IPerge* 368; cf. *IG* XII 1, 66 (Artemis Pergaia, Rhodes).

not only gave her name to the city of Smyrna (modern Izmir, not far from Ephesus), but also to a part of Ephesus which she seized.[58] Strabo specifies Myrina and Cyme as cities which had been in some sense Amazon foundations,[59] as well as Smyrna and Ephesus – not to mention the tombs that recur as Amazon legacy. For, as Strabo tartly observes, there were many writers on these Amazon traditions, but a very few who claimed to locate them in history. They were important, but part of prehistory and myth.[60]

To the north of Ephesus, the port city of Cyme (now abandoned) regularly showed a portrait of its Amazon founder on its coinage (Plate 3). The Amazon – named Cyme – was already established by the end of the archaic period, as Hecataeus of Miletus attests. The city's most famous son – the historian Ephorus of the fourth century BC – supported his city's claim to Amazon foundation. To that end he engaged in tortuous interpretation of Homer, so that the poet (also claimed for Cyme by some) could also be made to support the city's Amazon past.[61] Interestingly, the female portrait that featured throughout the history of coinage there shows no clear Amazon traits – no weapons, no special clothing or headgear, beyond a simple headband. We see a fairly mature woman, handsome and stern enough – a Greek lady, one might think.[62] As with Theseus' Amazon at Athens and probably the Amazon refugees at

---

[58] Strabo 14.1.4.
[59] A city of Aeolis, with a namesake on Lemnos: see Chapter 9.
[60] Strabo 11.5.4, 12.3.21.
[61] Strabo 12.3.22, unpersuaded by Ephorus' Homeric games. See also Steph. Byz. s.v. Amazoneion (Hecataeus); Hesychius 634.
[62] Further, Oakley 1982, 3; Matthaei 2013, 63–5. Similarities with Mesembrian coins are insufficient to show their female head also to be an Amazon, otherwise unattested there.

Ephesus, it seems that the city of Cyme claimed an Amazon who had somehow made the transition to Greek-style culture. Ephorus explains Amazons as ordinary females who had been mistreated by their men and so were driven to expel them by force when the opportunity arose.[63] Cyme the Amazon was not Greek, but she belonged to a tradition wherein Amazons were ordinary women at the end of their tethers, as the coin portrait shows her. It remained entirely possible to imagine her as part of the Amazon diaspora, driven from Themiscyra by Heracles, as at Ephesus.

We might wish to know more about the circumstances in which Apollo was said to have raped an Amazon named Gryne, in a grove at the Aeolian town of Gryneion. It was located not far from Myrina, and indeed Aeolian Cyme, and retained some renown for its oracle and fine temple of Apollo.[64] While Myrina here is not to be confused with its homonym on the island of Lemnos, the tale of Amazon Gryne sits within a sweep of Amazon connections down this coast, to Smyrna and onwards into Caria. While Apollo's tendency to rape is familiar enough (foiled, for example, by the metamorphosis of Daphne), our Gryne is the only Amazon said to have been subjected to such an assault by Apollo, whose relations with Amazons seem generally protective, beside his sister Artemis. We may wonder what was said at Gryneion itself, where a very different creation-tale was available, centred on the actions of Grynus, a descendant of the noble Telephus, with no Amazon involved, it seems.[65]

[63] Schol. Ap. Rhod. 2.965 = *FGrH* 70 F60a.
[64] Further, Hansen and Nielsen 2004.
[65] Problematic allusions appear in Hellenistic and Latin poetry (including Virgil), but the tale of Gryne as raped Amazon is nowhere explicit until

The Amazons of Halicarnassus

We meet another Amazon tradition in the region of Caria, south of Ephesus – among the rulers of Halicarnassus (modern Bodrum). Herodotus was a proud son of the city, though he travelled extensively – to Athens, southern Italy, and elsewhere. In general he ignores Amazons – a fact obscured by his repeat of the Sauromatian tale[66] and brief reference to Athenian pride in victory over the Amazons.[67] His own analysis of the history of Asia Minor has no place at all for Amazons. There is no word about them or their foundations. At the start of his *Histories* he even omits Amazons from his list of conflicts between Asia and Europe, though he includes Medea and other myths – no doubt raising eyebrows in Athens. His omission of Amazons is all the more remarkable in view of his account of the Battle of Salamis. There he has the Persian King Xerxes declare his best captain to be Artemisia I of Halicarnassus – 'My men have become women, and my women have become men'. She had fought ruthlessly and survived the defeat – Amazonian enough.[68] There were probably Amazon traditions at Halicarnassus well before Herodotus completed his work around 425 BC. We first see them clearly, however, at Halicarnassus in the next century – on the tombs of their rulers, the Hecatomnids, the family of Mausolus.

About 350 BC battling Amazons were shown prominently amid the sculptures of Mausolus' huge tomb at Halicarnassus – the original Mausoleum, reckoned

the late antique commentaries of Servius (on Verg. *Aen.* 4.345), who also recounts the tale of Eurypylus' son (on Verg. *Ecl.* 6.72) with Courtney 1990 for cautionary remarks on earlier texts.

[66] Chapter 6.   [67] Hdt. 9.27.4, quoted p. 195.
[68] Hdt. 8.88; cf. 7.99; Ar. *Lys.* 674–7; *Thesm.* 1200.

among the seven wonders of the world. It is usual to tag Mausolus' family as 'Carian' on account of their local antecedents, but they were embedded in Greek culture, too. The fabric of the Mausoleum displayed an appropriate mix of influences, though it is Greek enough in conception and execution. A great frieze of Amazons – once resplendent in colours of blue and red – ran along the top of its great podium, on which stood a gigantic pyramidal structure, stepped and crowned with the spectacular four-horse chariot of Mausolus and his sister-wife Artemisia II. They were interred beneath this mass of masonry. As so often in Greek art, Amazons are shown in battle with warriors who seem Greek – very possibly Heracles' destruction of the Amazons in Themiscyra. The few slabs which have survived in good condition give some idea of the Amazons' contribution to the great tomb. While the Greeks are all on foot, often helmeted and sometimes heroically nude, their Amazon opponents appear in their familiar short dresses, showing their limbs and the shape of their bodies. The Greeks have swords and solid shields (hoplites of a sort), while the Amazons carry their light crescent-shields and a familiar range of weapons – axe, bow, javelin-spear. While some weapons are sculpted, others appeared in metal, now lost. Some of the Amazons are shown on horseback.

Death was so central to Amazon myth that we cannot be surprised to find Amazons on the Mausoleum. Their own tombs apart, Amazons featured similarly on the burial monuments of lesser persons too. At Athens, for example, we see a similar Amazon frieze on the large tomb from Kallithea, now displayed in Piraeus

Museum (Plate 27). And again in evident tomb-decoration in Athens' National Museum (Plate 14). These sculptures were contemporary – a fashion, perhaps – but Amazons had appeared in such contexts well before.[69] However, there was more at stake in Halicarnassus, as signalled by an astonishing recent discovery at Mylasa (modern Milas) in the Carian interior. There, remains of a supposed Roman temple were revealed as the top of another vast tomb – to rival the Mausoleum itself, albeit badly damaged by robbers. The identity of the deceased is unlikely to be agreed, but all accept that we have here a tomb created at much the same time as the Mausoleum, for a member of Mausolus' family. Amazons were painted in battle on the walls of the burial chamber – all but invisible now.[70] Homer had already placed Amazons in the general area, defeated by Bellerophon in Lycia.[71]

However, Amazons had a special importance for Mausolus' family on account of the cult of Zeus at Labraunda – the key cult of their regime. The splendid Labraunda was the family's homeland, high on a terraced mountainside that overlooks the extensive plain of Mylasa far below. The symbol of Zeus's cult there was a double axe. The cult-statue showed Zeus brandishing the axe on high in his right hand – the image was reproduced on the coins of Mausolus' dynasty. Crucially, this was an Amazon axe. Heracles had taken it from the Amazon queen Hippolyte, when he sacked Themiscyra, along with her belt. He had then given the axe to Queen Omphale of

---

[69] See the Kallithea Tomb (Plate 27), with Palagia 2016.
[70] Işık 2019 with Summerer 2021.   [71] Further, Keen 1998.

Lydia. From there it found its way to Caria. Like the Amazon belt, this axe was a powerful talisman, imbued with the might of an Amazon queen and touched by Heracles himself. Still greater supernatural power was close, as Plutarch tells the story:[72]

> When Heracles killed Hippolyte and took the axe together with her other weapons, he made a gift of it to Omphale. The Lydian rulers after her used to carry it as one of their sacred objects, until Candaules came to power. He passed it to one of his companions to carry, dishonouring it. But when Gyges revolted and was at war with Candaules, Arselis of Mylasa came to aid the revolt with an army. Arselis destroyed Candaules and his companion, and conveyed the axe to Caria with the other booty. There Arselis had made a statue of Zeus, placed the axe in its hand, and called the god Labraundian. For the Lydians call an axe a 'labrys'.
>
> (Plutarch, *Moralia*, 301f–302a)

The story illustrates the talismanic power of the Amazon axe among the rulers of the region. Elsewhere too the so-called labrys was significant – at the town of Labrys in south Russia,[73] and probably at Amisus, where we find the Thermodon river depicted as a reclining god, holding up the double axe.[74] The talismanic axe appeared regularly on the fabric of the wide realm created by Mausolus' family. Clearly, Amazons had a special place in Mausolus' Caria, at home on the Mausoleum and the walls of its counterpart in Mylasa. Less clear is whether the Amazon axe was especially important for the women

---

[72] See Hellström 2009, who also notes other Carian deities with such an axe.
[73] p. 161.   [74] Robert 1980; cf. Summerer 2000–1.

of the family, who were very prominent in the dynasty. It is quite possible that Artemisia I of Salamis fame (who may or may not have been linked to Mausolus) claimed a connection to the Amazon axe.

For this axe seems at home with women. From Hippolyte it went to Omphale and her successors, until dishonoured by a man and taken to Caria by the mysterious Arselis, who may be an Amazonian woman at the head of an army. Candaules, who dishonoured the axe, had also dishonoured his wife and so sparked Gyges' uprising. In the early chapter of his *Histories* Herodotus recounts the story of Candaules' wife,[75] with no word of an Amazon aspect, as usual, but Plutarch's details seem to chime with Candaules' disrespect for females. Herodotus at least flags up the gender issues in Carian history and society.[76]

All these claims to Amazon roots, with all their variety, demonstrate that Greeks appreciated the benefits of such antecedents. However famous a city, cult, or symbol might be, an Amazon association brought kudos. Amazons were a people of Asia Minor who had a strong place in traditions across the Greek world, and so linked these Greeks of Asia to the old centres of Greek culture and identity in the heartlands, at Athens and elsewhere. They also brought with them a sense of deep antiquity, taking origins back into the time of heroes, before mundane history. Their special relationship with important deities made their creations – cities and the rest – more than a human phenomenon. The gods were at hand. Similarly, as Pausanias (a man of the region) draws attention to the

[75] Harman 2018.   [76] Carney 2005.

validation that Amazons brought even to the great sanctuary at Ephesus:

All the cities worship Ephesian Artemis, as men also do privately, holding her in special honour among the gods. In my view, the reasons for that are both the report that the renowned Amazons founded the cult with their statue, and that this sanctuary was created in most ancient antiquity. Three further factors contributing to its fame are the size of the temple, excelling all other human constructions, the success of the city of the Ephesians, and the brilliance of the goddess there.

(Paus. 4.31.8)

Even so, Amazons need not be protagonists in such tales. A local historian in Bithynia – for example – wrote of the foundation of Pythopolis there, named after Pythian Apollo at Delphi and founded by Theseus. The city's river was named Solois at the time of Theseus' creation of the new city, it was said. No Amazon to be seen – until we hear of the passion inspired in Theseus' companion – a youth named Solois – by the Amazon he was shipping back to Athens from Themiscyra. The Amazon had done nothing to found the city. However, as the story goes, the youth had committed suicide in unrequited love by throwing himself into the river, and Theseus had recalled a Delphic oracle, so that he created the city and named the river after the youth. The Amazon's contribution was simply to be irresistible to the youth, and unyielding to his advances.[77]

At Lagina, outside the city of Stratonicea, whose huge remains lie not so far from Mylasa, we find one of the greatest puzzles of Amazon iconography, around which

---

[77] Plut. *Theseus*, 26 reporting Menecrates' account.

there has been enormous scholarly debate.[78] A large frieze of Amazons features there at the cult-centre of Hecate, who tends to represent the darker side of Artemis, the moon, and more. It was sculpted around 100 BC, and some scholars have for that reason sought to make Roman expansion key to its story. While that may be doubted, and the date itself is fluid enough, most scholars seem to agree that the frieze depicts a story of reconciliation or at least a break from battle between Greek warriors and armed Amazons, complete with images of their foregoing fighting. Here again we seem to have a story of Amazons who have given up the fight, at least for now. At the cult-site the frieze probably showed Hecate's control of the story, which may very well be a tale of the cult's very creation, which would be important to cult and city alike, explaining the large outlay of resources that its creation will have demanded. As in different ways elsewhere in Asia Minor and beyond, Amazons had been brought into local culture by the goddess through the agency of Greeks.

---

[78] Baumeister 2007; cf. Herring 2022, with extensive bibliography and a range of suggestions.

8

The Pride of Athens

~

Amazons had a special place in the history and identity of Athenians. As Theseus created their new city, they said, a huge Amazon army had marched from the Black Sea to destroy the emerging Athens.[1] After months of siege, the Amazons were rebuffed. They withdrew under truce, but never made it home. Amazon tombs were the main memorials of the imagined event, in the city, in its region, and on the route northwards at least as far as Thessaly. Some said that male forces had supported them, but this was very much an Amazon affair. Athenians claimed not only that they had defeated the Amazons, but also that they had destroyed them for good. In fact, this became one of the key achievements that Athenians imagined in their distant past. At the Battle of Plataea in 479 they are said to have included their Amazon success among the victories which gave them a right to pick their spot in the Greek battle lines; at least that is how Herodotus presents their argument some fifty years later in his *Histories*: 'We also have a fine success against the Amazons who once upon a time invaded our land, Attica, from the river Thermodon'.[2] Athenians boasted of other achievements too, notably their victory on the beach at Marathon in 490. However, Athenians took great pride in their

[1] On this Hellanicus is often miscited, muddled with Tzetzes' Byzantine poetry; cf. Plut. *Thes.* 26.1.
[2] Hdt. 9.27.4; Steinbock 2013, 55.

Amazon success, which appears repeatedly in our texts as well as in the public and private art of the city. In his *Life of Theseus* Plutarch assures his readers that the Amazon invasion was 'no trivial or womanish affair'.[3]

Almost a century after Plataea, Athenians were still eager to revisit their defeat of the Amazon invasion. Lysias harped on the victory in a list of key Athenian successes in the distant past – much as the Athenians at Plataea are said to have done. He stresses that the defeat of the Amazons had been a victory for justice.[4] This was part of a public funeral, a speech given at Athens each year over those who had died in war for their city.[5] As at Plataea, we see Athenian pride in dealing with the Amazons. Lysias stresses the injustice of their assault, as also with the other enemies he summons from the past. The Amazon motive, he insists, was naked imperialism, with an ambition encouraged by divine support, technology (iron weapons and cavalry), and consequent local success in Asia Minor. Their ambitious invasion had been driven by word of Athens' fame. Lysias wrote this speech (if he is indeed its author) soon after Athens' own imperial disaster – the great defeat in 404, which Athenians could trace to their own ambitious imperialism, not least overseas in Sicily. In fact many imperialists had already made such a mistake, including Herodotus' Croesus of Lydia, who had destroyed his own empire in his greed to expand still further. No coincidence that an unusually historical vase showed Croesus on one side, and Theseus' Amazon story on the other. A chastened Croesus sits enthroned on a log-pyre, intent on suicide. On the other side, Theseus and a friend

---

[3] Plut. *Thes.* 27.1.   [4] Quoted above, pp. 48–49.   [5] See Todd 2007.

carry away from Themiscyra the Amazon who will die for Athens and help the Athenians to victory and the destruction of her own people (Plate 8, attributed to Myson and dated c. 525–475).[6]

For Lysias, there was also a broader injustice in Amazons, who enjoyed advantages from their father which was out of step with democratic ideals, if not so much with Athenian realities. Gender entailed a deeper injustice here, too. By defeating and ultimately destroying Amazons, the Athenians could claim to have supported nature and the proper order of things. Their victory had rescued a form of truth from the imperialistic deviance generated by Ares and his provision for his overambitious daughters. As Penthesilea had been foolish to face Achilles in battle, the Amazons should have been content with their success against weaker foes in Asia. At the same time, Lysias is careful to stress the glory in defeating this peculiar and dangerous phenomenon. Athenians of those far-off days had been real men, like those who had now died for the city which marked their deaths with Lysias' speech.

Athenians did not tire of Amazons. The philosopher and rhetorician Isocrates would soon return to the theme in at least four speeches. Again, the Amazons are grouped with Thracian and Peloponnesian aggressors, as at Plataea and in Lysias' speech. However, Isocrates presents them as companions of Scythian invaders, not a force alone. Lysias had mentioned warlike allies, but he had left Amazons as the principals in the invasion. Where Lysias had stressed that these women were (in Homer's words) matches for men, it seems that Isocrates stressed Scythian allies to avoid any

---

[6] Arafat 1997. Vases rarely show historical events.

diminution of the Athenian achievement as a victory over women. Scythians were also from the Black Sea region, and favoured horses and archery in the manner of Amazons. Their long hair may have mattered too. It was in Isocrates' day that Amazons had been explained away as a male force of fine warriors, who shaved, grew their hair, and dressed in a Thracian manner. To some, that kind of rationalisation made more sense than an impossible female expedition – against Athens or anywhere else.[7]

Isocrates' version seems to respond to a potential flaw in Athenian claims to victory over an army of females. In any event, his version tends to confuse the geopolitics, and to do so deliberately. For by bringing Scythians to the fore, he makes the invasion a European affair:

The most outstanding of the wars was the Persian. However, but no less striking are the ancient signs of the deeds done in ancestral conflicts. For, while Greece was still modest, there came into our land Thracians, with Eumolpus, son of Poseidon, and Scythians with Amazons, the daughters of Ares – not at the same time, but when each were rulers of Europe. They hated the whole Greek race. They made complaints against us, in particular, thinking that thus they risked trouble with one city, while getting power over all the cities at once.

(Isocrates 4.68)

He imagines that these peoples complained of Theseus' activities. Where Lysias had asserted Amazon injustice, Isocrates presents Amazons as part of a strategy to rule all Greece, so that Athenian victory was a benefit to Greece as a whole. Elsewhere Isocrates says that the Amazons

---

[7] Palaephatus, *On the Incredible* 32, envisaging Athens, no doubt. Date arguable.

claimed that their invasion was sparked by Hippolyte, their fellow Amazon, who had broken their laws by falling in love with Theseus and becoming his partner:

And Scythians with Amazons – Ares' offspring, who made the expedition over Hippolyte, who had broken the laws laid down among them, loving Theseus, going off with him, and cohabiting.

(Isocrates 12.193)[8]

Our author conceals the larger story, where Theseus had gone to Themiscyra (on his own expedition or with Heracles). Instead, we have a love story, in breach of a peculiar local law of no appeal to Athenians. Hippolyte is a Helen, except that Helen had broken the more serious laws of marriage among Greeks. No doubt our author expected his audience to recall the bloody demands of Amazon law – a girl must kill in battle before sex and cohabitation. In her passion for her romantic Athenian hero, Hippolyte was spared such bloodshed. As Lysias had stressed, justice was on the Athenian side. All the more so, since Hippolyte in this way becomes another of the persecuted females who finds protection from tyranny at Athens – a further source of pride for the city.[9]

Justice and the Supernatural

Aeschylus puts these ideas in a supernatural framework, when he brings Amazons to the fore in the conclusion of his *Oresteia* trilogy, first staged in 458.[10] Again the Amazon

---

[8] From the *Panathenaicus*, a speech of the early 330s.
[9] Cf. Euripides' *Medea* and *Heraclidae*; Tzanetou 2012.
[10] Harding 2008, 95 sees the poet inventing rather than repeating/adapting tradition, but we cannot know as much. Cf. Shapiro 1991.

invasion was unjust – they had invaded 'through envy of Theseus' – the words of Athena herself, the city's protectress.[11] The goddess proceeds to foretell the Areopagus lawcourt, which specialised in homicide cases, for the drama ends with the trial of Orestes for matricide. Invading Amazons play a powerful role, as she explains. During their siege, they built up this hill to match the neighbouring acropolis, held by the Athenians. They also named it after their father, Areopagus, the 'Hill of Ares'. Most important, she says that it is to be a place of reverence and fear, a deterrent for Athenians which will restrain them from murder under good laws. Fear (*phobos*) was key to Theseus' victory and its commemoration in the city. On an autumn day each year, Athenians celebrated Theseus' sacrifice to Fear (the deity Phobos) before leading his army into battle with the besieging Amazons. An oracle had inspired the sacrifice, it was said.[12] The gods had guided Athens to victory, and redirected the horror of battle against these daughters of Ares, who had received sacrifice from them on his hill. The nature of these offerings is not specified, but we should suppose rites of blood at least – especially if Scythians were involved. Herodotus writes of their gory human sacrifices to Ares in Scythia.[13] As often, Amazons are steeped in death – appropriate to a homicide court that commanded the death penalty. Hippolyte might have risked death by breaking the alien law about Amazon killer-brides, but the Amazon invasion would channel these ideas and energies for the good of the city, by the divine ordinance set out by Athena herself. Amazon injustice

[11] *Eumenides* 686.   [12] Plut. *Thes.* 27.2.   [13] Hdt. 4.60.

would contribute to a future of ultimate Athenian justice on the hill they had named for their father.

Well over a century after Aeschylus' drama, Amazons mysteriously featured at the battle of Chaeronea in 338. This was the home town of the learned Plutarch, who also provides much of our data on Amazons in Athens, which he also knew well at first hand. Chaeronea was a key battle, where Macedon established power over Greece, including Athens. At last an army from the north had gained control of Athens, as Amazons and others had attempted. There was a supernatural flavour to their evocation at this vital juncture – in two ways, as Plutarch relates. First, he claims that a river Thermodon ran past the battlefield – it had become known as the Haimon – a name which might evoke bloodiness, perhaps stained by the battle itself.[14] Another story[15] said that Thermodon appeared on a stone, complete with explanatory inscription – it was found as the Athenians and others pitched camp. The river appeared as a god, carrying a wounded Amazon, for river-gods supported their peoples. Heracles was also present – destroyer of Amazons, with and without Theseus, but also ancestor of Macedon's kings. The Athenians and other Greeks had their camp by his sanctuary there. An uncertain Plutarch insists that the gods were at work, with suitable oracles besides. Macedon's victory meant for him the loss of Greek freedom. At last the Amazon ambition had been attained. The implied link back to Theseus' victory at Athens was strengthened by talk of Amazons buried by

[14] Plut. *Dem.* 19.2; cf. *Thes.* 27.2; Paus. 9.19.3.
[15] Plutarch reports it from Duris of Samos (c. 300 BC), where there was similar Amazon etymology at Panaima.

the river as they tried to get home from that defeat.[16] Of course, Alexander had participated in the battle – the beginning, it seems, of his involvement with Amazons. When Demosthenes gave an oration for the dead, he was brief on Amazons, whom he located now beyond the Phasis, east from Themiscyra – a hint of tales to come about their survival in the Caucasus and distant east.[17]

An Amazon Queen for Athens

Until the Amazons arrived from the distant north and east, Theseus' Amazon was in effect queen of Athens. She is variously named Antiope, Hippolyte, or something else. Antiope seems favoured outside the city, but in Athens she was usually called Hippolyte or simply 'the Amazon'. She was transformed into a great lady of the city. In real life, other non-Greek women had become the partners of important Athenians, in the city and elsewhere. A vase shows our Amazon being schooled in her new life by an imposing Theseus, with a Greek woman, who lays a friendly arm on her shoulders. She pays close attention, sitting in her Amazon clothes and hat – soon to be exchanged for Greek garb (Figure 1). She bore Theseus a son, Hippolytus, whose tragedy illustrated the fault lines in his parents' relationship, as we shall see. Her transformation seemed complete, with uneventful months or more in the city.

However, all that changed when the Amazons invaded. She had retained her capacity for battle and went to war beside Theseus, fighting for the city which was now her own and, arguably, was fighting to protect her. Sadly, she

---

[16] Plut. *Thes.* 27.   [17] Dem. 60.8, notably brief, as Plato, *Menex.* 239b.

Figure 1 Theseus instructing his Amazon on her new life in Athens. Private collection: CVA Japan 1, 16–17.

would be killed in the fray at the Itonian Gate, where her monument commemorated the event.[18] Molpadia had killed her, with arrow or javelin, and was also commemorated in the city.[19] There seems to have been a central clash between Molpadia and Theseus, perhaps straight after his Amazon was killed.[20] A mid fifth-century Athenian vase shows Theseus battling between two Amazons, where one is named as his partner, here Antiope, so that the other must be Molpadia (Plate 7).[21] She is also the Amazon killed by Theseus on the so-called Elgin throne – a large ceremonial

---

[18] Known as the 'Amazon's stele': Ps.-Plato, *Axiochus*, 364d–365a; cf. Lalonde 2019 on the warrior Athena Itonia, esp. 173–5.
[19] Her name suggests music and Apollo, among other gods; cf. Eumolpus. It was a short step from the lyre to the bow.
[20] Plut. *Thes.* 27.4; Paus. 1.2.1.
[21] Attributed to Polygnotus: Matheson 1995, 171–2.

seat in Hymettian marble.[22] There the image is well paired with the tyrannicides, Harmodius and Aristogiton (Plate 28). Around 513 BC they had famously attempted to kill the tyrant of Athens, Hippias, son of Pisistratus, who soon left the city for Persia. They had opened a new phase in the emergence of Athenian democracy, rather as Theseus' defeat of the Amazons had done, under his very democratic monarchy. His killing of Molpadia the Amazon marked the end of her unjust regime and assault upon the city. In their different ways, both the tyrannicides (who had only managed to kill the brother of Hippias the tyrant) and Theseus had advanced the city's democratic state, so that the two images were pillars of the story of Athens.

Theseus' Amazon wife had died too for Athens. While some preferred to imagine that she had survived and brokered the truce that ended the war, that seems hard to accommodate in the narrative.[23] Meanwhile, it has been suggested that a vase-painting shows the stele (a grave marker?) of Theseus' Amazon (Plate 9).[24] Certainly, the manner of the Amazon nearby might suit mourning.

Amazons in Athens

Athens' Amazon story had left memorials and images across the city, including the two dead queens, and Athenians killed in the fighting too. Some of this needed special

---

[22] See Palagia 2018 on the image of Molpadia's death. Possibly the image has contributed to Theseus' killing of another Amazon (tagged as Andromache) on a late red-figure vessel in the British Museum, *ARV²* 1052.29, showing battle in Themiscyra.

[23] Plut. *Thes.* 27.4.

[24] Rotroff and Lamberton 2014, 135–6 on *ARV²* 1073.7.

research, as pursued by the local historian Cleidemus in Athens in the fourth century.[25] However, the broad tradition was known widely in Athens, key to civic identity, as we may infer from Aeschylus' references to the Amazon role in the creation of the Areopagus and its court, though there were other tales too. Of course, the sanctuary of Theseus featured Amazons, probably on the exterior of the building and certainly in paintings kept inside. Pausanias saw them as images of Athenians fighting Amazons, no doubt led by our hero.[26] It had been developed in the 470s to house the remains of Theseus 'found' on Scyros – the oversize bones were brought forcibly to Athens by Cimon and lodged in the sanctuary.[27] An annual festival was preceded by a sacrifice for the Amazons,[28] which recalled the ritual of the truce that ended the fighting.[29] For close by was the so-called Horcomosium ('Place of Oath-swearing'), where Theseus' Athenians and surviving Amazons had sworn the truce that covered the Amazons' departure. Clearly Amazons were remembered as warriors with whom a truce could be agreed under divine oversight. However, the truce did not diminish the Athenian sense of victory.

Cimon and his associates were also behind the construction of the Painted Stoa (Stoa Poikile) – a colonnade erected in the heart of Athens around 460.[30] It featured a series of important paintings, probably on boards. Lost

[25] Plut. *Thes.* 27; McInerney 1994.   [26] Paus. 1.17.2; cf. 5.11.2.
[27] Walker 1995, 21.
[28] See Robertson 1992, 132 for Artemis and Apollo.
[29] Plut. *Thes.* 27.5, abandoned by Roman times.
[30] Wycherley 1957, 45 n. 2; Plut. *Cimon* 4, using the stoa's first name –
Peisianakteion: schol. Dem. 20.112.

long ago, we rely on Pausanias' description of what remained towards AD 200. He describes four principal paintings of Athenian victories. First, over the Spartans (the problematic Battle of Oenoe). Second, defeat of the Amazons, at least some on horseback.[31] Third, victory at Troy. Fourth, Marathon, with the Persians already in flight. The ensemble echoes Athenian claims at Plataea and the lists of the funeral orations of Lysias and the rest – complete with Amazons. The paintings made the stoa a victory monument, where Athens' ringing success against the Persians at Eurymedon (about 466) was evoked and perhaps even shown in a painting removed by Pausanias time, some six centuries after the stoa was built. We happen to know that the children of Heracles – refugees from Eurystheus – were also depicted in the stoa, so that the building was a material expression of the rhetoric of Lysias and the rest in its ethics too – the city was a force for good.[32]

The well-preserved temple of Hephaestus and Athena (the Hephaestion, commonly misnamed the Theseion) stands on the elevated north-western side of the Agora.[33] Its deities were an important couple at Athens – in their strange way the parents of Erichthonius. Its sculpted metopes show famous deeds of Theseus and Heracles in two distinct sets. We see Heracles' quest for the queen's belt. Probably Theseus' Amazon victory was planned too, but

---

[31] Cf. Ar. *Lys.* 677–9 and its scholion.
[32] Schol. Ar. *Plutus* 885. Modern attempts to use the paintings to support the hypothesis that Amazons evoke Persians are misplaced, pace Castriota 1992 and others.
[33] Built over decades from the 460s or so: Shear 2014, esp. 143–5; cf. Wycherley 1957, esp. 68–71.

the programme is incomplete – some metopes were never sculpted. For, while there was some scope for dispute about which of the two heroes had put an end to the Amazons, that seems not to have been an issue in Athens or elsewhere, where the two seem either to operate in parallel or to collaborate against Amazons. That fundamental harmony is confirmed by the sculptural programme here and on the Athenian treasury at Delphi around 490 (the date is hotly debated).[34] Heracles was an expansive force for all Greeks, centred on the Peloponnese and the wide frontiers while Theseus combined distant adventures with a similar enforcing of civil order in Attica and its environs. The two heroes went well enough together, as the temple's designers evidently thought.

The city's Amazon images and its public rhetoric furnish valuable context for developments on the acropolis.[35] Again, Theseus and Amazons featured prominently.[36] The Parthenon tends now to be understood as a victory monument, and rightly so. Victory at Salamis in 480 had driven the Persians from Athens, but the city had been ravaged and burnt. From the early 440s the construction of this new temple for Athena marked recovery, progress, and Athenian imperial success. As we have seen, Athenians liked to interpret their success as ethical – victory against injustice, in defence of themselves and others, perhaps of civilisation itself. Closer examination of the Parthenon and its various Amazons reveals more about this celebration of victory. On its exterior, the metopes of the west side of the temple are badly damaged, but display Amazonomachy,

---

[34] Boardman 1982 claims conflict even so.   [35] Shear 2014, 79–135.

[36] See Shear 2014, 119; an exceptional Amazon victory would need better preservation.

which is always the defeat of Amazons.[37] No coincidence, surely, that Amazons had been based to the west, on the hill of their father Ares. We have seen how Athenians characterised the Amazon invasion in terms of unjust law and practice concerning sex and marriage – for them part of Amazon aggression and the more general deviance of Amazon society. A glance around the rest of the exterior shows kindred images. After all, military and civic success demanded ordered reproduction, ensuring a strong army of citizen soldiers. In that sense the Parthenon projected success into the future, as well as celebrating victories of past and present.

The metopes[38] on the north side of the temple showed Aphrodite reconciling Menelaus and Helen at the fall of Troy. On the south side were rapist Centaurs disrupting the wedding of Theseus' companion, Pirithous, very likely with images of Ixion's attempt on Hera. The metopes on the east showed the victory of the Olympians (including Athena) over the Giants – riotous revolutionaries against Olympian rule, noted for their rapist habits. In their rampant chaos, the Giants were another threat to marriage and ordered reproduction, duly crushed. Athena alone appears with a winged Victory in attendance – here the assertion of order was especially hers. It was her strong physical resistance to attempted rape that created Erichthonius, who gave the Athenians their prized autochthony – in their justice they had not taken the land of others.[39] Athena manages to be a warrior-woman who asserts traditional order without threatening it, in Athens at

[37] Some see Persians, e.g. Yeroulanou 1998, 409, with bibliography.
[38] Schwab 2005.   [39] Calame 2011; cf. Harrison 1977, 417.

least.[40] She dominates both pediments of her temple, born on the east, and besting Poseidon for the patronage of Athens on the west.[41] The recurrent themes of victory, lawful marriage, and ordered reproduction on the temple's exterior are further echoed inside, where a large Victory stood in the palm of Athena's gold and ivory cult-statue. Holding a spear in her other hand, Athena also had a huge shield at her side – very much the warrior. This shield showed the Amazon battle scenes again, in relief on its outer surface, around its circumference. Roman-period slabs – pulled from the sea off Piraeus – are taken to show good reproductions of scenes from this shield (Plates 29 and 30). On the inside of the shield (perhaps painted)[42] was the Olympians' defeat of the Giants again – located opposite the Amazons as on the metopes outside.[43] The great shield protected the militant goddess, and so her Athenians too, as well as such refugees as they sheltered. Her support against the Amazons was assured.

We may be sure that there were more Amazons on Athens' public buildings than we know. Elsewhere on the acropolis, at the entrance to the great rock, was the temple of Athena Nike (Athena Victory). This was specifically Athena as goddess of military victory. The building was completed in the 420s.[44] Amazons, of course, demanded inclusion. We know almost nothing about the temple's sculpture, in fact, but there is a good case to be made for an echo of the Parthenon, with Theseus

[40] She might be alluring too: in Byzantium, Nicetas Choniates drooled over her image: see Jenkins 1947, 31.
[41] Paus. 1.24.5 – remains are scant.   [42] Wycherley 1957, 124.
[43] Pliny, *NH* 36.18; Palagia 2019, 332–46.   [44] Shear 2014, esp. 348.

fighting Amazons on the west pediment of this temple, with Athena in a battle with Giants again on the east pediment opposite, as with the Parthenon metopes.[45] It would be good to know how Athenians handled the Amazon themes on temple(s) of Ares, who is routinely tagged as their father in Athenian rhetoric.[46] In Hellenistic times, when King Attalus I of Pergamum monumentalised his own victories on the Athenian acropolis about 200, he of course included Amazons.[47]

Amazons and the Creation of Athens

Athenian pride in Theseus' defeat of the Amazon invasion is very clear from the fifth century onwards. The victory expressed Athens' claim to stand for Greeks at large, collectively and individually, not least as a place of refuge against tyranny. Athenian victory at Marathon was soon followed by the collective defeat of the Persian invasion of Xerxes, and the Athenian adventures in imperialism that ensued. Athenians liked to recall their prehistoric exploits against Amazons and others, at a time when their city was vulnerable – coalescing under Theseus. Certainly, there was scope for comparisons and looser associations between the various enemies across the centuries. However, far too much has been made of Amazons as quasi-Persians. The lack of any text to that effect should be warning enough, while modern inferences from Athenian art in support of the hypothetical connection are thin and flimsy. When artists wished to show Persians, they had no need to present

---

[45] Shear 2014, esp. 355.   [46] See Stewart et al. 2019, esp. 694.
[47] Paus. 1.25.2; Stewart 2004.

them as Amazons – we find both among the images of the Stoa Poikile, with much else besides. Meanwhile, great claims have been advanced for a shift at Athens away from Heracles to Theseus as the archaic period becomes the fifth century. Again, there is a measure of plausibility, for the developing democracy presumably thought and expressed changes in the use of the far past. And yet, again, there is no real evidence about that, nor about any change in attitudes to Amazons in these decades. In the extant texts and images, we have seen coherence and continuity in the public rhetoric and representation of Amazons at Athens, at least until the later fourth century. Athens emerges almost as an Amazon foundation, created with the demise of Amazon power, like the Sauromatians of the north and many a city and cult of Asia Minor.[48] Monuments and their stories set Amazons at the beginning of the Areopagus, in particular. More generally, Amazons had challenged Theseus' new Athens, militarily and ethically. Athens had held its own against them, and better, a fine springboard for its future.

Amazons also offered Athens connections with its immediate neighbours. For the story of the invasion entailed not only Athens and Attica, but also Boeotia, Euboea, Megara, and the Argolid. We have a scatter of details, each of which suggests larger traditions, local and lost. Boeotian tales emerged at Chaeronea, while a late archaic pediment from near Lake Copais hints at more – its dying Amazon might have tried to fight Heracles.[49] On Euboea, we hear of Amazons, wounded at Athens, and sent there for treatment

[48] Paus. 7.2.7 suggests that Pindar shifted the beginnings of Artemis Ephesia to the Amazons who besieged Athens.
[49] Hansen and Nielsen 2004, 443.

at Chalcis: the dead were buried at an Amazoneum there.[50]
Theseus had been shown carrying his Amazon on the pediment of Apollo Daphnephorus in neighbouring Eretria.[51]
The Megarians claimed the burial of another Hippolyte
(sister of Theseus' Amazon) in a tomb built in the shape of
an Amazon shield. She had led a breakaway group from
carnage at Athens, in death and despair south of the city.[52]
Pindar shows how Aegina resonated with the Amazons on
its fabric.[53] And the Argolid boasted not only Hippolytus at
Troezen, but also his recovery at Epidaurus, while Amazons
featured on Hera's temple at Argos, with the Amazon belt
on show in Mycenae.[54] In their different ways (with tombs
to the fore, as usual with Amazons) these traditions and their
deeper associations made Athens central to a web of traditions, anchored in the memorials of the Amazon siege in the
city itself, including the monuments of Amazons and burials
of those Athenians who had died in defeating them. From
Homer onwards these monuments were charged with
a supernatural and militant energy, while links to Amazons
of Argonautic and Trojan tales are likely enough to have
played a role, especially into Thessaly.[55] The very existence
of relics, stories, and likely rituals seemed to confirm the
reality of the mighty clash through which the new Athens of
Theseus had emerged strong and proud.

[50] Plut. *Thes.* 27; Paus. 1.41.7. [51] Plut. *Thes.* 27.
[52] Paus. 1.41.7. Plutarch names it the Rhomboid, perhaps another way to
perceive an elongated crescent.
[53] Chapter 4. [54] p. 109.
[55] Plut. *Thes.* 27, with Mili 2015, 121; Paus. 1.41.7.

9

Artemis vs. Aphrodite

Greek Women Go Amazon

~

The potential Amazon in Greek women is especially clear in myth set on the island of Lemnos in the northern Aegean – the 'greatest evil' in Greek culture, as some ancients had it. It began with Lemnian neglect of Aphrodite, though an Amazon presence in Lemnos' earliest tales suggests still deeper roots, as we shall see. Ancient outrage centred upon a murderous conspiracy of the women of the island. When their men abandoned them for Thracian girls, they were as furious as Aphrodite had been when she was neglected. As the tale was often told, the goddess had inflicted upon the women of the island an awful smell, repugnant to their men. This smell had driven the men of Lemnos to keep well away from their wives, who were now overwhelmed with jealous hatred of their menfolk and new girlfriends, as Aphrodite had intended. The women of the island conspired and agreed on a deadly plan for violent revenge. So, at the same moment and without warning, the Lemnian women slaughtered all their menfolk – husbands, fathers, sons, brothers, and all. No men survived on Lemnos.

Women's killing of men might suggest Amazons,[1] but it was the aftermath that really made Amazons of these

---

[1] The Danaids who killed their husbands are also Amazonian in their way: p. 128; Zeitlin 1978; 1990, esp. 113.

otherwise traditional Greek women. For they had to take over the roles of their men – farming, politics, and more. Their ruler was of course a queen, named Hypsipyle. She had taken over the throne of her father (a King Thoas)[2] and ruled Lemnos in his place, while an assembly of females might be gathered for key decisions. All went smoothly enough, but the women knew that their greatest test would come when battle was required. The island's history guaranteed that sooner or later raiders would come, most likely from the nearby mainland of Thrace. Such raids were a fact of life on Lemnos, and they would certainly happen again. Fortunately, when that day came, it was the Argonauts who arrived instead. However, the women knew nothing of the Argo and its crew of Greek heroes, so they bravely marshalled in their husbands' battle-gear – all the more bravely because they knew their limitations. Of course, they were terrified as the ship drew closer and battle loomed at the port of Myrina.

Our fullest version of events is the *Argonautica* of Apollonius Rhodius, which tells that there was no battle at all in the end. While the women realised that these 'raiders' were fine Greeks, the Argonauts were delighted to find the opposing army to be a bevy of relieved and very hospitable women. They made love, not war. And so the women had children, and males returned to Lemnos. The Argonauts had declined a tempting offer to settle there, and sailed on to the Black Sea in quest of the Golden Fleece. So wrote Apollonius Rhodius, in his romantic epic

---

[2] Sometimes Hypsipyle saves her father: e.g. Apollod. 1.15, while the stink is not in all accounts.

on the quest, composed at Ptolemaic Alexandria around 300 BC.[3]

However, there were other versions, which we have only in fragments, if at all. According to some, there was actual fighting as the women went to battle.[4] Well over a century before Apollonius, on the Athenian stage, the tragic poet Sophocles had offered a darker version, with bloodshed: in his play *Lemnian Women* he wrote that the women fought hard. And the ancient scholar who preserves this version also informs us that Aeschylus – in another play, his *Hypsipyle* – had offered a rather less romantic notion than the Ptolemaic version. For Aeschylus had the women – armed – refuse to let the Argonauts land on Lemnos until they had sworn an unusual oath – that they would have sex with them and then leave.[5] Aeschylus' Lemnian ladies seem also to have shaved their heads, whether in mourning or seeking to appear more masculine.[6] In Amazonian tales the recognition of warrior women was a recurrent issue, settled by stripping off the armour of the dead, as was routine in victory. In Sophocles' version, for example, the bodies of women who had died in the hard fight may well have revealed that this was not a force of men, as the Argonauts would have assumed at first. Myths usually have different versions. The earlier versions of the Athenian playwrights made more of the Amazon theme

---

[3] Some said the Argo stopped at Lemnos on the way home, as did Pindar (for an audience at Cyrene: Calame 2003) and Myrsilus of Methymna, on Lesbos near Lemnos: Jackson 1990.

[4] Other versions have not survived well or at all: further, Wright 2019, 21 on Aeschylus' plays.

[5] Schol. Ap. Rhod. 1.769–73.   [6] Aeschylus *TrGF* fr. 41.

which echoed not only the founder of Myrina, but also Athenian preoccupations about battle with Amazons and even oaths of agreement with Amazons too, such as Theseus had famously made at Athens.[7]

In any event, the women kept their bloody secret, claiming that their men had simply left for the Thracian mainland opposite and the Thracian females there – a clever half-truth for the Argonauts, who were perhaps preoccupied and not so very interested. All was well enough, but the Lemnians had been through a terrible time. The lesson was never to neglect Aphrodite, who had of course engineered the whole series of events to show the catastrophe that neglect of her might bring. That was remembered on Lemnos, but it was a lesson for all Greeks, and others besides, already in place as archaic Greece emerged into history, as Homer indicates.[8] This was a myth with outlandish features (more below), but its essentials concerned the ever-present issue of how men and women might and should behave towards each other, and of course the gods besides.

Athenian settlement on the island (from around 500 BC) ensured that the myth had currency well beyond the northern Aegean. Meanwhile, strands of the story reached also into the Peloponnese, where Hypsipyle would become a slave in Argos. There she unwittingly creates the Nemean Games, when her help for a great expedition against Thebes brings death to the infant boy in her charge – part of the foundation myth of these games, first attested around 406 BC in Euripides' fragmentary play

---

[7] On the Horcomosium there, see p. 271.
[8] *Iliad* 7.467–75, 23.746–7. Masciadri 2008 gathers texts on Lemnian traditions.

Hypsipyle, though probably a much older myth.[9] An Amazonian queen was better with soldiers than with babies, perhaps.

In the fourth century BC it was said that Lemnos had an ancient law specifically against the neglect of Aphrodite. Failure to make the proper sacrifices to her was punishable by death. Presumably the law was taken to embody the lesson that the Lemnians had learned the hard way, whether or not the law itself was a historical reality. Our source is a certain Asclepiades – obscure enough,[10] but his biography is fascinating. He was a Greek of Thrace from the small town of Tragilos, who went to study in Athens. His homeland was deep in Thrace, not far from modern Serres. We are told little or nothing about what these sacrifices were, and where Aphrodite's cult-places may have been on the island.[11] Around AD 300 a writer from Lemnos, named Philostratus,[12] takes the Lemnian women's murder of their men to explain a remarkable festival of Hephaestus there, during which there was no fire for as much as nine days. Whatever we make of his account (he is prone to satire), there is no reason to doubt that the famous Lemnian evil served to explain a substantial part of the island's rituals and traditions.[13] As the most prominent deity of the island by far, Hephaestus had to have a place in the bloody myth. His marriage to Aphrodite demanded as much.

[9] On the play, Wright 2019, 202–3.   [10] *FGrH* 12 F14.
[11] Perhaps schol. Stat. *Theb.* 5.59, with Burkert 1970, 3 n. 5.
[12] Bowie 2009.
[13] Philostratus, *Heroicus* 53.5–7; cf. Burkert 1970 for sober discussion.

Lemnian Cults and Contexts

It would be good to know the tales that surrounded Lemnian Myrina, or Myrrhine.[14] We have seen this Amazonian female near Troy: her tomb was a landmark on the plain of Homer's *Iliad*. But it is not until much later, in the first century BC, that we hear of her in any detail – in a fantastical tale of her attempt at world domination in the very distant past, including dealings with the people of Atlantis.[15] That rococo account is typical of the Amazon concoctions of this later period, but its inclusion of a long list of Myrrhine's civic foundations in Asia Minor may very well sweep up an assortment of actual local traditions, for example in Cilicia, where coinage attests an Amazon place in civic identity. Regrettably, Lemnos does not get a mention in any case. Nor does the other Myrina of the region, which no doubt also claimed her as founder, located across the sea on the coast of the western Aegean. Lemnos was known overwhelmingly for the slaughter of men, which put Amazon foundation in the shade. Accordingly, we have scant information too about an early goddess who bears the island's name. This goddess Lemnos continued to receive cult on the island well into Greek times, perhaps as a mother-goddess of its land, a kind of Cybele, as usually imagined.[16]

---

[14] Martin 1987, esp. 87 on the evocations of the name in *Lysistrata*.

[15] Diod. 3.54–56; cf. Dionysius of Chalcis *FHG* 4 F 2. An Athenian tradition (surely) made its founder a daughter of an early Athenian ruler (schol. Ap. Rhod. 1.601), while an obscure etymology recorded (and dismissed) by the Byzantine *Etymologicum Magnum* (s.v. Myrina) inferred that the name of the town meant 'flowing' or even 'weeping'.

[16] Steph. Byz. s.v. Lemnos, with Hansen and Nielsen 2004, 756–8.

Much clearer is the Thracian part in Lemnos' past, which recurs in the tale of slaughter and elsewhere. We should recall that Amazons were considered Thracian from early on, so that Myrrhine would likely be Thracian and speak a Thracian language. Meanwhile, a visit to modern Myrina immediately explains why the island was so strongly linked to Thrace, and not much to the coast of Asia Minor to its east. At the outskirts of the town, around Avlonas, the distant cape of Mt Athos in Thrace (the third prong of Chalcidice) looms from the sea to an extent that seems impossible, given its great distance across the water. On most days of the year it appears almost close enough to touch. Ancient writers exaggerated only a little when they wrote that Athos cast its shadow on Myrina.[17] Furthermore, Greeks believed that the first settlers on Lemnos were a Thracian people, the Sintians. They were sometimes credited with the invention of weapons, not unlike the Amazons on occasion.[18] For Greeks, there was a roughness about them, which perhaps suited the god they tended – the fire-god Hephaestus, as we shall see. He is key to understanding Aphrodite's rage.

In principle, Aphrodite's importance on Lemnos might seem assured, and any neglect of her unlikely. For the fire-god Hephaestus was her husband. He had been thrown from Olympus by his furious parents, though even our

---

[17] Ap. Rhod. 1.604, after Sophocles *TrGF* fr.776. See Huxley 1980, 190.

[18] Thuc. 2.98. Hellanicus of Lesbos *FGrH* 4 F71a (and 71b–d on weapons) apparently made them somehow Greeks at first, who intermarried with Thracians already on Lemnos when they turned up, so that they became a people of Greek-Thracian ethnicity. Since Hellanicus came from nearby Lesbos, that might be considered almost local tradition. In general, Blakely 2006.

earliest texts differ on whether he was thrown down by his father Zeus or his mother Hera.[19] His impact on Lemnos was volcanic in every sense, taken by Lemnians to explain the striking geology of parts of the island, where the remains of prehistoric volcanoes are evident still.[20] The fire-god was immortal and survived the cataclysm, but the Sintians of Thrace were needed to bring him back to health. The crash to earth left the god with a damaged leg, if he had not been born lame – as some said, the reason why his mother had rejected him so violently. The fiery crash was a key moment in Lemnian religion too, for this was now Hephaestus' island, and Lemnos' northern city took his name. This was Hephaestia,[21] across the island from Myrina in the south-west. The two towns maintained a separate identity on the island, but we shall see how they also had much in common. Meanwhile, the crash and Sintian therapy mark the beginning of the island's claim to offer cures, particularly through the mysterious quality of its very earth, whether or not this was caused by the fiery fall itself.

In the ruins of Hephaestia the damaged classical statue of her son, Eros, has survived to remind us of her powerful presence, if the myth were not enough.[22] But there was a local problem on Lemnos, which contributed to Lemnian anxiety about her neglect. For there was the sea-nymph

---

[19] For different versions (including a crash into the sea), see e.g. *Iliad* 1.590–4; Plato, *Republic* 378d (Zeus); *Iliad* 18.395–405; Hesiod *Theogony*, 927–8 (Hera); *Iliad* 18. 136ff; Masciadri 2008; West 2017.

[20] In fact, Lemnos' volcanoes died well before human habitation there: West 2017.

[21] Not Hephaestias, as often given but without authority in Greek texts.

[22] A starting point for study of Lemnian archaeology might be Kypraiou 2000.

Kabeiro, at the centre of the local mystery cult of the Kabeiroi – the 'Great Gods', as they were also known.[23] These were very ancient forces on the islands off Thrace, attested on Lemnos by extensive remains on a sea-washed promontory not far from the town of Hephaestia. Kabeiro presided there, while her divine sons had been fathered by the fire-god himself. The cult was of great importance on Lemnos, but there was no role for Aphrodite here. Here at least Kabeiro threatened to overshadow her, and even take her husband, offspring, and all. Perhaps worse, Aphrodite's more usual rival – the virginal Artemis – was also very important on the island in her own right. Artemis even took a leading role in the medical traditions on Lemnos, which had begun with the fire-god's crash into the island's very earth.

Artemis and Lemnian Earth

Several islands of the Aegean were renowned in antiquity for the special properties of their earths. The special earth of Lemnos was the most famous, highly prized for its medical effectiveness. While myths revolved around Lemnian earth, Greek medics sought to establish a more scientific sense of what this earth might be and how it might be used to medical effect. In Roman imperial times two of the best Greek medics (Dioscorides and Galen) wrote enough on the subject to give us a picture of the extraction, processing, and uses of the wondrous substance. Modern analysis has further explained the value of the special earth, acknowledged and exploited across

[23] Blakely 2006; 2013; Zelnick-Abramovitz 2018.

221

the centuries down to recent times. It is rich in alum, still used as a styptic and astringent, for example in staunching wounds.[24] Its value in treating venomous bites was prized in particular.[25] However, the ancient medics also make clear that the Lemnian earth was central to religious life and practice on the island, especially to its north around Hephaestia. Its presiding deity was Aphrodite's greatest rival, Artemis.

In the second century AD, Galen of Pergamum made determined efforts to investigate the earth on the island itself, where he visited twice.[26] He was the greatest doctor of his age. His account of this research shows clearly that Myrina had little to do with the earth, but at Hephaestia it was central to the duties of the priestess of Artemis in and outside the town. On a specific day each year, it seems, the priestess processed to a holy site in the wilds. She took a cart, which she then brought back to town, loaded with raw earth. Most likely the event was a civic procession, accompanied by the great and the good of Hephaestia. For this was no small matter. At Hephaestia, on his second visit to Lemnos, Galen quizzed the local intellectuals, and discovered a local publication on the earth. He tells us how the priestess worked on the earth at the temple of Artemis there. He missed the festival, but he was able to purchase a quantity of earth-tablets, refined and stamped by the priestess with the image of a goat – a favourite creature of the goddess and denizen of the wilds. Other forms of the earth were also available, used for cleaning

---

[24] Photos-Jones and Hall 2014; Photos-Jones et al. 2015.
[25] Especially Dioscorides, 5.97, a no-nonsense student of medicinal materials, around AD 80.
[26] Galen, *Simples* 12.169–77 is his story.

and painting, on which Galen is careful to make distinctions that earlier writers had not attempted. The good stuff was *sphragis*, he insists, the special product of Artemis' priestess.[27] Ancient medics had to reckon with a slew of false substances and potions, so that Galen's concern is intense for the good of his patients and his own reputation. The trouble of two trips to Lemnos had been worthwhile. The priestess's stamp was a form of guarantee that this was the real deal – not just Lemnian earth, but specifically the kind known as *sphragis*, with Artemis' seal. Its remarkable powers were appropriate to its supernatural associations. In fact, we should note that seal-stones and the like had an independent history in the development of ancient medicine, somewhere between science and magic.[28] Galen may have heard of a woman of Lemnos called Theoris, infamous in classical Athens. She was remembered as an especially deadly woman of the island, executed on the grounds of poisoning and witchcraft.[29] In any case the wondrous earth was well suited to the inventor-magician Hephaestus[30] and the sense of rare and mysterious powers on his island, where the transformation of Greek women into temporary Amazons seemed to echo the divine craftsman's ability to turn the earth and its minerals into works of wonder almost beyond human imagination.

The earth around Hephaestia was notably red. So red that even serious writers thought that the priestess mixed goat-blood into her tablets, until Galen scotched the

---

[27] Galen, *Simples* 12.170.
[28] Marganne 1997; Dasen 2011 compares a reddish hematite example, bearing the image of a she-goat, now in Paris.
[29] Collins 2001.   [30] Faraone 1987.

rumour. The striking red colour needed no additions, and was readily accommodated too in the tale of the fire-god's tumultuous crash. Locals seem to have placed his fall on a bare and burnt-looking hill, clearly visible from Hephaestia. Archaeology has not helped much, but our texts give some sense of this sacred landscape. On the blasted hill was a sanctuary of the fire-god, the civic patron. There is talk of a labyrinth there, such as a special craftsman might create, like Daedalus' on Crete.[31] The earth for *sphragis* may well have been taken from there. If Artemis had a sanctuary on the fire-god's hill, Aphrodite had yet more reason to rage. However, nothing has yet been found there, and her extramural sanctuary may well have stood at nearby Kotsinos, whose name is derived from its red earth. There the modern church of the Virgin of the Spring of Life attracts attention on a small hill, with an underground passage nearby. Artemis may have been here. Certainly, it is intriguing that a legendary 'Amazon' from the fifteenth century is commemorated with a modern statue precisely there – Maroula, a girl who took up her dead father's sword and led the fight against invading Turks, as the story goes. Meanwhile, we see a similar focus on Artemis at Myrina, without the red earth and the fire-god, as it seems. For an extramural sanctuary of Artemis has been identified at Avlonas, up the west coast of the island from Myrina, in which another temple of the goddess seems likely enough. From Avlonas there is an especially good view of Mount Athos and Thrace, together with a coastal

---

[31] Pliny, *NH* 36.86 on the mysterious labyrinth, with Doob 2019, 22–4: cf. Laoupi 2008 for intriguing possibilities. Pliny is clear on the antiquity of *sphragis*, *NH* 35.33 (as pigment).

view of striking hill formations. The Thracian factor on the island offers some explanation for Artemis' importance there, aside from the goddess's appropriateness to the wild landscape around its coasts, in particular, where Artemis tends to recur in Greek culture. In Thrace, we are told, the principal deity was 'Artemis the Queen'.[32]

Philoctetes and the Smells of Aphrodite

Artemis' special earth – the *sphragis* – was known as a powerful treatment for venomous bites. The myth of Philoctetes had many aspects, including its confirmation of this curative power.[33] For the Greek hero had been bitten by a snake on an islet near Lemnos en route to besiege Troy. The bite was commemorated by a bronze statue set on a likely islet there, showing Philoctetes, bandages and all.[34] The bite had soon festered and produced such an appalling stink that the Greek invasion force marooned the wretched man on Lemnos. The gods were at work again. For they knew that Troy could not be taken without Philoctetes and his bow, a relic of Heracles himself. After some ten years of fruitless siege the Greeks came back for him. They found that his awful wound had been cured. Lemnos itself had cured him. As a Lemnian claimed, the wound had healed as soon as Philoctetes set foot on the island.[35] The Athenian

---

[32] Herodotus 4.33.
[33] Galen, *Simples* 12.173. On the tragedies about him, see Dio Chrys. *Oration* 52, with Wright 2019, 65–6. On Sophocles' extant *Philoctetes*, see Morwood 2008.
[34] Appian, *Mithr.* 77.
[35] Philostratus, *Heroicus* 28.5: he proceeds to list the medical uses of the curative earth.

tragedian Sophocles, whose play *Philoctetes* has survived for us, shows a harsh and lonely environment, where the injury is healed by a local herb, presumably bringing the earth's curative properties to the wound. In short, the land had dealt admirably with the unbearable stink of Philoctetes' suppurating leg, which seemed to echo the Sintians' healing of lame Hephaestus himself on the island.

Greek myths do not often make so much of an appalling stink. It is especially interesting, then, that Aphrodite's chosen punishment of the Lemnians was also an intolerable smell, in most versions at least. She was usually known for her alluring scents, the perfumes of seduction and sex. But this was a stink, designed to drive Lemnian men to Thracian girls and Lemnian women to a shared jealous rage that would lead them to mass murder – 'the greatest evil'. Crucially, the cleansing powers of Artemis' earth show a rationale for Aphrodite's unusual mode of vengeance. The Lemnians had devoted their attentions to Artemis. Now Aphrodite chose to demonstrate that nothing earthly – not even Artemis' much-vaunted *sphragis* – could withstand her divine powers. As usual in myths that highlight human imbalance with regard to these goddesses, the lesson was that both must be honoured and balance maintained.

We may also reflect on Artemis' goat on her special earth. For the animal was a byword in Greek culture for a stinking smell (not least in humans), as well as sexual desire.[36] Had Aphrodite not transformed the Lemnian

---

[36] On the smell, see Kitchell 2014, 77; cf. Aristophanes, *Peace* 810–12, the armpits of Gorgons and Harpies, with S. D. Olson ad loc.; Diosc. 1. Tortuous claims that smelly plants may be involved are best ignored.

women almost into the goats they seemed to venerate so much? Clearly, they were still human females, but they stank like goats and perhaps had the desire of goats, which drove their jealousy. We have seen elsewhere the tendency in Greek religion to interweave females and animals, including goats, as in the myth of Embaros' daughter at Munychia.[37] We know that actual priestesses of Artemis were known by the names of animals associated with her.[38] If we are right to suppose as much, we might better appreciate the humour that Athenian audiences evidently found in the Lemnian myth, which recurred on the Athenian comic stage through the fifth and fourth centuries BC.[39] After all, a lame god was an easy target, especially married to the physically perfect Aphrodite.[40]

There was something idiosyncratic in stamping a substance of cleansing cure with the image of a beast renowned for its repulsive smell. So why was this the image on *sphragis*? Artemis had other creatures which would have been less peculiar, such as a deer perhaps, like the stag we see with her on a small dedication (as it seems to be) found at Hephaestia – or even a bear. An answer is suggested by the myth of the discovery of the oracle at Delphi, where Artemis had a place beside her twin brother, Apollo, the god of the oracle. At Delphi a goat had revealed the oracle, dizzied by its vapours.[41]

---

[37] Further, Papadopoulou 2014.

[38] Suidas s.v. Embaros; cf. Eustathius, *Commentary on Iliad* 2.772, with some variations in detail. Priestesses include 'Bear', 'Filly', 'Bee', and 'Fawn'; Faraone 2003.

[39] Aristophanes, frr. 372–91, among other comic authors. Note also Euripides' *Hypsipyle*: Wright 2016.

[40] Further, Hall 2018.

[41] On the Delphi myth: Diod. 16.26; Paus. 10.5.7.

We must wonder whether a goat appeared on Lemnian *sphragis* not simply because it was a favourite of the goddess,[42] but also because the discovery of the curative earth had been enabled by a goat, as at Delphi.

Lessons Learned

Aphrodite's strategy had created an Amazonian microcosm on Lemnos, which was a road to perdition. As elsewhere, an all-female society could be maintained, but it had no future without reproduction – even if an effective army could be formed. Amazons might prefer Artemis, but they also needed Aphrodite if they wanted a future. At the same time, the Lemnian tale presented more positive features of the women's experience. Apollonius stresses that women on Lemnos enjoyed their new roles. For some at least, the traditionally male tasks of farming and the like had been distinctly preferable to the closeted lifestyles of Greek ladies. At a political level, Apollonius shows the women with political structures and debate of a kind that was not so very different from the previous example of their menfolk. In short, his Ptolemaic version left no doubt that women could run an orderly state and take difficult decisions. Queen Hypsipyle presides, but opens discussion in such a way that she accepts the decision to consort with the Argonauts that was not her own immediate preference. Here perhaps there is a hint of something different. For old women in her assembly win the debate, stressing the

---

[42] Goats were at home in at least some of her sanctuaries, see Arrian, *Anabasis* 7.203–4; Aelian, *HA* 11.9 (goats, deer, and hares).

need for sex (alias Aphrodite) for the island's future. Their wisdom reproduces that to be expected of senior male citizens, but we also recall – perhaps inevitably – the more usual conversations between queens or other great ladies and the old females in their households – aged nurses, in large part. In that sense there was a measure of female domesticity, perhaps, in the women's handling of state problems, but far more important is the fact that the debate came to the right decision (as we are shown it), and the queen appears as a fine example of restrained monarchy. One wonders how far our author was guided by his own political context at Alexandria, where queens ruled with their royal brothers. We should not expect such sympathy on the comic stage at Athens, where women's joint action and political organisation seem to have given a lot of amusement.[43]

Throughout the Lemnian myth, questions of responsibility remain unresolved, as often. Clearly, Aphrodite had caused this series of events. In Apollonius' poem she is present at every turn, and will be key to Jason's success in obtaining the Golden Fleece, ensuring the vital help of the besotted – yet dangerous – princess Medea. The goddess wielded a power much mightier than the sword, an irresistible force at least as strong for women as for men. As Jason strides to the palace of Queen Hypsipyle, the goddess is displayed upon his starry cloak:

> Next, deep-tressed Cytherea (Aphrodite) was shown,
> wielding Ares' swift shield. And from shoulder
> to elbow on her left, her tunic hung loose at its fastening

---

[43] In Aristophanes' *Lysistrata* and *Ecclesiazusae*, amongst other plays, probably including those on the Lemnian theme.

beneath her breast. The reflection was plain
to see in the bronze shield opposite her body.

(Ap. Rhod. 1.42–6)

Aphrodite is Jason's badge of sexuality, tinged with danger. We are reminded of her famous affair with Ares the
war-god. On Lemnos, the island of Hephaestus, the allusions were rampant, for it had been her husband the fire-
god himself who had punished the adulterous pair.
Already in Homer, Hephaestus had used a special net of
his devising to capture the lovers during sex and drag
them in front of the other Olympians, to make them
a laughing-stock. Do we have some sense here that
Aphrodite's punishment of the Lemnians had also been
payback for Hephaestus' crafty mockery of her?
Certainly, mention of Ares recalls the union of love and
war, both between the goddess and the war-god and in the
bloody events on Lemnos, including the development of
the story from battle on the beach to sex in the women's
beds. The women had been ready to try battle, and had
then tried sex, which brought them the victory they
wanted. The Argonauts were to leave – however much
they were tempted to stay. But Aphrodite had returned in
the form of the children that would follow, including the
queen's two heroic sons. Myth was little concerned with
the years they would need to grow up, for the goddess
would ensure that there would be no problem. Love and
war are elided, and the women consigned to the former,
with new Lemnian men to take care of the fighting. The
goddess had turned the war-god's mighty shield into
a mirror, taken from battle to the beauty of the boudoir.
The Amazonian episode was well and truly over, and

a kind of justice had been enforced by the jealous goddess.[44]

Artemis is nowhere to be seen in all this, for she had assured more than enough honour on Lemnos. As she states at the outset of Euripides' *Hippolytus*, she must not interfere against a vengeful Aphrodite. The balance between them was a kind of partnership, which both should uphold. But that did not remove responsibility from humans in a world which was, after all, always under divine command and construction. Gods and goddesses could be brutal in upholding their perceived rights and status, but the Lemnians had brought disaster upon themselves. They had been punished and a more balanced future was all but guaranteed. The myth explained and underpinned the need on Lemnos to find due honours for Aphrodite as well as Artemis and the more local Kabeiro.

Greeks, Barbarians, and Amazons

The mythology of ancient Greek religion and cults comprised a wealth of local traditions, while also maintaining a substantial coherence and universality across Greek culture around the Mediterranean, Black Sea, and beyond. Different emphases and inconsistencies were accommodated within this extensive kaleidoscope of beliefs and practices. Local identities and pride ensured that there were disagreements about the true version of a myth across space and time, but that was a tolerable friction within this elastic system. Our Lemnian women are a case in point. On the island itself, the local geography and religious traditions

---

[44] In other poetry, McCarter 2012.

were entwined with Aphrodite's rage and punishment of the islanders. And yet we have had to work quite hard to establish the local situation of the myth – with Kabeiro, a prominent Artemis, and the rest. These local factors were almost as uninteresting for Greek culture in general as they were crucial on Lemnos itself. We must also acknowledge, however, that in this instance there is an important complication to the familiar pattern of local vs. universal in Greek myth – Athens.

Substantial Athenian intervention and settlement from around 500 BC brought the budding Athenian empire into the frame. A strong indication is Herodotus' mention of Brauron in Lemnos' distant past. It was said that in early times raiders from Lemnos had abducted Athenian girls from the coast of Attica at Brauron – the site of a great extramural sanctuary of Artemis herself. The raiders had deliberately targeted her festival there, thronged with pubescent females.[45] Bloody disaster would ensue, which would become a justification for the Athenian seizure of the island in historical times. The clear attempt to interweave Athenian and Lemnian prehistory leaves us to reflect upon the potential Athenian contribution to Lemnos' Amazonian traditions.[46] While Amazons were dear to Artemis, they were also fundamental to the Athenians' identity. Early Athens passed a great initial test when Theseus' new city resisted an Amazon invasion, and so – in many versions – brought an end to the Amazon

---

[45] Echoing the fire-god's attempted rape of Athena: Parker 1996, 154, 241; cf. 1993.

[46] Hdt. 6.138–40 with a second set of killings; the victims were strong-willed Athenian women (those snatched from Brauron) and their offspring.

state at Themiscyra, to which the invaders did not manage to return alive. While we are in no position to detail the interplay of Athenian interest in Amazons with the Lemnian tale of independent women going to battle, we know that there was substantial and difficult interaction between Athenian and Lemnian culture, so that the issue of Amazons was surely part of that murky history.

While that also helps to account for the Athenian taste for plays about Lemnos and its women, the more universal point is that these Lemnian women were Greeks, even if the island's Thracian connections are given due weight. There is a wider lesson in Aphrodite's punishment of the Lemnians, beyond human relations with the divine. That is, when men treat their women badly (as did the Lemnian men who abandoned their spouses for Thracian girls merely by reason of the smell that had afflicted them), death and disaster may be the result. The women could manage well enough without the men, which seems to support the broader idea that women do not need men. And if women's martial efforts are in question, other men may be found to take the place of errant husbands. Such a lesson was not limited to Lemnos, nor even to Amazonian tales. We may consider Argos, and Queen Clytaemnestra's murderous response to Agamemnon's behaviour, for example, and her attempt to replace him with Aegisthus. But the Lemnian women had been more successful, while their Amazonian state and army recall other Amazon traditions, as at Cyme, for example. When Greeks tried to rationalise myths of Amazons, they sometimes argued that these were normal women abandoned or mistreated by their menfolk. Under such pressure such women had ventured to establish an all-female community, whether or not divinely inspired. The lesson to the Lemnians had been not to neglect Aphrodite, but the warning to Greek men in general was more universal – not to mistreat their women. And that general advice took the relevance of Amazons well beyond the ethnography of distant regions, where Amazons might be imagined as various kinds of barbarian, and brought it back to the heart of Greek culture. In rare cases Greek women might be Amazonian (notably, Atalanta),[47] but they all might go Amazon under unacceptable pressure. The gap between barbarian and Greek woman suddenly disappears. For it is precisely the Amazon potential in Greek women that kept the whole concept of Amazons, with its various aspects, powerfully relevant to real Greeks, not only in works of erudition, but in everyday life too. Of course, the lesson was by no means a female call to arms (however that might be imagined), for it was the male-dominated establishment that put Amazons on great public buildings or on the equipment of drinking-parties. However, as the 'Lemnian evil' showed, the mistreatment of women – including Aphrodite herself, an embodiment of sexual relations – threatened chaos and disaster, even if opinions would vary sharply as to what might constitute mistreatment.

[47] Barringer 1996.

10

Alexander the Great and the Amazon Queen

~

Alexander the Great's encounter with an Amazon queen was a highlight of his eastern conquests, and a landmark in later tales about Amazons. She wanted to bear his child, preferably his daughter. So she made a special journey to see him for sex, with an entourage of 300 of her cavalry-girls, dressed to impress. Or so the more creative claimed, around 300 BC and for centuries thereafter. The claim was hard to ignore. But from the first it was derided by many. A few tried to make some sober sense of it – the rationalising urge that dogs myth. In any case, the episode demanded attention. Indeed, it breathed new life into Amazon myth. The astonishing encounter brought Amazons out of extinction and placed them under the spotlight in the excitement that surrounded Alexander's remarkable exploits in the new world to the east. Among these exploits was now an Amazon queen – sexy as ever they were – and real, very much flesh and blood. Alexander's role model Achilles had fallen for the dying Penthesilea. Too late. Now Alexander himself could put that right with another, living queen of the Amazons. Later, the queen might even look like Cleopatra of Egypt, with a variety of Romans striving to be a new Alexander.

Once Alexander had 'found' Amazons, the hunt was on for the place(s) where they might live – in regions that were distant and obscure to Greeks, of course. Wilder parts of the Caucasus mountains attracted attention, somewhere between the Black Sea and the Caspian. An informed view of the geography might see a missing link here between the traditional Amazon homeland at Themiscyra (long since destroyed) and the Amazonian lands towards the Don. A less careful vision might regard all these remote locations to be more or less the same place – the far north-east. It is intriguing to follow the geographer Strabo as he struggles to make sense of Amazon tales and places, while explicitly rejecting the reality of Amazons at all levels. By the time he wrote (around AD 25), Roman forces had started to penetrate these Caucasian regions, eager to mimic Alexander and even discover Amazons of their own – hopefully stripping the bodies of the enemy dead in their search for women warriors.[1]

The story of Amazon sex did not stand alone. Alexander the Great was enmeshed in many a tale of sexual high jinks, in fact and fiction. Already his father, Philip II, had combined a partying disposition with a string of diplomatic marriages to enhance and enlarge his Balkan realms. Alexander also indulged his extensive tastes, about which different authors offered different perspectives from the first, well before the burgeoning fictions of the late antique *Alexander Romance*.[2] These different accounts played into larger questions about the man himself, on which the biographer Plutarch has left us a *Life*,

---

[1] Plut. *Pomp.* 35. On later Roman parades of victory over Amazons, see Beard 2007, 43, 122–3.
[2] Further, Stoneman 2007; 2008. Ogden 2020, 150 observes that Amazons are kept at a distance in the extraordinary *Romance*. Nawotka 2017, 17 sees the author's wish to clean up this aspect of Alexander's sexual record, which he reduced to diplomatic negotiation.

written with half an eye to Julius Caesar. There was debate about Alexander's character, especially his mastery – or lack – of the self-control that was considered vital for any good king.[3] Inevitably, there was controversy, too, about where truth met fiction in the many reports of his activities. How did he respond when an Amazon queen offered him sex? Her offer was the stuff of many a young Greek's fantasy. So, what happened? And was this truth or fiction – or perhaps the ever-popular middle way, where rationalisation might seem to save us from the problem?

Stories of Alexander's sexual antics with the queen were already rife on his death at Babylon in 323 BC. Many were quick to dismiss the nonsense. We are told that the writer Onesicritus (who marched with Alexander) had spoken of the Amazon episode, only to be mocked by one of the Macedonian generals. He (Lysimachus) asked a question of the writer that was simple, yet devastating and hilarious – 'Where was I at that time?'[4] Always close to Alexander, the general had seen no Amazon queens. Onesicritus had a penchant for such creativity.[5] The quip became famous, but even so Amazon tales were touted by the more imaginative writers with Alexander's army, and by others who followed them. However, there was always a sense of fiction and fantasy.[6] Inevitably so, since Amazons were usually consigned to a distant past, if not to complete unreality. And yet there was a kind of

---

[3] See e.g. the debate on a constitution for Persia, Hdt. 3.80–2.
[4] Cf. Strabo 11.5.4. On Cleitarchus, Lane Fox 2018, 95–8.
[5] The quip: Plut. *Alex.* 46; the penchant: Arrian, *Anab.* 6.2.6; Aulus Gellius, *NA* 9.4.
[6] Baynham 2001 assembles views. It should be stressed that a Scythian princess is not an Amazon, with rationalising speculations.

logic in the match: an Amazon queen in search of a super-child by Alexander the Great.[7] Succession was a dominant concern as soon as Alexander died, so that his possible children were a major issue. At the same time, however, no one seems to have suggested a search for a pregnant Amazon. No child of the great mating seems to have been envisaged. By and large, Greeks understood that the union was a fantasy, albeit a wonderful one.

We know the queen as Thalestris (or Thallestris, or Thalestria). It is an unusual name for an Amazon, since it does not suggest the themes usually raised by Amazon names, all conflict and horses. In contrast, the name Thalestris evokes flowery fertility. We may infer that the name has been invented only for this encounter and the notion of reproduction with Alexander. No surviving text names the queen, until we find her enthusiastically embraced by Diodorus Siculus around 30 BC, though she had probably acquired the name well before his day. Myth plays a large part in his extensive history, especially in its early portions. However, where Amazons are concerned, he is regularly sensationalist. No surprise, then, that he expresses no doubts about the queen's visit:

As Alexander turned back towards Hyrcania, the queen of the Amazons came to him. Her name was Thalestris, and she was queen of the land between the rivers Phasis and Thermodon. She was outstanding both in beauty and in bodily strength. Among her fellow Amazons she was admired for her courage. She arrived with 300 Amazons equipped with weapons of war, after leaving most of her army on the borders of Hyrcania. King Alexander

---

[7] A son would be returned to him, as a thoughtful tradition notes: Curtius (6.5.17–21) builds this into his Roman vision of a not-very-enthusiastic Alexander.

marvelled at her unexpected presence, the bearing of the women, and Thalestris. When he asked what need had brought her, she revealed that she had come to make a baby. She said that he was the best man alive, on account of his exploits, while she was outstanding among women in strength and courage – so it was likely that a child born of two pre-eminent parents would excel the rest of mankind in quality. Delighted, the king accepted her offer and spent thirteen days in her company. He then sent her back to her own land, honoured with notable gifts.

(Diod. 17.77.1–3)

So Diodorus tells the tale, some 300 years after Alexander's death. On his version the queen is assertive and clear, even business-like. Her blunt directness owes a lot to Greek notions of other warrior peoples, like the Scythians or the Spartans, who similarly do not mince their words.[8] Hers is the language of a male warrior, as also is her physique and courage (the Greek word here, *andreia*, can also mean manliness). She does not mention beauty among her qualities, but Diodorus finds another way to make that clear, too, if we had been in any doubt on the matter. The geography is loosely described, but makes sense enough. The Amazon army had come from the Black Sea homeland eastwards through the Caucasus mountains to Hyrcania, by the shores of the Caspian. This was a region with a harsh reputation, well into Roman imperial times.[9] The Amazon army and its queen had no fear. But Diodorus' vision was already out of date by the time he wrote. There were no Amazons between the Thermodon and Colchian Phasis, as both Xenophon

[8] Spartans and Scythians share austerity and much else, despite modern claims that (all) Greek and (all) Scythian cultures are polar opposites in Greek minds: further, Braund 2004.
[9] Famously, Virgil, *Aeneid* 4.365–7.

and Roman generals had demonstrated. In fact, Diodorus knew that, and even mentions the Amazon presence there as a thing of the distant past in the second book of this same work.[10] Evidently, the story was too good to overlook – and perhaps few cared about Thalestris' point of departure when it was her arrival that was so startling.

Queens were in fashion in Diodorus' day, while the offspring of queens were also important. For Cleopatra VII of Egypt made a great impression in Rome as well as Alexandria,[11] with Julius Caesar as well as Mark Antony – who had a liking for queens. She committed a famous suicide in 30 BC, but she had also brought a massive military to Antony's cause – not quite an Amazon, but in a world where Romans aspired to be Alexander, the similarity was obvious enough.[12] Moreover, her son by Caesar was important enough to be murdered by the new emperor Augustus, determined to be Caesar's only heir.[13] Elsewhere Cleopatra was also echoed in the story of Cleophis – also bedded by Alexander, it was said, but otherwise unknown.[14]

How were more sober authors to handle this extraordinary episode? The historian Arrian offered a middle way of sorts, a kind of rationalisation, whose origins he does not explain (though he indicates that it was not his own invention). Arrian is usually regarded as the best of our historians of Alexander, though he wrote in the second century AD and is not beyond challenge. Thalestris does

---

[10] Diod. 2.52, where these Amazons peaked around the time of the Trojan War.

[11] Gruen 2003.

[12] Propertius 3.11 brings Cleopatra together with Penthesilea and other powerful women.

[13] Meiklejohn 1934.   [14] On Cleophis, see Ogden 2010, 150–1.

not appear in his account, nor any other Amazon queen. Instead, he offers the remarkable image of a pageant of half-naked females, on horseback and in Amazon kit. There were 100 of these young women, complete with the characteristic axes that Amazons had famously carried. These girls were flesh and blood. They had been sent, he says, by a regional governor as Alexander's army made its way back from India through Iran, crossing the Nesaean plain – already a very special place. It was renowned for its alfalfa pasture and excellent horses – the great herds of the Persian kings.[15] However, the reality of the place did not quite match the dream: there was some disappointment that only a mere 50,000 or so mares were found. There had been talk of far more. Arrian writes that it was on this plain – as some had said[16] – that Alexander encountered Amazons. Their association with horses provided some plausibility.[17] There were dreams aplenty in his army – full of riches and wonders in these strange and distant lands, barely known at all in Greece. Why should there not be Amazons on this plain of horses? But Arrian is clear that these alluring girls were not real Amazons. This was indeed a pageant – and a gift of welcome. Wilder accounts could make actual Amazons of them, should that be wanted.

These 'Amazons' were returned, untouched, says Arrian. Alexander was worried about their effect on discipline – a recurrent theme around Amazons.[18] If the whole story has some basis in fact (and it may not), the governor had

[15] Between Behistun and Ecbatana: Polybius 10.27 with Briant 2002, 420.
[16] For the full range of texts, see Baynham 2001; Ogden 2010, esp. 146–50.
[17] On horses and Thalestris, see also Ogden 2020.
[18] Cf. Jason on Atalanta: p. 42.

misjudged the king. Had his gift been a response to Greek hunger for Amazons? It is clear enough that the more guileful of local rulers saw an opportunity to use such notions to their own advantage. Earlier, Pharasmanes, ruler of the Chorasmians, south of the Aral Sea, had tried to lure Alexander into his personal schemes by offering a hare-brained expedition to a region somehow between the Colchians of the eastern Black Sea and the land of the Amazons. He claimed that these Amazons lived somewhere in his vicinity. Wisely, Alexander had declined, but Pharasmanes' attempt illustrates not only the machinations of local informants, but also the potential impact of Amazon myth on real-world decisions.[19] Although Alexander had grown up with Achilles and his Amazon, he evidently retained a strong sense of military priorities, as Arrian tells it. The king could resist the Amazons promised by Pharasmanes as well as the flesh-and-blood pageant on the Nesaean plain. It would be good to know more about what his officers and men had to say on the matter, especially as the remarkable tomb at Vergina illustrates the fact that an Amazon concern was not peculiar to Alexander. For a decorative shield was found in the tomb, still on display in the museum there, which almost certainly depicts Achilles killing Penthesilea – yet another example of an Amazon image in a funereal context.[20]

Striving for historical truth, the worthy Arrian was conflicted on the subject of Amazons.[21] He is disposed to accept the reality of Amazons in prehistory, on the

[19] Arrian, *Anab.* 4.15; Bosworth 2000, 41–2.
[20] The damaged scene is barely visible under normal conditions: see Borza and Palagia 2007, esp. 114.
[21] Arrian, *Anab.* 7.13.

feeble grounds that early poets wrote about them so often. His own background in north-western Asia Minor may have guided him too. Amazons were legion in his native Bithynia. As a proud son of Nicomedia, and keen student of Bithynian traditions, Arrian was in no position to dismiss the reality of Amazons past. In his work on Bithynia (we have some fragments), Arrian himself had written of Amazons in early times there – as local traditions demanded.[22] He was impressed too by the Athenians' insistence upon Amazons in their prehistory, especially as so much of the Greek culture he championed was centred in his day upon Athens. Probably he wrote of Alexander late in his life, after he had been Hadrian's governor in the huge province of Cappadocia – still more full of Amazons.[23] This province included the eastern Black Sea, on which he wrote his *Periplus* for Hadrian around AD 132. It included Themiscyra itself and the river Thermodon. For all his concern with myth in this *Periplus*, Arrian gives only the briefest of passing references to the Amazons: '... the Thermodon, on whose banks the Amazons are said to have lived'. Amazons are consigned to prehistory. Arrian will not have forgotten the fun that his great model – Xenophon – had had with locals interested in the possibility of living Amazons in his army.[24] They had been led astray at the sight of a girl performing military dances for them at Xenophon's

[22] On the work and its context, see Bosworth 1972; note esp. *FGrH* 156 F48–50, and earlier Demosthenes of Bithynia, who even claimed that Paphlagonian Amastris was named after an Amazon (*FGrH*) 699 F11 (=Steph. Byz. s.v.). On Bithynian myth, see further Braund 2020 on Achilles.

[23] See Bosworth 1972 on the limited evidence.

[24] Arrian, *Periplus* 13; Xen. *Anab.* with Braund 2019.

command. We may catch an echo of the pageant for Alexander on the Nesaean plain.

As Strabo had insisted, it was absurd to claim that Amazons had persisted into the historical period, especially if they were located in known regions. Arrian notes that Xenophon had marched across the plain of Themiscyra without seeing a single Amazon there, in their supposed homeland. Arrian saw that none of his best sources said a word about any Amazon encounter with Alexander. On balance we can understand the historian's cautious preference for a kind of rationalisation. In this way he retained the colour of Amazons, while illustrating Alexander's good sense and self-control. Also, Alexander's humour. When he sent the cavalry-girls home, he allegedly quipped that he would come and have sex with their queen. This soldierly remark may have sparked the Thalestris story. It certainly helped Arrian to navigate his Amazon dilemmas. We should pause, too, and observe how this Amazon story drew humour from Alexander and his general, Lysimachus, as we are told. For an abiding curiosity of Amazon myth is the co-existence of opposite moods and responses – of comedy and tragedy, creation and extinction, truth and fiction.

We are fortunate that Plutarch (c. AD 100) had been at least as sceptical as Arrian, a few decades before, in his *Life* of Alexander.[25] Looking through works on Alexander he named names. By listing authors who told the Thalestris story and those who did not, he demonstrated that it was a sensationalist minority that wrote of the Amazon queen.

[25] Plut. *Alex.* 46.

Even the imaginative Duris of Samos said nothing of Alexander's supposed frolic. That was all the more telling, given Duris' inclusion of a mysterious Amazon story in his account of the battle of Chaeronea in 338, two years before the Macedonian crossed into Asia.[26] Also listed without the story is Chares of Mytilene, whose role was to receive visitors to Alexander, as Plutarch quietly notes. His silence on any Amazon visit was striking.[27] Plutarch also notes the torpedo of a question ('Where was I, then?') which Lysimachus launched. Plutarch observes too that Alexander himself wrote nothing about Amazons, even though he wrote in great detail about broadly comparable matters, including a nomad king's offer of his daughter – grist for the rationalising mill.[28]

The Thalestris story was a wonderful fiction, avoided by all but the wildest of writers. Local attempts to deploy notional Amazons might be more historical, but their convenience for rationalising must make them suspect too. Alexander's Thalestris – and possibly the other 'Amazons' on offer to him – illustrate the strength and adaptability of the old myths. Why should Alexander – a new Achilles – not have a version of Penthesilea? Who could say for certain what strange peoples and creatures dwelt in the far-off world that he had smashed into? A Thalestris might be imagined among the rest – a superwoman in search of the superman, to create a special child. However, Theseus' experience showed the risks involved for parents and child – if a son, at

---

[26] See p. 201 on Chaeronea.
[27] Plut. *Alex.* 46.1; all the more so, since Chares was elsewhere criticised as a flamboyant writer: *P.Oxy.* LXXI 4808 with Lane Fox 2018, 92.
[28] Cf. Arrian, *Anab.* 4.15.

least. Achilles had wanted his Amazon, but had killed her at the same moment. Theseus' example might suggest that he had done the best thing. As far as we may judge, Alexander himself showed no desire to breed with an Amazon. However, as usual with Amazons, stories of these independent, sexy, and dangerous women remained attractive and current – all the more so when hooked onto the astonishing legend of Alexander himself.

Mountain Orgies: Amazons and 'Garglers' of the Caucasus

Once Alexander had 'found' living Amazons, there was new pressure to explain how these all-female societies were able to reproduce. There is a striking silence on the matter in the various earlier texts that have survived for us, where Amazons are repeatedly daughters of Ares, with only the rarest name of an Amazon mother, primarily the nymph Harmonia.[29] Are we to see this neglect as further evidence of the male creation and domination of Amazon myth (in texts and in general)? Or are we seeing a neglect of the mother that aligned with usual tendencies in actual Greek society? Very likely, both. And of course we have already noted the lack of interest in most Amazon individuals, whose names tend to be used and reused by our sources with only a very few exceptions, most notably the epic Penthesilea. Amazon names recurrently chime with aspects of Amazon myth that were readily transferrable from one Amazon to another – Antianeira, Hippolyte, and more.[30]

---

[29] Harmonia and Ares: see schol. Ap. Rhod 2.992 (Pherecydes, 3F 15).
[30] The enthusiastic inventions of the vase-painters do not affect the point.

In later times, our fullest account of Amazon reproduction is provided by the geographer Strabo, who – as we have seen – found even ancient Amazon tales absurd. One wonders what was said on the subject in his native city of Amasia. Its name might encourage an Amazon tradition, especially as it lay only a little south of the Themiscyra plain. However, Strabo spent most of his life hobnobbing with the elite of the Roman empire – a long life that ended under the emperor Tiberius, around AD 25 or so. Evidently, he felt obliged by the weight of Amazon myth to report some of the claims he had heard about them.

At one point Strabo relays talk of an Amazon arrangement for reproduction – far away in a remote corner of the Caucasus mountains, which seemed to chime with what had been said about Thalestris' visit to Alexander.[31] These mountains were complex and little known – a region where anything might be imagined. Indeed, Greek culture had long considered mountains to be places for wild cults of all kinds, most notably the rites of Dionysus. Somewhere in the Caucasus mountains, it was said, lived a group of Amazons, who carried out all the usual male tasks (ploughing, herding, and especially horse-training). Some of them liked to hunt and exercise for war. Meanwhile, in a neighbouring valley, there was another people, apparently all male. They were named Gargarians. The name evokes gargling in Greek. It was probably formed in a way similar to 'barbarian', from non-Greeks' use of an alien language.[32] The plurality of small and localised languages around the Caucasus no doubt helped the story. It was said that for two months

---

[31] Strabo 11.5.1.
[32] See e.g. Vlassopoulos 2013, 37 and the works he cites. Later, Plut. *Pomp.* 35 gives other names for the Amazons' men, Gelae or Legae.

each year, in spring, the Amazons and these 'Garglers' gathered in the high country between them. They spent these months in religious ritual and anonymous sex. Two months were time enough. We may recall that Alexander – some said – spent two weeks in bed with his Amazon queen. Their sex was appropriately heroic. In due course, when the Amazons had given birth to children, they gave the baby boys to the 'Garglers' and kept the girls, who would be brought up as Amazons. In that way the problem of Amazon reproduction was solved: Amazon babies were born (with no sign of hostility to motherhood, we may note) and male influence was kept away from their all-female microcosm. In effect, the 'Garglers' were sperm donors. Spring was breeding season in this high corner of the Caucasus: there was something animalian about this nameless and seasonal path to children. And yet this was also a mode of reproduction that required none of the savagery imagined by Diodorus and others.

However, this fine story is clearly located in a very specific place, and concerns a group of Amazons, far away from Themiscyra.[33] These are the Ceraunian ('Lightning-bolt') mountains of the Caucasus, a name far more familiar elsewhere – in the western Balkans, by the Adriatic.[34] They seem to be the westernmost spurs which become the hills and flatlands towards the Taman peninsula. The imagined geography is shaky, but these Amazons are placed towards the Sauromatians and especially Labrys. Some limited coherence, then, albeit

[33] Strabo 11.5.4 notes that some tried to trace the relationship back to Themiscyra, whence they said the Garglers had also come.
[34] On Caucasian associations in these Adriatic mountains, see Braund 1994, 34.

centuries after Herodotus wrote of Amazon traditions in this general area.

In relaying this fantasy, Strabo invokes the writers who travelled with one of the new Alexanders of Rome – the general Pompey, who had conquered swathes of the east in the 60s BC, and had investigated even the Caucasus in part. As a boy Strabo had been brought to Rome as a direct result of these Roman campaigns, which perhaps tempered his distaste for Amazons. He names one of Pompey's authors and confidants as a principal source – Theophanes of Mytilene. Another named source was Metrodorus of Scepsis, who came from the eastern coast of the Hellespont and had prospered (rather like Strabo's family) under Pompey's principal opponent, King Mithridates VI Eupator. Metrodorus' remarks were no doubt part of his standing obsession with Trojan legends, wherein Amazons were prominent enough from the first. He and the other authorities that Strabo names were all writers of the later Hellenistic world, at least two centuries after Alexander. We struggle to connect their fancies with the ancient myths of Amazons. For those had been rooted in a Greek culture that was much smaller in its extent and reach. Alexander and others – Greek and Roman – had given some licence to those writers who shifted Amazons from Themiscyra into the high Caucasus.

Unleashed Imaginations

Amazons had been the stuff of fiction and fantasy ever since they first emerged in archaic times. While their myth had been framed by epic tales and communal traditions, the partying environment of the symposium already offered a context that could encourage wilder imaginings. The medical tradition affords a glimpse of sensational stories about Amazons that circulated by the end of the fifth century. Presumably the extraordinary scenes on vases of the fourth century – with Amazons fighting griffins and the like (Plate 31) – owe something to these lost texts. Alexander's exploits had permitted (even demanded) some reconsideration of Amazon reality. Had Alexander even had sex with an Amazon queen – and at her request? In any case, Greek novelistic fiction was developing fast through the fourth century and onwards. Alexander's exploits were well suited to that process – his Amazon frolic as much as any other episode. Meanwhile, the new Hellenistic kingdoms created by his generals – especially the Ptolemies at Alexandria – supported and financed the scholarly organisation, examination, and reworking of traditional myths, including those of Amazons. As in Diodorus' case, the expanding Roman empire would bring to bear a whole set of new impulses to this frothy mix. All the more so, since pre-Roman cultures in Etruria and southern Italy had their own Amazon traditions. We do well to bear in mind that even the famous Amazon vases painted by Exekias in sixth-century Athens were deposited in burials of Etruria.

Creating a new Amazon history, Diodorus offers a whole dynasty of Amazon queens, with daughters succeeding their mothers through the generations. No doubt much of this was taken from earlier texts, but he can be outspokenly innovative at times. For example, he relishes his claim that the Amazons of Libya were much earlier than those of the Black Sea, though these early Amazons were largely forgotten.[35] His is the first extended history of Amazon monarchy that we have, though he points to predecessors who are beyond our knowledge and may themselves be fictitious. His Italian context in space and time may explain that unusual framework, which looks like an expanded version of the Amazon dynasty at Caulonia in the Greek colonial environment of southern Italy. His Amazons look quite different from those in the fragmented traditions of the Aegean coastlands that had multiplied from early archaic times. Diodorus had managed to bring these together within a history that was more coherent, though not more inclusive or convincing. In his monarchical conception, a series of strong queens had established Amazon society with laws that kept men in submission and busy with woolworking – the ultimate female task. This Amazon society was not an all-female state, such as we tend to find earlier, but the inversion of his own society in regard to gender roles and power relationships. The women were prepared for war, trained and practised in hunting from an early age. The girls had their right breast cauterised for that purpose, while the men's subjugation was ensured by the mutilation of their limbs. This was a harsh and imperialist culture, whose gods were Ares and Artemis in famously bloody guise – as Artemis Tauropolus. Yet Diodorus tries to offer a history of the generations of Amazons which is also in part a rationalisation. He asserts that these Amazons were not literally daughters of Ares, but gained and suited that name by virtue of their prowess, though he soon allows that Penthesilea was indeed a real daughter of Ares.[36]

[35] Diod. 2.52. [36] Diod. 2.45.

In the Greek east of the Roman empire sensationalist fictions came to overwhelm serious treatments of ancient traditions about Amazons. This was a world in which Amazon duels were staged in the amphitheatre to amuse the crowds. The old tales were very familiar, so that only the determined rationaliser might find something to say. Even in the sixth century AD, the prolific historian Procopius not only tried his hand at yet another account of the peoples and places around the Black Sea, but also attempted to explain the phenomenon of Amazons in terms that were rational and respectful enough, but not so far from what had been written many times over the centuries before. He declares that Amazons had never existed. Women with male qualities were a freak of nature, and in any case were unattested in the Black Sea region. He holds that the myth arose from a large expedition of non-Greeks which camped by the river Thermodon. The expedition included women, but these stayed at the camp while their men set off to conquer the wider region. When these men were completely destroyed in the attempt, the women – against their will – had no choice but to defend themselves with such equipment as their men had left. They were all destroyed too, but their attempt gave rise to the myth of Amazons. Procopius infers all this from what he regards as natural, and current experience with the Huns in this part of the world with whose forces women participated. Inevitably perhaps, Procopius talks of women discovered among the Hun dead when their bodies were stripped. As our author admits, there was not much new in his version of the truth.[37]

[37] Procopius, *Wars* 8.3.5–11.

Truth was valued, however much contested, but sheer fantasy was potentially more enjoyable and fresh. In his *Heroicus* – mystical, mysterious, and satirical – Philostratus (c. AD 200) had offered a bizarre version of Achilles' conflict with Amazons. It forms the concluding part of an imaginary conversation, in which a Phoenician is regaled with tall and terrifying tales – told by a strangely sophisticated gardener (the Vine-dresser), who claims to have heard these reports from the ghostly Protesilaus (the first Greek to die at Troy in Homer's *Iliad*, killed as he jumped ashore).[38] These tales were told at Protesilaus' sanctuary at the entrance to the Hellespont – a real and respected location on the way to the Black Sea, but this dialogue-on-dialogue was complete fiction – a vehicle for learned controversy, heavily laced with dark, intellectual humour. For the Vine-dresser suggested that he had reliable reports from the ghostly Protesilaus about the ghostly Achilles on the island of Leuke, off the Danube delta in open water. The island and the sanctuary of Achilles that occupied much of it were the real setting for these clever games of truth and fiction. Leuke is now called Snake Island across a range of the region's languages.

In this highly inventive fantasy, Amazons complete a chain of stories that give prominence to remarkable women including a certain Hiera of Mysia,[39] herself an Amazon-like warrior, as well as a hapless Trojan girl whom Achilles tears to pieces in his hatred of Troy. The Phoenician is told that Achilles had not fought the Amazons at Troy, because they had not come there.

[38] *Iliad* 2.695–709.   [39] The name means Sacred in Greek.

The clash came on Leuke. In 'fact', the story goes, the Amazons had heard of Achilles' sanctuary on Leuke and had decided to make the great voyage there from the Thermodon, across most of the Black Sea. Their purpose was impious greed – they wanted the riches and mares of the little island and Achilles himself, for purposes not quite specified. There is only a hint at their sexual desire for the hero. So they had vessels built to ship their horses with them on this absurd project. There is humour here for the well-informed reader. The island was (and is) tiny,[40] so that horses were unlikely there and were certainly useless for military purposes. Amazons were famously incapable at sea: Herodotus' well-known tale of Sauromatian origins relied on their ignorance of ships, so that the voyage was more than unlikely. The whole absurd plan also neglected the powers of the ghostly hero. In 'fact' Achilles soon had the horses (mares) kill and eat their Amazon riders, with body parts and dying Amazons scattered in and around his sanctuary. Sated and crazed, the horses jumped into the sea and died. The Amazon ships were made to strike and sink each other, and Achilles cleansed his island by bringing the waves across its surface, to wash away the gory Amazon remains that the horses had not consumed.

These are bestial Amazons, as their attempt upon the holy sanctuary shows. It was their custom to fatten up those shipwrecked on their shores, in order to sell them as meat to the cannibals of Scythia. And they kept men out of their land. It is in this context that Philostratus pauses to relate at some length their means of reproduction. First, they set off

---

[40] Some 0.7 × 0.7 km at its widest points.

to the Halys River (to their west on the south coast of the Black Sea), to buy goods and have sex, wherever they might find it there. There may be a suggestion of prostitution – the exchange of sex for goods. In due course they treat their babies very differently. Males are dumped at the borders of their territory, to be picked up as slaves. Females are considered Amazons, nurtured and loved by their mothers. The learned author introduces a new (as it seems) version of Amazon breast-lore. Here they have both breasts and do not mutilate them at all. The 'problem' of the obstructive right breast is 'solved' simply by not breastfeeding, so that the breast does not come to hang in the way. The baby females are brought up on the milk of horses, instead. Our author makes much of their equine associations, including even their end as horse-food on Achilles' island. He exploits too Herodotean details of Scythian cannibals and horse-milking – all part of his clever literary game. It is characteristic of the *Heroicus* that it prizes novelty at every turn.

Its claims about Amazons may well have no general currency beyond the text itself. For his clever games our author has taken familiar Amazon themes – horses, breasts, motherhood, and the rest – and given them a new twist, while sweeping aside venerable traditions of Achilles and Penthesilea at Troy and more besides. The devotees of Artemis have been turned into bestial monsters at last, but in an extreme and iconoclastic fiction that transformed these fine women of traditional Greek culture into cheap, immoral hucksters – amusement for would-be intellectuals.[41]

---

[41] The modern hunt is on again for Persians: Maclean and Aitken 2002, lxxx.

Clearly, we have only some of the many texts written about Amazons, rather as our vision of Amazon sculptures is partial and often fragmented. However, although we are guided primarily by the pieces that have survived for us, Alexander's Amazon story was a landmark in the development of Amazon traditions and fictions, while the Amazon phenomenon was caught up too – as all else – in the larger processes of historical and cultural change that we have glanced at. There is a palpable tendency away from the attractive challenges of conquered and creative Amazons towards unrooted and unlimited fictions of all kinds. With Alexander's discoveries, Amazons had come to life again, amid new horizons. The old civic, cultic, and artistic traditions concerning Amazons were well embedded and persisted strongly enough, bolstered by the great monuments, Homeric epics, and the rest. However, away from collective, more institutional Amazon traditions, there were now also new Amazons, about whom almost any fiction might be offered, without reference to tradition, but also referencing such earlier ideas (as with Philostratus' *Heroicus*) or setting out to subvert them, as Diodorus Siculus sometimes explicitly seeks to do, in the form of a new Amazon history. Of course, Amazons were fictional from first to last, but the nature of those fictions changed, especially pivoting around Alexander's world-expanding exploits.

11

Conclusions
Amazon Realities

⌁

We have seen how the legendary Amazons of Greek prehistory were key figures in the real world of Greek society and culture from its discernible beginnings around 700 into the Roman period, over half a millennium later – and beyond. We have followed the development of their legend from tales rooted in local traditions and cults into an expanded Greek world, marked by Alexander's campaigns to the east. Through the archaic and classical centuries, down to the fourth century, Greeks had treated Amazons with a potent mix of reverence, lust, and the pride of conquest. By the end of the fourth century, however, that mix contained ingredients which are hard to find earlier – notions of living Amazons, abiding in obscure locations, no longer battling Greeks, but at war with griffins and other fantastical beasts. While the old traditions stayed strong, sensationalism now had a role in myths that had always been extraordinary enough. In result, tales of Amazons become more brutal into the Byzantine era. Our primary concern has been the Amazons of archaic and classical times.

Amazons were a myth made by and for men, created and consumed by a male-dominated world. Almost nothing suggests that women of this world took a significantly different view of Amazons. But how much can we make of

that in a world where women's voices are so seldom heard?
We know little or nothing about what women thought on
any subject in classical antiquity, except where these women
were queens or enjoyed another form of wealth and privil-
ege. Certainly, Amazons (as we have them) show no concern for other women, but their example was open to many
interpretations, including the viability of a certain kind of
militant female independence – with its competing
(dis)advantages. The life-experiences of Greek women
surely gave them some particular perspectives on Amazon
myth, but we hear next to nothing of such views.
Overwhelmingly, Amazons were part of a shared prehistory
that was common to Greek men and women alike. Tales of
Amazons of yore mattered among Greeks because they
connected with so much in their real-life world. They
exemplified an alternative order, in which women were in
control of their own lives, but the price for that was a grim
existence and early, violent death. Commitment to warfare
was vital to independent survival, while their descent from
Ares the war-god helped them to meet that need. They had
the physical and mental potential for pitched battle among
heroes and their derring-do. Self-belief runs through
Amazon stories, but overconfidence was also a danger, for
Amazons had built an imperialist state in prehistory – fit to
attack the greatest army that King Priam had seen in Asia
Minor before the Greeks arrived at the gates of Troy. As
Greeks surveyed this great prehistory, they saw that states
rose and fell. The more insightful among them saw imperialism and excessive ambition as key reasons for the failure of
empires – under Croesus, Cyrus, and others. Amazons
would fail for such reasons too, as most clearly in their
doomed march upon Theseus' Athens, far from the regions

they had managed to control. Women, as well as men, could catch the blight of imperialism.

Amazons had to be major warriors, for Greeks would rejoice in conquering them – there was no glory in defeating women who were not a special threat. Amazons would be slaughtered and their state destroyed, though some avoided immediate destruction, always resourceful. At Troy, Achilles would kill Penthesilea, as he had killed Hector and so many other, male warriors. Heracles had smashed Amazon society at Themiscyra, as other Greek heroes claimed also to have done, with and without him – Telamon, Iolaus, and more, including Theseus. The great hero of Athens would also repel their siege of his newly formed city. While each of these Greek conquests had its nuances, together they show a single pattern. In heroic prehistory, Greeks always won their battles with Amazons (albeit taking casualties). Greeks were the cause of Amazon demise. Greeks had come to settle in and around the Amazon homeland at Themiscyra. Greeks had imagined Amazons in a setting well suited to their lifestyle, and familiar to Greeks from early archaic times. From the 430s Athenians were farming the fields of the Amazons, whence they had marched to destroy the nascent city of Theseus. In real time there was no longer an Amazon community on the southern shores of the Black Sea. Greeks had put an end to it before history began. Amazons had enjoyed success until they encountered heroes who were still better in battle – Greek supermen. In the view of Greek men it was not simply or primarily because of their female gender that Amazons were defeated. These women were matches for men, with a record to prove it – accomplished warriors. To defeat

Amazons was a major achievement for men, even Greek
men, including supermen. Achilles and Heracles would
both become gods soon after their Amazon conquests. At
Athens, even the most self-satisfied acknowledged that
Amazons had maintained a siege for months before
departing under truce – a great achievement of the city,
as Athenians boasted.

It is tempting to imagine – albeit in the absence of
direct evidence – that Greek females might enjoy the
success of these women warriors, with whatever qualifica-
tion. Amazon independence could surely appeal to the
closeted women of ancient Greece. However, we may
wonder how many were willing to accept the price for
such independence – a short life aimed at the ghastly
violence of the battlefield. In any case, Amazons were
enemies to the women of Greece as well as its men. At
Troy, Amazons had fought for Greek defeat, champion of
the male-dominated city of Priam. At Athens they would
have sacked the city, not improved the lives of its women.
Real Athenian women might desire more independence,
but hardly at the expense of their city, families, and lives.
As the male myth had it, Amazons were not gender warriors, struggling for the rights of women in general.

Greek male perspectives are better attested, and indicated
by the uses of Amazon images in art – private as well as
public. The Greek conquerors of Amazons were renowned
for much more besides. Tales of conquering Amazons
formed part of more extensive heroic records, which made
role models of Heracles and the rest. In the male culture of
the gymnasium such heroes embodied a whole ideology of
struggle, training, and competition for glory, whether in
sport, in battle, or in life more generally. At the symposium,

men spoke and sang, in celebration of heroic achievements, past and present. Images on the vases of these gatherings illustrate recurrent themes of heroism, pleasure, and success – with Amazons often enough on show. They tend to appear in battle – so-called Amazonomachy, or 'Amazon-fighting'. But all the men present knew that they would be the victors, even when images might seem to show the outcome to be in doubt. They also expected Amazons to be especially alluring – shown as nubile females in their prime, strikingly beautiful in every sense. Their costumes are attractive too – variously exotic, revealing, and alluring. For Amazons wield weapons of love and lust as well as those of war. The would-be Greek hero of the gymnasium and symposium must deal with opponents who challenged not only their skills in war, but also their sexual psychology. The age-old heroes had shown the way, but also the problem. Heracles had not been overwhelmed by the sexual allure of his Amazon queen. On Lemnos, too, it was Heracles who recalled the Argonauts from the beds of the Lemnian women to their heroic quest for the Golden Fleece, at least in Apollonius' version. Theseus had abducted his Amazon (or had he?) and precipitated a major conflict, with all its echoes of Paris, Helen, and Troy. Achilles' weakness was not only his heel, but also his vulnerability to the stunning attractions of Penthesilea. Her death would be followed soon enough by his own – still disturbed and wounded in his soul. In the real world Amazon tales warned men that women were potentially a special danger – they might seem weaker, but were they? Here lies a kind of magic in Amazons, who had no use for other kinds, by contrast with Medea, Circe, and other powerful females of the heroic age. The queen's talismanic belt elevated her above other

Amazons, but (like the Golden Fleece) it seems to have bestowed no specific magical powers. The sexual allure of Amazons was magic enough.

We begin to understand how Amazons had a strong relevance to Greek society around relationships between men and women, while their dual powers of force and seduction also brought them into an important Greek conversation about the nature of power and empire. In Greek society the patriarchal family was the normative building-block, but Amazons were outside male control, which made such a family impossible – a threat. Where we hear anything of the Amazon family, sex and marriage depend on the bride's prior killing of at least one warrior in battle, with various ways to maintain female control at the expense of any male children. Most of that is late accretion. Amazon myth's key family relationship was that these were Ares' daughters, though we do not see him exerting authority over them, and rarely find him directly involved in their society. He could not save them. The heroes had shown that the Amazon threat was about female power, which could be handled with resolute self-control – probably. These women were a serious challenge to the would-be hero because they had unexpected skills for heroic pitched battle and for seduction – an exceptional combination, recalling the famous statue of armed Aphrodite at Sparta. For we have seen how Artemis and Aphrodite – virginity and sex – are rivals intertwined and arguably indivisible in Greek culture. The youth of the gymnasium had to deal with both in life, as his heroes had dealt with both in their exploits against Amazons and others. In addition, there was an implication that Greek men (and perhaps especially Athenian men – at Athens) were remarkable in that the end of Amazons was their achievement – first by Greek heroes and thereafter by Greek men who sought to sustain the victory in dealing with women of the real world thereafter. Elsewhere, the story was very different. Amazons had defeated men of the barbarian world, and were likely to succeed against them again and in future. The jingoism is clear enough, while we have observed also the warning to Greek men posed by aspects of the Amazon conception. Among Greeks, male abuse of women had been disastrous for men on Lemnos, with its Amazon traditions. For Ephorus at Cyme, the whole Amazon myth had arisen from male injustice to women. History shows that Amazons had long since ceased to exist, if ever they had. But they survived strongly as a cultural phenomenon at the heart of Greek society, especially in gender relations and in particular contexts from place to place across the Greek world and its many communities.

Amazons were resilient. Refugees from smashed Themiscyra had futures – but only with a substantial transformation. The Sauromatian tale illustrates a case, already in the fifth century. Herodotus' shipwrecked Amazons had avoided transportation to Greece – exceptionally difficult slaves-to-be. They used their sharp wits to establish a new Sauromatian people above the Black Sea, whose women rode horses, hunted, and fought in battle beside their menfolk – transformation, but better than slavery. Another shipwreck had brought Penthesilea's Clete to Italy, where she established a dynasty of queens and produced a son. At Athens, Theseus' Amazon had become a woman of Athens, so that she died in battle for the city and was honoured with a memorial tomb – even if her son

Hippolytus proved problematic. In Asia Minor itself, we not only glimpse tales of unknown Amazon involvement among the rulers of Troy, but find a long list of foundations attributed to Amazons. Ephesus, in particular, was a focus of asylum for Amazon refugees, whose futures lay with the Ephesian form of their goddess, Artemis. Variously under threat from Heracles and Dionysus, Amazons had been key to the creation of her great cult. The goddess had saved these Amazons, but also brought them into a new life which she managed. Up the coast at Cyme, the founding Amazon appears on civic coinage in a guise that suggests her complete transition to Greek womanhood, whether or not she retained her Amazon capacity, as did Theseus' Amazon at Athens. Amazons who escaped immediate death at Themiscyra and elsewhere were able to make new lives. However, their future retained features of their Amazon past, so that Amazon myth seemed to explain a variety of local customs and the very existence of significant cults and communities.

These transitions also show that the differences between Amazons and other Greek women could be overcome, so that the Amazon paradigm had all the more relevance to female lives in Greek society – in both male and female outlooks. In fact, Amazonian Greek women had a place in Greek culture, aside from Amazons. We have seen the Amazon-like Atalanta of Arcadia, with her own – deadly – transition to marriage. The women of Lemnos became warriors, marshalled for battle until they instead went to bed with the Argonauts, and returned to a more normative state through the machinations of Aphrodite. Telesilla and others took to the battlefield with the equipment of their absent men. Their stories also underpin local traditions in

Argos and elsewhere. Such traditions apart, transition between Amazon and Greek female was also explored in fiction. In the novel *Calligone*, the heroine of that name is an athletic girl from the Greek city of Olbia on the northwest coast of the Black Sea. In pursuit of her boyfriend, she takes on the guise of an Amazon, with the strength and attitude to strangle a man to death. Another Greek fiction – *The Uprising of the Amazons* – has Theseus' Amazon enraged by her man's Jason-like infidelity. She and other Amazons seek armed revenge. As these various traditions and fictions illustrate, Amazons and Greek women were different, but also similar enough in attitude and behaviour as well as their common biology.

The Thracian ethnicity of Amazons brought considerable coherence to their practices – their language, favoured weaponry, love of horses,[1] robust assertiveness, and more were characteristic of Thracians in Greek eyes. The women of Thrace had a name for violence, too. Greeks liked to portray Amazons with the famous fox-fur hats of Thrace, or the Phrygian caps of what Xenophon and others called 'Thrace in Asia'. We have seen how their Thracian presence at Themiscyra made sense in terms of a more general Thracian migration eastwards as far as the Caucasus, as imagined in prehistory. By contrast, modern attempts to apply alternative identities to Amazons have proved unconvincing. Something Scythian – even nomadism – has been claimed for them, because they appear sometimes in the skin-tight clothes of the archer, mounted or on foot. A Persian

---

[1] By late antiquity, their horses might eat flesh or breath fire: schol. Hom. *Iliad* 3.189.

identity is routinely foisted on them, because Themiscyra lies (just) within the Persian empire, as do the lands of so many other peoples. However, no ancient text says so, or supports the hypothesis that Amazons somehow evoked Persians at Athens after Marathon. Possibly there were Greeks who found some echo of the Amazon siege in the beach-battle at Marathon or in the brief Persian walkover under Xerxes, but even texts on these subjects are notably silent about anything of the sort. Greeks seem to have regarded Amazons as better-quality warriors than most of what Persia had to offer.

Daughters of Ares, Amazons showed all respect to the Olympian gods, as did Thracians and other 'barbarians'. Artemis was closest to them, herself a militant young female, a mistress of animals and the hunt, always equipped to kill with bow and javelin. Her twin brother, Apollo, was always close too, as at Delphi. However, deities of marriage and reproduction could only be at odds with the alternative Amazon lifestyle – Hera, in particular, who had undermined Heracles' attempt at a peaceful mission for the Amazon queen's belt. Aphrodite had a complex relationship with Amazons, as with Artemis – we have seen how Amazons could embrace and weaponise her powers too. Athena might seem a natural ally for Amazons, since she was the goddess most obviously a warrior. However, we have seen her mature beauty and maternal dimension as obstacles to affinity with Amazons, impossible in the light of their assault upon her city of Athens.

For principal issues and allegiances were played out in the display of Amazons on Greek public buildings, especially temples. In essence, a male choice. Women had important roles in the practice of Greek religion, but the design and financing of temples and the like were the decisions of male power and institutions. It was men who chose, for example, to show Amazons on the Parthenon – in defeat, of course. In their alternative life-style, Amazons could be bracketed with more monstrous mythical beings (Centaurs, and even Giants), but only insofar as these too were at odds with marriage and for-malised parenthood, vital for the communal future of any Greek city. While Amazons had more and less positive relations with different Olympian deities, this public art invariably projected their defeat and the failure of their lifestyle. For that reason, Amazons featured on temples of Hera and Athena as well as those of Apollo and Artemis. At Olympia Zeus presided over a world in which Amazons had their place, albeit in defeat at the hands of Greek heroes – Heracles, Theseus, and Achilles duly featured at his great temple there. For Amazons were part of their great stories, which in turn formed the prehistory of Greek culture, at the beginning of things. Amazons were special on account of their gender and lifestyle, but they belonged to the great tales of the distant past – daughters of a god, and players in the Argonautic and Trojan tales that, with Heracles' labours and more, made up the fabric of this imagined prehistory. The taming of Amazons was key in the formation of Greek culture, as public art sought to insist.

Amazon tombs were not only landmarks, but also fur-ther proof of their defeat. And yet, from Homer's Troy onwards, these were also monuments to Amazon strength and ambition, charged with the militant energy that Hector had sought to activate in his army. The tomb of Theseus' Amazon was in effect part of Athens' defences at the Itonian Gate, where she had been killed for the city. The new Athens had been baptised in Amazon blood, with the death too of the opposing Amazon queen – memorialised along like the dead on both sides. The Amazon siege ran through the fabric of the city, as Athenians understood well before Cleidemus tried to trace the detail in the fourth century. Death and its monuments combined with temple art and more to declare the security of a society that was dominated by men. Amazon relics offered yet more assurance, while also proclaiming the success and power that Amazons had enjoyed until their conquest by Greeks. The Amazon axe, in particular, evoked empire and a deep past for the ruling family of Mausolus in Caria, as no doubt the people of Labrys claimed in the wealthy lands of south Russia and the Bosporan kingdom. The axe, the famous belt, and the tombs of Amazons insisted that Amazons had existed long ago, while ensuring also their immortal memory in death and glory – the principal concerns of funerary art. Greeks took a range of views on the plausibility of real Amazons in the distant past. As our texts show, there was scope for humour too, centred on the atypical powers of these beautiful women warriors – rebooted by absurd claims that Alexander had found some living examples in alien lands. However, there was no doubt – across Greek culture and around the Mediterranean and beyond – about the many-sided significance of Amazons and their stories for Greeks, men and women alike.

Amazons had died in their beautiful, sexual prime, brave and inspired. In that sense they were a failure, and Greek men gloried in their conquest of these extraordinary opponents. Their images are stained with blood – from battle, not from bed and birth like most Greek women. In their pomp and in their domestication, Amazons had created cities, cults, and other phenomena of Greek culture – including their tombs. They were not forgotten. Small wonder that they recur in funerary art, battling against Greeks on the tombs of Greek men in Athens, Halicarnassus and elsewhere. Theirs was a story of lives lived among heroes – lives which had achieved immortality in memory. Key relics – the belt, the axe – confirmed the special powers of Amazons, and the continuation of their stories beyond death and domestication, as did their images and tales from Homer onwards. For flesh-and-blood Greeks – whatever their gender – Amazons and their stories had raised a wealth of questions about gender relations which survived the Amazons themselves, for it was in the context of such issues that the legend had become established.

Amazons were an ancient Greek myth, creation and treasure of a male-dominated society. This book has tried to explain how the myth played well with Greek men in their pursuit of social success and even heroism for themselves, their families and communities, both at human and at divine level, as they faced their divinities and mortality itself. The ultimate failure of Amazons is clear, and was necessary for this society, where the family ensured stability and committed male warriors for the future. That may seem disappointing to some readers of this book. The consolation, if needed, is not to indulge in desperate fantasies about real Amazons excavated in a far-off land, but to move away from the reductionism that has so limited modern work on Amazons. They were good warriors in myth, but their stories entail much more that is positive besides – intelligence, adaptability, resource-fulness, scientific prowess, remarkable construction skills, and a strong association with much of the supernatural. It has become quite usual in ancient studies to stress the male oppression of women, whose lives were indeed limited in most cases. Amazon myth is intriguing because it is a male-orientated myth which indicates that men had a far more nuanced view of Greek women than is often supposed. This myth not only acknowledges female potential in war but also insists on the wider capacities of women to run their own lives and societies, and to do that with notable success. The gap between Amazons and Greek women at large, as we have seen, was not only bridgeable, but bridged. Amazons did not depend on their descent from the war-god – their skills could be acquired by other women, as the fiction of Calligone indicates. An Amazon queen admires the statuesque phys-ique of this young lady of Pontic Olbia, who goes on to dress and behave in the manner of an Amazon, ready to strangle a man who distresses her. When Clytaemnestra butchered her husband Agamemnon in his very house, Aeschylus makes Apollo himself reflect on the less per-sonal and close-quarters death he might have found at Troy from Amazon arrows fired from afar. On Lemnos and elsewhere we have seen many instances of Amazonian behaviour among Greek women, which has somehow been overlooked or denied by those who have claimed that Greek women and Amazons are wholly different or even opposite to each other, as structuralist method tends to demand. The host of Amazon images from antiquity, painted and sculpted, show us – again and again – women who could easily be taken for Greeks, were it not for their clothing and gear in many cases. Occasional nonsense in antiquity about breast-mutilation and its consequences seems never to have found its way into Greek thought about Amazons in general, while modern interests in tattoos and lesbian lifestyles have no echo in our ancient texts and images in regard to Amazons. There can have been few Greeks – female and male – who did not admire the bodies of the Amazons they imagined and saw depicted all around their societies. And Amazons could even be brought into Greek society, albeit with difficulty. The resolution of Greek–Amazon conflicts might well become the creation of cities and cults, under the super-vision of the gods and goddesses who regulated and dir-ected the world of humans, as commemorated in the Horcomosium at Athens, which marked and memorial-ised the Amazons' withdrawal from their siege of the city under an exchange of oaths that confirmed the establish-ment of Theseus' new foundation.

The taming of Amazons by the greatest male heroes was more than the simple application of force, not least because the power of Amazons entailed much more than force and militarism. They were the offspring not only of Ares, but also of the nymph Harmonia, whose name bespoke an order and organisation that went beyond the demands of warfare and discipline into cooperation, social cohesion, and even forms of friendship and love. These women could fight very well, but they could also create culture in so many other ways. The results were stunning across the cities of the Greek world and their cults, from Massilia and Italy to the Black Sea, Ephesus, and Lagina, where tales of defeat became the creation of key locations and practices in Greek and local cultures, celebrated at the

great panhellenic centres. At Ephesus, Cyme, and elsewhere there was explicit acknowledgement of the divine
role in the bringing of Amazons into Greek and local
culture. Ares is hard to find, but Artemis is very clear at
times, as we have seen, no doubt with Apollo close at hand
as well as the all-powerful Zeus. Of course any suggestion
of female power was potentially controversial, nevertheless, so that men might also find humour in all this, and/or
insist that the myth was ridiculous and implausible. Clumsy
attempts to find real-life Amazons in Alexander's eastern
exploits encouraged that kind of response, together with
the fictional conflicts of Amazons, griffins, and the like.
Through such stories Amazon hunting was set aside from
war-training (such as young men routinely found in the
hunt) and turned into an other-worldly idiosyncrasy of
foreign parts, where griffins had long been imagined
towards north and east.[2] Griffins were familiar and formidable, but they were also redolent of faraway fictions that
had much less impact on Greek reality than the Amazon
myth that had played so great a role in Greek notions of the
prehistory and the creation of culture. Their strong association with griffins through the fourth century and beyond
was symptomatic of a new sense of Amazons, part of a shift
away from old traditions towards unrooted fictions. Of
course, old traditions subsisted, too, as usual in the ancient
world. Hallowed myth evolved alongside new fictions,
even assisted by the tastes of Hellenistic and later scholarship. Accordingly, while some chose to guffaw to an extent
that seems unusual before the fourth century (even in the
carnivalistic world of Athenian Old Comedy, for example),

---

[2] Further Braund 2024.

Amazons and even griffins might be chosen as appropriate decoration for the headgear of a princess of the colonial Greek world, as we see on the *kalathos* worn by a woman ('priestess' as this elite female has often been called) of the rich Bosporan elite of the fourth century BC. The *kalathos* was a stylised wool-basket which evoked female propriety, expressed through the traditional working of wool in the home. The great wealth of her burial, in its construction and contents, provides the context for the battle between Amazons and griffins that is depicted in gold (Plate 32 shows one of its scenes) upon the 'basket' she wore on her head in death. As elsewhere, Amazons were a deathly phenomenon. In this case, however, they struggle with mighty griffins, who take the place of the familiar Greek heroes. Evocations ranged too from Dionysus and potential afterlife, through Heracles and other conquerors of Amazons, to a broader sense of female courage and achievement. We cannot know which of these and other associations mattered most to those who placed the remarkable *kalathos* on the deceased woman's head, but we can be sure enough that – however much currents of thought and belief about Amazons were changing through the fourth century BC – Amazon myth remained powerful in the life of the region, and especially at the site of this burial (Bol'shaya Bliznitsa)[3] in the environs of Labrys, the city of the Amazon axe.

---

[3] In detail, Braund 2018, ch. 6. See Kalashnik 2014, 156–61 for excellent colour images. Amazons are clearly shown, with axes as well as swords, and even the characteristic Amazon shield (*pelta*). The funereal context leaves scant doubt that these are not Arimaspians, who are routinely claimed in Amazon scenes where griffins are present, despite the Dionysiac conflict with Amazons, well known in the Ephesus–Samos area. Further, Treister 2001, with comparanda nearby and as far afield as Tarentum.

However, there was a framework of continuity for these developments, especially as the great tales of the archaic world remained fundamental to Greeks. Key questions persisted, as we see with Quintus of Smyrna's poetic take on the fall of Troy, composed in the fourth century AD or thereabouts. He offers his sense of how Trojan women might have responded to seeing the initial victories of the Amazon queen Penthesilea. He shows the women inspired. So much so, that they start to move, and are drawn towards leaving the relative safety of the city, and to sally forth themselves to fight the besieging Greek men, just as the Amazons were doing so well. But a wise Trojan matron – named Theano[4] – cools their ardour with words of hard realism. Amazons had trained for battle all their lives. They were prepared for warfare in mind, body, and skills. The ladies of Troy could not fight like Amazons, inspired though they might be. Her words rang true for these Trojan women, who thought better of their enthusiasm for the battlefield. Quintus' episode illustrates an issue which had run through so much of Amazon myth, namely the potential of women to become Amazonian, including women who had lived lives that Greek society considered normal.

---

[4] Quintus, *Fall of Troy* 1.604–42.

BIBLIOGRAPHY

Angliker, E. 2022. 'The problem of local *epiclesis* abroad: A case study of the worship of Apollo Pythios on the island of Kea', *BICS* 65: 162–75.

Arafat, K. 1995. [Review of *Die Skulpturen des Asklepiostempels in Epidauros*, by N. Yalouris], *CR* 45(1): 197–8. www.jstor.org/stable/710456.

Arafat, K. 1997. 'State of the art, art of the state: Sexual violence and politics in late archaic and early classical vase-painting', in S. Deacy and K. Pierce eds, *Rape in Antiquity*, London, 97–119.

Arafat, K. 2013. 'Marathon in art', in C. Carey and M. Edwards eds, *Marathon: 2,500 Years On* (*BICS* suppl. 124), 79–89.

Arrington, N. 2015. *Ashes, Images, and Memories: The Presence of the War Dead in Fifth-Century Athens*, Oxford.

Aston, E. 2011. *Mixanthrôpoi*, Liège.

Aston, E. 2021. 'Labour III: The Cerynean Hind', in D. Ogden ed., *The Oxford Handbook of Heracles*, Oxford, 62–70.

Ballesteros-Pastor, L. 2009. 'Bears and bees in Themiscyra: A sanctuary for Artemis in the land of the Amazons?', in T. Fischer-Hansen and B. Poulsen eds, *From Artemis to Diana: The Goddess of Man and Beast*, Copenhagen, 333–40.

Bar, S., Greensmith, E., and Ozbek, L. eds. 2022. *Quintus of Smyrna's Posthomerica*, Edinburgh.

Barringer, J. 1996. 'Atalanta as model: The hunter and the hunted', *ClAnt* 15: 48–76.

Barringer, J. 2004. 'Skythian hunters on Attic vases', in C. Marconi ed., *Greek Vases: Images, Contexts, and Controversies*, Leiden, 13–25.

Baumeister, P. 2007. *Der Fries des Hekateions von Lagina. Neue Untersuchungen zu Monument und Kontext*, Istanbul.

Baynham, E. 2001. 'Alexander and the Amazons', *CQ* 51: 115–26.

Beard, M. 2007. *The Roman Triumph*, Cambridge, MA.

Bekker-Nielsen, T. and Jensen, M. 2015. 'Two Pontic rivers', *Cedrus* 3: 231–42.

Best, J. 1969. *Thracian Peltasts and Their Influence on Greek Warfare*, Groningen.

Bevan, E. 1987. 'The goddess Artemis, and the dedication of bears in sanctuaries', *ABSA* 82: 17–21.

Bichler, R. 2016. 'Persian geography and the Ionians: Herodotus', in S. Bianchetti and M. Cataudella eds, *Brill's Companion to Ancient Geography*, Leiden, 3–20.

Blakely, S. 2006. *Myth, Ritual, and Metallurgy in Ancient Greece and Recent Africa*, Cambridge.

Blakely, S. 2013. '*Daimones* in the Thracian sea: Mysteries, iron, and metaphors', *Archiv für Religionsgeschichte* 14: 155–82.

Blinkenberg Hastrup, H. 2017. 'Ephesus and the Amazons: Remembering or recreating the early history of a Greek polis in the 5th century BC', in E. Mortensen and B. Poulsen eds, *Cityscapes and Monuments of Western Asia Minor*, Oxford, 142–53.

Blok, J. 1995. *The Early Amazons*, Leiden.

Blok, J. 1997. 'A tale of many cities: Amazons in the mythical past of Greek cities in Asia Minor', in E. Lunbeck and S. Marchand eds, *Proof and Persuasion: Essays on Authority, Objectivity, and Evidence*, Turnhout, 81–99.

Blondell, R. 2005. 'How to kill an Amazon', *Helios* 32: 73–103.

Blundell, S. 1998. 'Marriage and the maiden: Narratives on the Parthenon', in S. Blundell and M. Williamson eds, *The Sacred and the Feminine in Ancient Greece*, London, 42–56.

Boardman, J. 1980. 'The Amazon's belt', *AJA* 84: 181–2.

Boardman, J. 1982. 'Herakles, Theseus and Amazons', in D. Kurtz and B. Sparkes eds, *The Eye of Greece*, Cambridge, 1–28.

Bodenstedt, F. 1977. 'Observations on some early electrum types of Mytilene and Phocaea', *Museum Notes (American Numismatic Society)* 22: 1–7.

Boehringer, S. 2007. *L'homosexualité féminine dans l'Antiquité grecque et romaine*, Paris.

Bol, R. 1998. *Amazones Volneratae: Untersuchungen zu den Ephesischen Amazonenstatuen*, Mainz.

Borowski, S. 2021. *Penthesilea und ihre Schwestern: Amazonenepisoden als Bauform des Heldenepos* (The Language of Classical Literature 35), Leiden.

Borza, E. N. and Palagia, O. 2007. 'The chronology of the Macedonian royal tombs at Vergina', *JDAI* 122: 81–125.

Bosak-Schroeder, C. 2020. *Other Natures: Environmental Encounters with Ancient Greek Ethnography*, Berkeley.

Bosworth, A. B. 1972. 'Arrian's literary development', *CQ* 22: 163–85.

Bosworth, A. B. 2000. 'A tale of two empires: Hernán Cortés and Alexander the Great', in A. B. Bosworth and E. Baynham eds, *Alexander the Great: Fact and Fiction*, Oxford, 23–49.

Bowie, E. 2009. 'Philostratus: The life of a sophist', in E. Bowie and J. Elsner eds, *Philostratus*, Cambridge, 19–32.

Bowra, C. M. 1957. 'Melinno's Hymn to Rome', *JRS* 47: 21–8.

Braund, D. 1994. *Georgia in Antiquity*, Oxford.

Braund, D. 1996. *Ruling Roman Britain*, London.

Braund, D. 1998. 'Herodotos on the problematics of reciprocity', in C. Gill, N. Postlethwaite, and R. Seaford eds, *Reciprocity in Ancient Greece*, Oxford, 159–80.

Braund, D. 2004. 'Herodotus' Spartan Scythians', in C. Tuplin ed., *Pontus and the Outside World: Studies in Black Sea History, Historiography, and Archaeology* (Colloquia Pontica 9), Leiden, 25–41.

Braund, D. 2010. 'Myth and ritual at Sinope: From Diogenes the Cynic to Sanape the Amazon', *Ancient Civilizations from Scythia to Siberia* 16(1–2): 11–23.

Braund, D. 2017. 'The goddess Bendis in fifth-century Athenian culture', *VDI* 3: 574–98.

Braund, D. 2018. *Greek Religion and Cults in the Black Sea Region: Goddesses in the Bosporan Kingdom from the Archaic Period to the Byzantine Era*, Cambridge.

Braund, D. 2019. 'Dancing around the Black Sea: Xenophon, Pseudo-Scymnus and Lucian's Bacchants', in D. Braund, E. Hall, and R. Wyles eds, *Ancient Theatre and Performance Culture around the Black Sea*, Cambridge, 470–89.

Braund, D. 2020. 'Between Bithynia and Borysthenes: From Achilles' racecourses on the river Kalpe to the arrival of Aphrodite in Hylaea', *AVesti* 29: 175–90.

Braund, D. 2021. 'In what sense was the Black Sea Thracian? Reflections on ethnic traditions from Thrace to Colchis and the Amazons', in V. Cojocaru and A.-I. Pázsint eds, *Migration and Identity in Eurasia: From Ancient Times to the Middle Ages*, Cluj-Napoca, 21–42.

Braund, D. 2022. 'Between Crimea, Rome and Asia Minor: Dyteutus as Orestes for the princeps', in D. Braund, A. Chaniotis, and E. Petropoulos eds, *The Black Sea Region in the Context of the Roman Empire*, Athens, 159–72.

Braund, D. 2024. 'Aristeas of Proconnesus', in G. Shipley ed., *Geographers of the Ancient Greek World, Cambridge*, 109–119.

Braund, D. forthcoming. 'The naked axeman, Ankaios', in J. Valeva et al. eds, *Alexandrovo Tomb*, Sofia.

Bremmer, J. 2008. 'Priestly personnel of the Ephesian Artemision: Anatolian, Persian, Greek and Roman aspects', in B. Dignas and K. Trampedach eds, *Practitioners of the Divine: Greek Priests and Religious Officials From Homer to Heliodorus*, Washington, DC, 37–53.

Bremmer, J. 2010. 'Hephaistos sweats, or How to construct an ambivalent god', in J. Bremmer and A. Erskine eds, *The Gods of the Greeks*, Edinburgh, 193–208.

Bremmer, J. 2014. *Initiation into the Mysteries of the Ancient World*, Berlin.

Briant, P. 2002. *From Cyrus to Alexander: A History of the Persian Empire*, Winona Lake.

Bron, C. 1996. 'The sword dance for Artemis', *GMusJ* 24: 69–83.

Brunet, S. 2014. 'Women with swords', in P. Christesen and D. Kyle eds, *A Companion to Sport and Spectacle in Greek and Roman Antiquity*, Malden, 278–91.

Bundrick, S. 2019. *Athens, Etruria, and the Many Lives of Greek Figured Pottery*, Madison.

Burkert, W. 1970. 'Jason, Hypsipyle and new fire at Lemnos. A study in myth and ritual', *CQ* 20: 1–16.

Calame, C. 2003. *Myth and History in Ancient Greece: The Symbolic Creation of a Colony*, Princeton.

Calame, C. 2011. 'Myth and performance on the Athenian stage: Praxithea, Erechtheus, their daughters, and the etiology of autochthony', *CPh* 106: 1–19.

Carney, E. 2005. 'Women and *dunasteia* in Caria', *AJPh* 126: 65–91.

Carpino, A. 2016. 'The "taste" for violence in Etruscan art: Debunking the myth', in S. Bell and A. Carpino eds, *A Companion to the Etruscans*, Malden, 410–31.

Carter, J. 1975. *The Sculpture of Tarentum*, Philadelphia.

Cartledge, P. 1981. 'Spartan wives: Liberation or licence?', *CQ* 31: 84–105 [repr. in *Spartan Reflections*, Berkeley 2001].

Castriota, D. 1992. *Myth, Ethos and Actuality: Official Art in Fifth-Century BC Athens*, Madison.

Chiarini, S. 2018. *The So-Called Nonsense Inscriptions on Ancient Greek Vases: Between Paideia and Paidiá*, Leiden.

Clay, J. S. 1980. 'Goat island: *Od*. 9.116–141', *CQ* 30(2): 261–4.

Cohen, A. 2010. *Art in the Era of Alexander the Great: Paradigms of Manhood and Their Cultural Traditions*, Cambridge.

Cohen, B. 1997. 'Divesting the breast of clothes in classical sculpture', in A. Koloski-Ostrow and C. Lyons eds, *Naked Truths: Women, Sexuality, and Gender in Classical Art and Archaeology*, London, 66–92.

Cohen, B. 2000. 'Man-killers and their victims: Inversions of the heroic ideal in classical art', in B. Cohen ed., *Not the*

Classical Ideal: Athens and the Construction of the Other in Greek Art, Leiden, 98–131.

Cole, S. G. 1998. 'Domesticating Artemis', in S. Blundell and M. Williamson eds, *The Sacred and the Feminine in Ancient Greece*, London, 24–38.

Collins, D. 2001. 'Theoris of Lemnos and the criminalization of magic in fourth-century Athens', *CQ* 51: 477–93.

Courtney, E. 1990. 'Vergil's sixth Eclogue', *QUCC* 34: 99–112.

Cousin, C. 2000. 'Composition, espace et paysage dans les peintures de Polygnote à la *lesché* de Delphes', *Gaia* 4: 61–103.

Craik, E. 2015. *The Hippocratic Corpus: Content and Context*, London.

Cuffel, A. 2007. 'Reorienting Christian "Amazons": Women warriors in Medieval Islamic literature in the context of the Crusades', in A. Cuffel and B. Britt eds, *Religion, Gender, and Culture in the Pre-modern World*, Basingstoke, 137–66.

Cyrino, M. 2013. 'Bows and Eros: Hunt as seduction in the Homeric Hymn to Aphrodite', *Arethusa* 46: 375–93.

Dalby, A. 1991. 'The curriculum vitae of Duris of Samos', *CQ* 41: 539–41.

Dan, A. 2011. 'Les Leukosyriens: quelques notes d'éthnographie sinopéenne', in D. Kassab Tezgör ed., *Sinope: The Results of Fifteen Years of Research. Proceedings of the International Symposium, 7–9 May 2009*, Leiden, 73–102.

Dasen, V. 2011. 'Magic and medicine: Gems and the power of seal', in C. Entwistle and N. Adams eds, *Gems of Heaven*, London, 69–74.

Davidson, J. 2001. 'Dover, Foucault and Greek homosexuality: Penetration and the truth of sex', *P&P* 170: 3–51.

Davies, M. 2001. *The Epic Cycle*, Bristol.

De Callataÿ, F. 2013. 'The Brussels tetradrachm of Aitna: Possibly the most precious ancient coin of the world', in P. Iossif ed., *All That Glitters: The Belgian Contribution to Greek Numismatics*, Athens, 82–94.

Devambez, P. 1976. 'Les Amazones et l'Orient', *RA* 2: 265–80.

Dewald, C. 1981. 'Women and Culture in Herodotus' *Histories*', in H. Foley ed., *Reflections of Women in Antiquity*, New York, 91–125.

Dickinson, O. 2005. 'The "face" of Agamemnon', *Hesperia* 74(3): 299–308.

Dillon, M. 2001. *Girls and Women in Classical Greek Religion*, London.

Doob, P. 2019. *The Idea of the Labyrinth from Classical Antiquity through the Middle Ages*, Ithaca.

Dowden, K. 1989. *Death and The Maiden: Girls' Initiation Rites in Greek Mythology*, London.

Dowden, K. 1997. 'The Amazons: Development and functions', *RhM* 140: 97–128.

DuBois, P. 1982. *Centaurs and Amazons: Women and the Prehistory of the Great Chain of Being*, Ann Arbor.

Dunbabin, K. 2016. 'The transformations of Achilles on late Roman mosaics in the East', in J. Audley-Miller and B. Dignas eds, *Wandering Myths: Transcultural Uses of Myth in the Ancient World*, Berlin, 357–96.

Eller, C. 2011. *Gentlemen and Amazons*, Berkeley.

Emerson, M. 2018. *Greek Sanctuaries and Temple Architecture: An Introduction*, London.

Fabbri, L. 2022. 'L'iconografia monetale dell'Amazzone eponima o fondatrice in età classica ed ellenistica', *Mètis* 20: 115–46.

Fabre-Serris, J. and Keith, A. eds. 2015. *Women and War in Antiquity*, Baltimore.

Facella, M. 2017. 'Beyond ritual: Cross-dressing between Greece and the Orient', in D. Campanile, F. Carlà-Uhink, and M. Facella eds, *TransAntiquity: Cross-Dressing and Transgender Dynamics in the Ancient World*, London, 108–20.

Fantuzzi, M. 2012. *Achilles in Love*, Oxford.

Faraone, C. 1987. 'Hephaestus the magician and Near Eastern parallels for Alcinous' watchdogs', *GRBS* 28: 257–80.

Faraone, C. 1997. 'Salvation and female heroics in the Parodos of Aristophanes' *Lysistrata*', *JHS* 117: 38–59.

Faraone, C. 2003. 'Playing the bear and the fawn for Artemis: Female initiation or substitute sacrifice?', in D. Dodd and C. Faraone eds, *Initiation in Ancient Greek Rituals and Narratives*, London, 43–68.

Fialko, E. 2017. 'Scythian female warriors in the south of eastern Europe', *Folia Praehistorica Posnanensia* 22: 29–47.

Figueira, T. 2010. 'Gynecocracy: How women policed masculine behavior in Archaic and Classical Sparta', in A. Powell and S. Hodkinson eds, *Sparta: The Body Politic*, Swansea, 265–96.

Finglass, P. and Kelly, A. eds. 2015. *Stesichorus in Context*, Cambridge.

Fleischer, R. 2002. 'Die Amazonen und das Asyl des Artemisions von Ephesos', *JDAI* 117: 185–216.

Fornasier, J. 2007. *Amazonen: Frauen, Kämpferinnen und Städtegründerinnen*, Mainz.

Fowler, R. 2013. *Early Greek Mythography*, Oxford.

Gaca, K. 2014. 'Ancient warfare and the ravaging martial rape of girls and women: Evidence from Homeric epic and Greek drama', in M. Masterson, N. Rabinowitz, and J. Robson eds, *Sex in Antiquity*, London, 278–97.

Gagné, R. 2021. *Cosmography and the Idea of Hyperborea in Ancient Greece*, Cambridge.

Gantz, T. 1993. *Early Greek Myth*, Baltimore.

Gardiner-Garden, J. 1986. 'Fourth-century conceptions of Maiotian ethnography', *Historia* 35: 192–225.

Genovese, C. 2013. 'I rilievi figurati dei Ninfei di Hierapolis di Frigia: il tema dell'amazonomachia nella decorazione architettonica dell'Asia Minore', *Quaderni di archeologia* 3: 123–30.

Gensheimer, M. B. 2017. 'Metaphors for Marathon in the sculptural program of the Athenian Treasury at Delphi', *Hesperia: The Journal of the American School of Classical Studies at Athens* 86(1): 1–42.

Gera, D. 1997. *Warrior Women: The Anonymous Tractatus de Mulieribus*, Leiden.

Gerber, D. 1978. 'The female breast in Greek erotic literature', *Arethusa* 11: 203–12.

Graf, F. 1984. 'Women, war, and warlike divinities', *ZPE* 55: 245–54.

Grassinger, D. 1999. *Die mythologischen Sarkophage. Teil I. Achill, Adonis, Aeneas, Aktaion, Alkestis, Amazonen* (Die antiken Sarkophagreliefs 12.1), Berlin.

Griffith, M. 1983. *Aeschylus: Prometheus Bound*, Cambridge.

Griffith, M. 2006. 'Horsepower and donkeywork: Equids and the ancient Greek imagination', *CPh* 101: 307–58.

Gruen, E. 2003. 'Cleopatra in Rome: Facts and fantasies', in D. Braund and C. Gill eds, *Myth, History and Culture in Republican Rome: Studies in Honour of T. P. Wiseman*, Exeter, 257–74.

Gruen, E. 2010. *Rethinking the Other in Antiquity*, Princeton.

Gutschke, F. 2019. 'Greek terracotta dolls: Between the domestic and the religious sphere', in G. Papantoniou, D. Michaelides, and M. Dikomitou-Eliadou eds, *Hellenistic and Roman Terracottas*, Leiden, 215–22.

Habicht, C. 1984. 'Pausanias and the evidence of inscriptions', *ClAnt* 3: 40–56.

Haft, A. 1990. 'The city-sacker Odysseus in *Iliad* 2 and 10', *TAPhA* 120: 37–56.

Hall, E. 1989. *Inventing the Barbarian*, Oxford.

Hall, E. 1993. 'Asia unmanned: Images of victory in classical Athens', in J. Rich and G. Shipley eds, *War and Society in the Greek World*, London, 108–33.

Hall, E. 2013. *Adventures with Iphigenia in Tauris: A Cultural History of Euripides' Black Sea Tragedy*, Oxford.

Hall, E. 2018. 'Hephaestus the hobbling humourist: The club-footed god in the history of early Greek comedy', *ICS* 43: 366–87.

Hansen, M. and Nielsen, T. 2004. *An Inventory of Archaic and Classical Poleis*, Oxford.

Harding, P. 2008. *The Story of Athens*, London.

Hardwick, L. 1990. 'Ancient Amazons: Heroes, outsiders or women?', *G&R* 37: 14–36.

Harlow, M. and Nosch, M.-L. eds. 2014. *Greek and Roman Textiles and Dress: An Interdisciplinary Anthology*, Oxford.

Harman, R. 2018. 'Metahistory and the visual in Herodotus and Thucydides', in A. Kampakoglou and A. Novokhatko eds, *Gaze, Vision, and Visuality in Ancient Greek Literature*, Berlin, 271–88.

Harrison, E. 1966. 'The composition of the Amazonomachy on the shield of Athena Parthenos', *Hesperia* 35: 107–33.

Harrison, E. 1977. 'Alkamenes' sculptures for the Hephaisteion: Part iii. Iconography and style', *AJA* 81: 411–26.

Harrison, E. 1981. 'Motifs of the city-siege on the shield of Athena Parthenos', *AJA* 85: 281–317.

Harrison, E. 1982. 'Two Pheidian heads: Nike and Amazon', in D. Kurtz and B. Sparkes eds, *The Eye of Greece*, Cambridge, 53–88.

Hasanov, Z. 2018. 'The cult of female warriors and rulers in the Scythian and Sarmatian cultures', *Annales Universitatis Apulensis Series Historica*, 22: 131–50.

Hayes, G. 2014. *Rationalizing Myth in Antiquity*, Oxford.

Heinen, H. 2012. 'Hypsikrateia/Hypsikrates: Travestie aus Liebe. König Mithradates Eupators Page und eine neue griechische Inschrift aus Phanagoreia/Rußland', *Jahrbuch der Göttinger Akademie der Wissenschaften* 2012: 215–38.

Hazewindus, M. 2019. *When Women Interfere: Studies in the Role of Women in Herodotus' Histories*, Leiden.

Hellström, P. 2009. 'Sacred architecture and Karian identity', in F. Rumscheid ed., *Die Karer und die Anderen*, Bonn, 267–90.

Henderson, J. 1991. *The Maculate Muse: Obscene Language in Attic Comedy* (2nd ed.), Oxford.

Henderson, J. 1994. '*Timeo danaos*: Amazons in early Greek art and pottery', in S. Goldhill and R. Osborne eds, *Art and Text in Ancient Greek Culture*, Cambridge, 85–137.

Hermary, A. 2020. 'Le trésor de Marseille à Delphes', *Annales de l'APLAES* 5: 23.

Hernández, P. 2010. 'Procles the Carthaginian: A North African sophist in Pausanias' *Periegesis*', *GRBS* 50: 119–32.

Herring, A. 2022. 'Depicting Amazons as local heroes in Hellenized Anatolia', *AJA* 126: 355–83.

Hölscher, T. 1998. 'Images and political identity: The case of Athens', in D. Boedeker and K. Raaflaub eds, *Democracy, Empire and the Arts in Fifth-Century Athens*, Cambridge, MA, 153–83.

Hölscher, T. 2000. 'Feindwelten – Glückswelten: Perser, Kentauren und Amazonen', in T. Hölscher ed., *Gegenwelten zu den Kulturen Griechenlands und Roms in der Antike*, Leipzig, 287–320.

Huxley, G. 1980. 'ΒΟΥΠΟΡΟΣ ΑΡΣΙΝΟΗΣ', *JHS* 100: 189–90.

Işık, C. 2019. *Die Wandmalereien in der Grabkammer des Hekatomneions: Beobachtungen zu Figurentypen, zur Komposition, Ikonographie und zum Stil*, Bonn.

Ivantchik, A. 2006. '"Scythian" archers on archaic Attic vases: Problems of interpretation', *Ancient Civilizations from Scythia to Siberia* 12: 196–271.

Ivantchik, A. 2013. 'Amazonen, Skythen und Sauromaten: Alte und moderne Mythen', in C. Schubert and A. Weiss eds, *Amazonen zwischen Griechen und Skythen*, Berlin, 73–88.

Jackson, S. 1990. 'Myrsilus of Methymna and the dreadful smell of the Lemnian Women', *ICS* 1: 77–83.

Jenkins, R. 1947. 'The bronze Athena at Byzantium', *JHS* 67: 31–3.

Jones, G. 2019. 'The sculptural poetics of Euripides' *Ion*: Reflections of art, myth, and cult from the Parthenon to the Attic stage', *Hesperia* 88: 727–62.

Jordan, P. 2014. *The Seven Wonders of the Ancient World*, London.

Kalashnik, Yu. 2014. *Greek Gold in the Hermitage Collection*, St Petersburg.

Kantiréa, M. 2014. 'Reconstituer l'histoire grecque sous l'Empire: A propos de l'asile au temps de Tibère', *Latomus* 73: 415–38.

Karlsson, K. and Carlsson, S. 2011. *Labraunda and Karia. Proceedings of the International Symposium Commemorating Sixty Years of Swedish Archaeological Work in Labraunda* (Acta Universitatis Upsaliensis, Boreas 32), Uppsala.

Kearns, E. 1990. 'Saving the Greek city', in O. Murray and S. Price eds, *The Greek City*, Oxford, 323–44.

Keen, A. 1998. *Dynastic Lycia: A Political History of the Lycians and Their Relations with Foreign Powers, c. 545–362 BC*, Leiden.

Kelaher, A. 2019–20. 'Apollo Daphnephoros and the Niobid Painter', *Mediterranean Archaeology* 32/33: 1–16.

Keuls, E. 1993. *The Reign of the Phallus*, London.

Kinns, P. 1989. 'Ionia: The pattern of coinage during the last century of the Persian empire', *REA* 91: 183–93.

Kitchell, K. 2014. *Animals in Antiquity, A to Z*, London.

Kopylov, V. and Larenok, P. 1994. *Taganrogskoye poseleniye*, Rostov-on-Don.

Kosmopoulou, A. 2001. 'Working women: Female professionals on classical Attic gravestones', *ABSA* 96: 281–319.

Kramberger, A. 2017. 'Bewaffnete Frauen vs. geschmückte Männer: Zum Problem des Genderings von Grabbeigaben am Beispiel der frühskythischen Bestattungen am Mittleren Dnepr', in C. Keller and K. Winger eds, *Frauen an der Macht? Neue interdisziplinäre Ansätze zur Frauen - und Geschlechterforschung für die Eisenzeit Mitteleuropas*, Bonn, 227–60.

Krentz P. 2002. 'Fighting by the rules: The invention of the hoplite *agon*', *Hesperia* 71: 23–39.

Kyle, D. 2014. 'Greek female sport rites, running, and racing', in P. Christesen and D. Kyle eds, *A Companion to Sport and Spectacle in Greek and Roman Antiquity*, Malden, 258–76.

Kypraiou, E. 2000. *Smouldering Lemnos*, Athens.

Lalonde, G. 2019. *Athena Itonia: Geography and Meaning of an Ancient Greek War Goddess*, Leiden.

Lane Fox, R. 2018. 'P.OXY. 4808 and historians', in K. Nawotka, R. Rollinger, J. Wiesehöfer, and A. Wojciechowska eds, *The Historiography of Alexander the Great*, Wiesbaden, 91–104.

Langdon, S. 2002. 'Trial by Amazon: Thoughts on the first Amazons in Greek art', in C. Callaway ed., *Ancient Journeys: Festschrift in Honor of E. N. Lane*, Stoa Consortium, 1–18.

Laoupi, A. 2008. 'The divine fires of creation: Homeric Hephaestos as a comet/meteor god', in S. Paipetis ed., *Science and Technology in Homeric Epics*, London, 325–40.

Larson, J. 1995. *Greek Heroine Cults*, Madison.

Larson, J. 2007. *Ancient Greek Cults*, London.

Leppin, H. 2015. *Antike Mythos in christlichen Kontexten*, Berlin.

Lippolis, E. ed. 1994. *Taranto: Le necropoli: Aspetti e problemi della documentazione archeologica tra VII e I sec. a.C* (Catalogo del Museo archeologico di Taranto 3), Taranto.

Lissarrague, F. 1990. *L'autre guerrier: archers, peltastes, cavaliers dans l'imagerie attique*, Paris.

Llewellyn-Jones, L. 2003. *Aphrodite's Tortoise: The Veiled Woman of Ancient Greece*, Swansea.

Loman, P. 2004. 'No woman no war: Women's participation in ancient Greek warfare', *G&R* 51: 34–54.

Loosley, E. 2018. 'Cultural imperialism at the borders of empire: The case of the "Villa of the Amazons" in Edessa', in G. Brooke, A. Curtis, M. al-Hamad, and G. Smith eds, *Near Eastern and Arabian Essays: Studies in Honour of John F. Healey* (Journal of Semitic Studies suppl. 41), 215–29.

López Martínez, M. 2022. 'The Pontic Princess Calligone, the Queen Themisto, and the Amazons in the Black Sea (P. Oxy. 5355 and PSI 981)', *APF* 68(1): 23–55.

Loraux, N. 1981. Le lit, la guerre. *L'homme* 1981: 37–67.

Loraux, N. 1986. *The Invention of Athens: The Funeral Oration in the Classical City*, New Haven.

Lowenstam, S. 1993. 'The pictures on Juno's Temple in the *Aeneid*', *CW* 87: 37–49.

MacLean, J. B. and Aitken, A. B. 2002. *Flavius Philostratus: On Heroes*, Munich.

McAllister, M. 1999. *Significant Otherness: Herodotos' Use of a Dominant Female Motif to Illustrate the Superiority of the Greeks*, Ottawa.

McCarter, S. 2012. 'The forging of a god: Venus, the shield of Aeneas, and Callimachus's *Hymn to Artemis*', *TAPhA* 142: 355–81.

McInerney, J. 1994. 'Politicizing the past: The "Atthis" of Kleidemos', *ClAnt* 13: 17–37.

Man, J. 2017. *Amazons: The Real Warrior Women of the Ancient World*, London.

Manetta, C. forthcoming. *Le tombe di Tracia*, Mainz.

Mango, C. 1985. *Le développement urbain de Constantinople (IVe–VIIe siècles)*, Paris.

Marazov, I. 2013. *Amazonka*, Sofia.

Marconi, C. 2016. 'The Greek west: Temples and their decoration', in M. M. Miles ed., *A Companion to Greek Architecture*, Malden, 75–91.

Marganne, M.-H. 1997. 'Les médicaments estampillés dans le corpus galénique', in A. Debru ed., *Galen on Pharmacology: Philosophy, History, and Medicine*, Leiden, 153–74.

Marks, J. 2005. 'The ongoing *neikos*: Thersites, Odysseus, and Achilles', *AJPh* 126: 1–31.

Marshall, C. 2017. 'Breastfeeding in Greek literature and thought', *ICS* 42: 185–201.

Martin, R. 1987. 'Fire on the mountain: *Lysistrata* and the Lemnian Women', *ClAnt* 6: 77–105.

Masciadri, V. 2008. *Eine Insel im Meer der Geschichten: Untersuchungen zu Mythen aus Lemnos*, Stuttgart.

Matheson, S. 1995. *Polygnotos and Vase Painting in Classical Athens*, Madison.

Matthaei, A. 2013. *Münzbild und Polisbild. Untersuchungen zur Selbstdarstellung kleinasiatischer Poleis im Hellenismus*, Munich.

Mattingly, H. B. 1996. 'Athens and the Black Sea in the fifth century BC', in O. Lordkipanidzé and P. Lévêque eds, *Sur les traces des Argonautes*, Paris, 151–7.

Mayor, A. 2014. *The Amazons*, Princeton.

Meiklejohn, K. 1934. 'Alexander Helios and Caesarion', *JRS* 24: 191–5.

Meyer, H. 1987. 'Ein neues Piräusrelief. Zur Überlieferung der Amazonomachie am Schild der Athena Parthenos', *MDAI(A)* 102: 295–321.

Miles, G. 2018. *Philostratus: Interpreters and Interpretation*, London.

Mili, M. 2015. *Religion and Society in Ancient Thessaly*, Oxford.

Moggi, M. 2005. 'Marpessa detta Choira e Ares Gynaikothoinas', in E. Østby ed., *Ancient Arcadia*, Athens, 139–50.

Moignard, E. 2015. *Master of Attic Black-Figure Painting: The Art and Legacy of Exekias*, London.

Morales, H. 2016. 'Rape, violence, complicity', *Arethusa* 49: 61–92.

Morwood, J. 2008. *The Tragedies of Sophocles*, Liverpool.

Moscati-Castelnuovo, L. 1999. 'From East to West: The Eponymous Amazon Cleta', in G. Tsetskhladze ed., *Ancient Greeks West and East*, Leiden, 163–77.

Munn, M. 2006. *The Mother of the Gods*, Berkeley.

Muntz, C. 2017. *Diodorus Siculus and the World of the Late Roman Republic*, Oxford.

Muratov, M. 2019. 'Paratheatrical performances in the Bosporan Kingdom: The evidence of terracotta figurines', in D. Braund, E. Hall, and R. Wyles eds, *Ancient Theatre and Performance Culture around the Black Sea*, Cambridge, 400–32.

Muth, S. 2008. *Gewalt im Bild. Das Phänomen der medialen Gewalt im Athen des 6. und 5. Jahrhunderts v. Chr.*, Berlin.

Nawotka, K. 2017. *The Alexander Romance by Ps.-Callisthenes*, Leiden.

Neer, R. 2001. 'Framing the gift: The politics of the Siphnian Treasury at Delphi', *ClAnt* 20: 273–344.

Neils, J. ed. 2005. *The Parthenon: From Antiquity to the Present*, Cambridge.

Nesselrath, H.-G. 2005. '"Where the lord of the sea grants passage to sailors through the deep-blue mere no more": The Greeks and the Western seas', *G&R* 52: 153–71.

Nesselrath, H.-G. 2014. 'Ancient comedy and historiography: Aristophanes meets Herodotus', in S. D. Olson ed., *Ancient Comedy and Reception: Essays in Honor of Jeffrey Henderson*, Berlin, 51–61.

Ní-Mheallaigh, K. 2020. *The Moon in the Greek and Roman Imagination*, Cambridge.

Nick, G. 2002. *Die Athena Parthenos. Studien zum griechischen Kultbild und seiner Rezeption* (MDAI(A) suppl. 19), Athens.

Nolan, E. 2021. 'Athenians, Amazons, and solecisms: Language contact in Herodotus', *AJPh* 142(4): 571–96.

O'Gorman, E. 2006. 'A woman's history of warfare', in V. Zajko and M. Leonard eds, *Laughing with Medusa: Classical Myth and Feminist Thought*, Oxford, 189–208.

Oakley, J. 1982. 'The autonomous wreathed tetradrachms of Kyme, Aeolis', *Museum Notes (American Numismatic Society)* 27: 1–37.

Ogden, D. 1997. *The Crooked Kings of Ancient Greece*, London.

Ogden, D. 2010. *Alexander the Great: Myth, Genesis and Sexuality*, Exeter.

Ogden, D. 2013. *Dragons, Serpents, & Slayers: A Sourcebook*. Oxford.

Ogden, D. 2020. 'The theft of Bucephalas', in M. D'Agostini, E. Anson, and F. Pownall eds, *Affective Relations and Personal Bonds in Hellenistic Antiquity*, Oxford, 143–61.

Østby, E. 1993. 'Twenty-five years of research on Greek sanctuaries: A bibliography', in N. Marinatos and R. Hägg eds, *Greek Sanctuaries: New Approaches*, London, 153–78.

Padgett, M. 2017. *The Berlin Painter and His World: Athenian Vase-Painting in the Early Fifth Century* BC, Princeton.

Palagia, O. 1994. *The Archaeology of Athens and Attica under the Democracy*, Oxford.

Palagia, O. 2016. 'Commemorating the dead: Grave markers, tombs, and tomb paintings, 400–30 BCE', in M. M. Miles ed., *A Companion to Greek Architecture*, Malden, 374–89.

Palagia, O. 2018. 'The Elgin Throne and the Tyrannicides', in P. Karanastasi, Th. Stephanidou-Tiberiou, and D. Damaskos eds. Γλυπτική και κοινωνία στη ρωμαϊκή Ελλάδα: καλλιτεχνικά προϊόντα, κοινωνικές προβολές [*Sculpture and Society in Roman Greece: Artistic Products, Social Projections*], Thessaloniki, 67–74.

Palagia, O. ed. 2019. *Handbook of Greek Sculpture*, Berlin.

Papadopoulou, C. 2014. 'Transforming the surroundings and its impact on cult rituals: The case study of Artemis Mounichia in the fifth century', in C. Moser and C. Feldman eds, *Locating the Sacred: Theoretical Approaches to the Emplacement of Religion*, Oxford, 111–27.

Parker, R. 1993. 'Artemis Lemnia', *ZPE* 99: 122.

Parker, R. 1996. *Athenian Religion: A History*, Oxford.

Parker, R. 2011. *On Greek Religion*, Ithaca.

Pembroke, S. 1967. 'Women in charge: The function of alternatives in early Greek tradition and the ancient idea of matriarchy', *JWI* 30: 1–35.

Penrose, W. D. 2016. *Postcolonial Amazons: Female Masculinity and Courage in Ancient Greek and Sanskrit Literature*, Oxford.

Persson, A. 1921. 'Les sculptures du téménos de "Marmaria" à Delphes', *BCH* 45: 316–34.

Petrakova, A. 2020. 'Exotische Utopien einer fernen Welt', *AVesti* 29: 278–90.

Petsalis-Diomidis, A. 2018. 'Undressing for Artemis: Sensory approaches to clothes dedications in Hellenistic epigram and in the cult of Artemis Brauronia', in A. Kampakoglou and A. Novokhatko eds, *Gaze, Vision, and Visuality in Ancient Greek Literature*, Berlin, 418–63.

Pfaff, C. 2003. *The Architecture of the Classical Temple of Hera*, Princeton.

Pfaff, C. 2013. 'Artemis and a hero at the Argive Heraion', *Hesperia* 82: 277–99.

Phillips, E. D. 1968. 'Saneunos the Scythian', *GRBS* 9(4), 385–8.

Photos-Jones, E. and Hall, A. 2014. 'Lemnian Earth, alum and astringency: A field-based approach', in D. Michaelides ed., *Medicine and Healing in the Ancient Mediterranean*, Oxford, 183–9.

Photos-Jones, E., Keane, C., Jones, A. X., Stamatakis, M., Robertson, P., Hall, A. J., and Leanord, A. 2015. 'Testing Dioscorides' medicinal clays for their antibacterial properties: The case of Samian Earth', *Journal of Archaeological Science* 57: 257–67.

Pirenne-Delforge, V. 1994. *L'Aphrodite grecque*, Liège.

Prinz, F. 1979. *Gründungsmythen und Sachenchronologien*, Munich.

Porter, J. R. 2020. [Review of Mayor 2014], *Academia.edu* 37418474: 1–109.

Rabinowitz, N. 2002. 'Excavating women's homoeroticism in Ancient Greece. The evidence from Attic vase painting', in N. Rabinowitz and L. Auanger eds, *Among Women: From the Homosocial to the Homoerotic in the Ancient World*, Austin, 106–66.

Redfield, J. 1977/8. 'The women of Sparta', *CJ* 73: 146–64.

Redfield, J. 2002. *The Locrian Maidens: Love and Death in Greek Italy*, Princeton.

Reguero, M. 2019. 'The rhetoric of weapons in Euripides' *Heracles*. Bow versus spear', *Mnemosyne* 73: 224–42.

Richter, G. 1942. 'Terracotta plaques from early Attic tombs', *BMM* 1: 85–9.

Ridgway, B. S. 1965. 'Wounded figures in Greek sculpture', *Archaeology* 8: 47–54.

Ridgway, B. S. 1974. 'A story of five Amazons', *AJA* 78: 1–17.

Riva, C. 2022. 'Violence, power and religion in the south Etruscan archaic city-state', in S. Rau and J. Rüpke eds, *Religion and Urbanity Online*, Berlin, https://doi.org/10.1515/urbrel.16039815.

Robert, L. 1980. 'Monnaie d'Amisos et le Thermodon', in *A travers l'Asie mineure*, Paris, 191–201.

Robertson, N. 1992. *Festivals and Legends: The Formation of Greek Cities in the Light of Public Ritual*, Toronto.

Robu, A. 2014. *Mégare et les établissements mégariens de Sicile, de la Propontide et du Pont-Euxin. Histoire et institutions*, Lausanne.

Rogers, G. 1991. *The Sacred Identity of Ephesos*, London.

Rogers, G. 2012. *The Mysteries of Artemis of Ephesos*, New Haven.

Roisman, P. 2005. *The Rhetoric of Manhood: Masculinity in the Attic Orators*, Berkeley.

Rolley, C. 1999 *La sculpture grecque 2. La période classique*, Paris.

Rotroff, S. and Lamberton, R. 2014. 'The tombs of Amazons', in A. Avramidou and D. Demetriou eds, *Approaching the Ancient Artifact: Representation, Narrative, and Function*, Berlin, 127–38.

Russell, T. 2016. *Byzantium and the Bosporus: A Historical Study, from the Seventh Century* BC *until the Foundation of Constantinople*, Oxford.

Russenberger, C. 2015. *Der Tod und die Mädchen: Amazonen auf römischen Sarkophagen*, Berlin.

Savostina, E. ed. 2001. *Amazonomachia? Bosporan Battle Relief*, Moscow-St Petersburg.

Schaps, D. 1982. 'The women of Greece in wartime', *ChP* 77: 196–211.

Schauenburg, K. 1960. 'Der Gürtel der Hippolyte', *Philologus* 104: 1–13.

Schmitt-Pantel, P. 2015. 'Dining in ancient Greece', in J. Wilkins and R. Nadeau eds, *A Companion to Food in the Ancient World*, Malden, 224–33.

Schwab, K. A. 2005. 'Celebrations of victory: The metopes of the Parthenon', in J. Neils ed., *The Parthenon: From Antiquity to the Present*, Cambridge, 158–97.

Schubert, C. and Weiss, A. eds, 2013. *Amazonen zwischen Griechen und Skythen*, Berlin.

Serwint, N. 1993. 'The female athletic costume at the Heraia and prenuptial initiation rites', *AJA* 97: 403–22.

Shannon-Henderson, K. 2019. *Religion and Memory in Tacitus' Annals*, Oxford.

Shapiro, H. A. 1983. 'Amazons, Thracians, and Scythians', *GRBS* 24: 105–14.

Shapiro, H. A. 1991. 'Theseus: Aspects of the hero in archaic Greece', *Studies in the History of Art* 32: 122–39.

Shear, J. 2013. '"Memories will never grow old": The politics of remembrance in the Athenian funeral orations', *CQ* 63: 511–36.

Shear, T. 2014. *Trophies of Victory Book Subtitle: Public Building in Periklean Athens*, Princeton.

Sinn, U. 1993. 'Greek sanctuaries as places of refuge', in N. Marinatos and R. Hagg eds, *Greek Sanctuaries: New Approaches*, London, 70–87.

Sofaer, J. 2006. *The Body as Material Culture*, Cambridge.

Sourvinou-Inwood, C. 1987. 'A series of erotic pursuits: Images and meanings', *JHS* 107: 131–53.

Spawforth, A. 2006. *The Complete Greek Temples*, London.

Stafford, E. 2011. *Herakles*, London.

Stamatopoulou, Z. 2017. 'Wounding the gods: The mortal Theomachos in the *Iliad* and the Hesiodic Aspis', *Mnemosyne* 70(6): 920–38.

Steinbock, B. 2013. *Social Memory in Athenian Public Discourse: Uses and Meanings of the Past*, Ann Arbor.

Steiner, D. 2015. '"Wolf's justice": The Iliadic Doloneia and the semiotics of wolves', *ClAnt* 34: 335–69.

Stephens, S. 2015. *Callimachus: The Hymns*, Oxford.

Stewart, A. 1995. 'Imag(in)ing the other: Amazons and ethnicity in fifth-century Athens', *Poetics Today* 16: 571–97.

Stewart, A. 2004. *Attalos, Athens, and the Akropolis*, Cambridge.

Stewart, A., Driscoll, E., Estrin, S., Gleason, N. J., Lawrence, E., Levitan, R., Lloyd-Knauf, S., and Turbeville, K. 2019. 'Classical sculpture from the Athenian Agora, part 2: The friezes of the Temple of Ares (Temple of Athena Pallenis)', *Hesperia* 88: 625–705.

Stoneman, R. 2007. *Il Romanzo di Alessandro*, Milan.

Stoneman, R. 2008. *Alexander the Great: A Life in Legend*, New Haven.

Stoneman, R. ed. 2022. *Alexander the Great: The Making of a Myth*, London.

Stoyanova, D. and Damyanov, M. 2021. 'Late archaic and early classical monumental architecture on the island of St. Kirik, Apollonia Pontike', in D. Braund, V. Stolba, and P. Ulrike eds, *Environment and Habitation around the Ancient Black Sea*, Berlin, 7–38.

Stoyanova, D. 2022. *Строителна керамика и архитектурна теракота от Аполония* Понтика *[Construction Ceramics and Architectural Terracotta from Apollonia Pontica]*, Sofia.

Stutz, L. and Tarlow, S. eds. 2013. *The Oxford Handbook of the Archaeology of Death and Burial*, Oxford.

Summerer, L. 2000–1. 'Amazonendarstellungen auf Münzen und Terrakotten von Amisos', *Talanta* 32/33: 27–39.

Summerer, L. 2005. 'Amisos: Eine Griechische Polis im Land der Leukosyrer', in D. Kacharava, M. Faudot, and E. Geny eds, *Pont-Euxin et polis*, Paris, 129–65.

Summerer, L. 2021. Review of Işık 2019, *BMCRev* 2021.10.32.

Sutton, R. 1997–8. 'Nuptial Eros: The visual discourse of marriage in Classical Athens', *JWAG* 55–56: 27–48.

Thomas, R. 2000. *Herodotus in Context: Ethnography, Science, and the Art of Persuasion*, Cambridge.

Thonemann, P. 2020. 'Lysimache and Lysistrata', *JHS* 140: 128–42.

Todd, S. 2007. *A Commentary on Lysias*, Oxford.

Tokhtas'yev, S. 2006. 'The Bosporus and Sindike in the era of Leukon I: New epigraphic publications', *Ancient Civilizations from Scythia to Siberia* 12: 1–22.

Topper, K. R. 2015. 'Dionysus comes to Thrace: The metaphor of corrupted sacrifice and the introduction of Dionysian cult in images of Lykourgos's madness', *Arethusa* 48: 139–71.

Treister, M. 2001. 'Hammering techniques in Archaic Greece', in J. Hargrave ed., *Hammering Techniques in Greek and Roman Jewellery and Toreutics*, Leiden, 17–77.

Tsagalis, C. 2008. *The Oral Palimpsest: Exploring Intertextuality in the Homeric Epics*, Washington, DC.

Tsantsanoglou, K. 2012. *Of Golden Manes and Silvery Faces: The Partheneion 1 of Alcman*, Berlin.

Tsiafakis, D. 2000. 'The allure and repulsion of Thracians in the art of Classical Athens', in B. Cohen ed., *Not the Classical Ideal: Athens and the Construction of the Other in Greek Art*, Leiden, 364–89.

Tsouvala, G. 2021. 'Female athletes in the Late Hellenistic and Roman world', in R. Ancona and G. Tsouvala eds, *New Directions in the Study of Women in the Greco-Roman World*, Oxford, 139–72.

Tuplin, C. 2010. 'Re-visiting Dareios' Scythian expedition', in J. Nieling and E. Rehm eds, *Achaemenid Impact in the Black Sea*, Aarhus, 281–312.

Tyrrell, W. 1984. *Amazons: A Study in Athenian Mythmaking*, Baltimore.

Tzanetou, A. 2012. *City of Suppliants: Tragedy and the Athenian Empire*, New York.

Van der Meer, L. 1995. *Interpretatio Etrusca: Greek Myths on Etruscan Mirrors*, Amsterdam.

Van der Meer, L. 2004. *Myths and More on Etruscan Stone Sarcophagi (c. 350–c. 250 BC)*, Louvain.

Van Wees, H. 2013. 'Farmers and hoplites: Models of historical development', in D. Kagan and G. Viggiano eds, *Men of Bronze Hoplite Warfare in Ancient Greece*, Princeton, 222–55.

Veness, R. 2002. 'Investing the barbarian? The dress of Amazons in Athenian art', in L. Llewellyn-Jones ed., *Women's Dress in the Ancient Greek World*, Swansea, 95–110.

Visser, M. 1982. 'Worship your enemy: Aspects of the cult of heroes in ancient Greece', *HThR* 75: 403–28.

Vlassopoulos, K. 2013. *Greeks and Barbarians*, Cambridge.

Von Bothmer, D. 1957. *Amazons in Greek Art*, Oxford.

Walker, H. 1995. *Theseus and Athens*, Oxford.

Warden, P. 2009. 'The blood of animals. Predation and transformation in Etruscan funerary representation', in S. Bell and H. Nagy eds, *New Perspectives on Etruria and Early Rome: In Honor of R. De Puma*, Madison, 198–219.

Weber, M. 2008. 'Neues zu den Amazonen von Ephesos', *Thetis* 15: 45–56.

West, M. 2003. '*Iliad* and *Aethiopis*', *CQ* 53: 1–14.

West, S. 2017. 'Mysterious Lemnos: A note on ΑΜΙΧΘΑΛΟΕΣΣΑ (*Il.* 24.753)', in C. Tsagalis and A. Markantonatos eds, *The Winnowing Oar: New Perspectives in Homeric Studies*, Berlin, 215–27.

Willemsen, S. 2011. 'Amazons in pre-Roman Italy', in P. Lulof and C. Rescigno eds, *Deliciae Fictiles* IV, Oxford, 44–9.

Wiseman, T. P. 1993. *Remus*, Cambridge.

Wiseman, T. P. 2004. *Myths of Rome*, Exeter.

Wright, M. 2016. *The Lost Plays of Greek Tragedy, Vol.* 1, London.

Wright, M. 2019. *The Lost Plays of Greek Tragedy, Vol.* 2, London.

Wycherley, R. E. 1957. *Athenian Agora, Vol.* III: *Literary and Epigraphical Testimonia*, Princeton.

Yeroulanou, M. 1998. 'Metopes and architecture: The Hephaisteion and the Parthenon', *ABSA* 93: 401–25.

Zeitlin, F. 1978. 'The dynamics of misogyny: Myth and myth-making in the *Oresteia*', *Arethusa* 11: 149–84.

Zeitlin, F. 1990. 'Patterns of gender in Aeschylean drama', in M. Griffith and D. Mastronarde eds, *Cabinet of the Muses*, Atlanta, 103–15.

Zelnick-Abramovitz, R. 2018. 'Kabeiroi, manumitted slaves and *xenoi*: The manumission inscriptions from Lemnos', *Dike* 21: 87–115.

Ziskowski, A. 2014. 'The Bellerophon myth in early Corinthian history and art', *Hesperia* 83: 81–102.

Zorman, M. 2008. 'CTH 3: The conquest of Zalpa justified', in VI *Congresso Internazionale di Ittitologia Roma*, 2005, Rome, 861–70.

INDEX

Achilles, 13, 16, 21, 59, 65, 72, 89, 91, 94, 98, 125, 254
Acmon, 85, 172–73
Admete, 110
Aegina, 88
Aeneas Tacticus, 177
Aeschylus
  Eumenides, 57, 200
  Persians, 28
  Prometheus Bound, 100
  Suppliants, 128
Aethiopis, 59, 90, 91, 92, 93, 95, 98, 296
Alexander the Great, 13, 52, 74, 202, 235
Amage, 158
Amazo, 180
Amazons
  age, 19, 30, 38, 60, 61, 63, 70
  as astronomers, 118
  as builders, 27, 102, 173
  as city founders, 174, 179, 180, 186, 192, 218
  as farmers, 17, 99, 166
  as horsewomen, 48, 51, 64, 75, 142, 169, 189, 206
  as hunters, 33
  as Persians, 27, 28, 206, 210
  beauty, 19, 24
  breasts, 25, 60, 70, 126, 147, 148
  children, 19, 20, 22, 67, 70, 71, 72, 142, 184, 235, 246, 248, 255

dancing, 26, 54, 123, 181, 182, 184
  See also clothing, training, weapons/armour
Amisus, 171
Andromache, 97, 110
Antiope, 202
Aphrodite, 22, 42, 43, 44, 46, 73, 75, 77, 95, 213
Apollo, 41, 161, 187
  See also Delos, Delphi
Apollonia Pontica, 100, 117
Apollonius Rhodius, 168, 214, 230
Ares, 19, 38, 44, 49, 96, 99, 173, 230
Argive Heraion, 114
Argos, 44, 216
Arimaspians, 138
Aristophanes
  Ecclesiazusae, 21
  Lysistrata, 12, 64, 75, 154
  Thesmophoriazusae, 155
Arrian, 240, 243
Artemis, 7, 21, 30, 41, 55, 107, 119, 123, 172, 177, 183, 221, 225
Artemisia, 155
Asclepiades of Tragilos, 217
Asclepius, 80, 151
Atalanta, 41, 42
  See also Tegea
Athena, 23, 208
Athens, 29, 48, 49, 79, 115, 184, 195–212
  Acropolis, 207

298

Index

weapons/armour, 33, 35, 51, 215
 axe, 15, 55, 56, 98, 100, 116,
  161, 189, 190, 241, 268, 273
 bow and arrow, 5, 14, 22, 41,
  43, 53, 54, 55, 57, 94, 128,
  136, 147, 189, 203, 225
 breastplate, 151
 club, 24, 107
 helmet, 59, 83, 93

javelin, 53, 54, 119, 147, 168,
  189, 203
 shield, 44, 96, 136, 242
 shield, crescent, 15, 56, 189,
  212, 273
 spear, 14, 54, 94
 sword, 54, 273
wolves, 131, 169
woolworking, 31, 32, 120